"Ever wonder why people have lucky numbers or why certain times, such as 11:11, seems to stamp life's significant events? With charm, wit, and a touch of humor, Jones and Flaxman dig deep into how numbers play a significant role in our lives. From ancient philosophy to today's science of information theory, Jones and Flaxman uncover the secret life and history of numbers. Could there be more to numbers than meets the eye? Do number lie at the core of the human experience? Is there a bigger picture? Could God actually be numbers? Jones and Flaxman investigate these questions and more in *11:11 The Time Prompt Phenomenon*. Never have I read a better exposé of the history, science, and philosophy behind numbers; a truly enjoyable and enlightening read. Jones and Flaxman had my number!"

—Edward Malkowski, author of *The Spiritual Technology of Ancient Egypt*

"In this digital age we are literally enveloped by numbers and, not surprisingly, the eternal fascination with numbers is stronger than ever. Marie D. Jones and Larry Flaxman provide an invaluable primer on the intriguing history and meaning of numbers, the lore of mystical numerology, time synchronicities, sequences, ratios, codes, Pythagorean secret societies, sacred geometries, and much else. Absolutely a fascinating read guaranteed to leave you counting for more!"

—Robert M. Schoch, PhD, author and editor of books including *The Parapsychology Revolution* and *Pyramid Quest*

"Through this most interesting book we learn how the repetitions of specific numbers, seen in the time of day for example, might be time prompts alerting us to pay attention. With the vast majority of the Western world asleep to our multidimensional existence, perhaps the time prompt phenomena is indeed a wakeup call from the universe of numbers, saying it's time to break out of the prison of the physical world, and move into the eternal now. A book that is right on TIME!"

—Robert R. Hieronimus, PhD, author of *The United Symbolism of America*

"It seemed to begin sometime in the 1980s. Every other person who wrote to us or approached us after a lecture appearance asked, 'I keep seeing 11:11. What does it mean?' In *11:11: The Time Prompt Phenomenon* Marie D. Jones and Larry Flaxman have accomplished a small miracle. They have made the mystery and wonder of numbers accessible to the average reader. In a brisk, easy-to-read style, they reveal that numbers truly possess the power to shape, form, describe and transform our lives and offer every one of us the key to the universe."

—Brad Steiger and Sherry Hansen Steiger, authors of *Conspiracies and Secret Societies*

"*11:11 :The Time Prompt Phenomenon* is a fun, fast moving, informative discussion of numbers as both a spiritual and scientific concept, and of the fundamental significance of numbers as they have been viewed throughout the ages of humanity. I recommend it as a thoroughly enjoyable read, after which you may never look at numbers the same way again."

—Laird Scranton, author of *The Science of the Dogon* and *Sacred Symbols of the Dogon*

11:11
The Time Prompt Phenomenon

11:11
The Time Prompt Phenomenon

The Meaning Behind Mysterious Signs, Sequences, and Synchronicities

By *Marie D. Jones* and *Larry Flaxman*

New Page Books
A Division of Career Press
Pompton Plains, NJ

11:11 THE TIME PROMPT PHENOMENON
EDITED AND TYPESET BY GINA TALUCCI
Cover design by Ian Shimkoviak, bookdesigners.com
Printed in the U.S.A.

To order this title, please call toll-free 1-800-CAREER-1 (NJ and Canada: 201-848-0310) to order using VISA or MasterCard, or for further information on books from Career Press.

The Career Press, Inc., 220 West Parkway, Unit 12
Pompton Plains, NJ 07444
www.careerpress.com
www.newpagebooks.com

Library of Congress Cataloging-in-Publication Data

Jones, Marie D., 1961-
    11:11 : the time prompt phenomenon : the meaning behind mysterious signs, sequences, and synchronicities / by Marie D. Jones and Larry Flaxman.
        p. cm.
    Includes bibliographical references (p.   ) and index.
    ISBN 978-1-60163-047-6
    1. Symbolism of numbers. 2. Coincidence. I. Flaxman, Larry. II. Title.

BF1623.P9J63 2009
133.3'35--dc22

                                                    2008044103

To Mary Essa and Max

Acknowledgments

Marie and Larry would like to thank Lisa Hagan, agent extraordinaire, friend, and ally, for her unwavering belief in our work. Also, to Michael Pye, Laurie Kelly-Pye, and the entire staff at New Page Books; we are honored to be a part of your amazing roster of authors, and look forward to more books with you! Thanks to our dear friend and Web guru Suzanne Weaver for creating an incredible online presence for us and putting up with our constant changes and requests! Thanks also to the wonderful staff at Warwick Associates; especially Diana and Simon, for helping us get the book into the right hands!

Marie would like to thank:

My mom, Milly, and my dad, John, for their continued support, love, and input in my life. Thanks to my sis, Angella, and my bro, John, and to my extended family: Winnie, Efren, and kin; Alana (and Robin, too!); Aaron; the Avakians; The LaContes; the back-East contingency; and especially to MomMom who is watching over me when she is not gambling in that big casino in the sky. To my friends, colleagues, and cheerleaders: Andrea Glass, Marit Flowers, Ron Jones and his family, Jeeni Criscenzo, John True, Nick Redfern, Lisa Collazo of writewhatyouknow.com, Ginger Voight (you GO girlfriend!), the gang at "Finding Your Voice," my PDSD colleagues, my longtime pal Helen "Sparkle" Cooper (we sold our souls for THIS?), and all the rest of you who know exactly who you are. Thanks to everyone who has ever listened to me on the radio, e-mailed me with support, and, best of all, paid for one of my books! Thanks most of all to my number one guy, Max, who is my reason for being, and to my friend and partner Larry Flaxman for going with me on this amazing roller-coaster ride. May our partnership flourish and grow, now that we've proven we can meet a deadline!

Larry would like to thank:

My mom, Sheila, for inspiring my thirst for knowledge, encouraging me to follow my dreams, and instilling my love for the literary arts. My dad, Norman, for his fatherly advice, sage opinions, and pushing me to be the best that I can be in every facet of my life. My brother, Jon, for always being there for me, and providing comic relief when called upon. Thanks to my wife, Emily, for being supportive, understanding, and putting up with my various hobbies, interests, and pursuits. Dodo, for being, well, Dodo. Thank you to all of my ARPAST friends and colleagues—you guys and gals are truly like my second family! To all of the friends, fans, and even critics that I have gained in this field—thank you! You folks keep me grounded, vigilant, and on my toes. The most important thank you goes to my beautiful daughter, Mary Essa (aka "The Honey"). I never imagined that a smile or laugh could bring me such happiness. It seems that every time my eyes would start to glaze over from writing, you would "page" me from your room with that angelic voice calling "Dada." I love you so much—you truly have me wrapped around your little finger! And last but certainly not least, thank you to my dear friend and partner Marie Jones for writing *PSIence*, believing in my abilities, and undertaking this exciting adventure with me. It's going to be a hell of a ride!

Contents

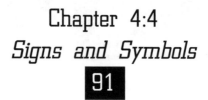

INTRODUCTION

The Measure of Reality

Throughout recorded history, human beings have had a predilection for names. From the earliest cave art to the baubles of modern civilization, we define our existence by giving names to things. Words, categories, and identities are built upon these names. It is these names that fundamentally create and manifest our reality—or at least the superficial illusion of reality. Through this perpetual process we become the words that we use to describe our lives and ourselves. We become our stories, and our stories become us.

However, beneath the words and names, beneath the images we create to make ourselves stand out from others, and beneath the perceptions and opinions that serve as the structure of our reason for being alive, there are numbers...countless, boundless numbers.

From the day we were born, our entrance long ago plotted in the stars and given cosmic significance that will shape our future destiny, we take on the power of numbers and make them our own. Or, perhaps, the greater truth is that numbers take us on.

We live according to times, dates, and measurements. We exist because of intricate resonances that come together in mathematically miraculous ways to create our genetic coding. We function by the clock and the calendar. We define our goals and regrets by the age of our bodies, the number of years we have been alive, and the number of candles that burn upon our birthday cake each year. As we have acknowledged the importance of names, numbers have likewise become fundamental to our reality. Our personal and collective destinies as humans are rife and rampant with the significance and proliferation of numbers. Yet it is not just numbers that seem to be at the heart of the invisible grid of reality upon which we move and exist. There are also sequences, patterns, equations, and even synchronicities of time and space that move into a common and mathematically determined rate of vibration in order to open a new dimension of reality...or perhaps allow a new, clarified perception of the reality, which we are already experiencing.

Times. Dates. Measurements.

Sacred geometry is at the heart of many of our most esoteric systems of ancient knowledge—from the building of the pyramids to the construction of chapels according to power points (ley lines) along the lines of the earth that appear to be aligned with some otherworldly pattern of amazing mystical precision. Who designed this pattern? Where did it come from? Did these creators have a name for them?

Who Thought Up the Math?

Even today, science is all about numbers, whether we speak of the biology of species, or the mechanisms by which an earthquake shatters a slip-strike fault after years of increasing pressure. Whether attempting to explain the physics of a black hole or the rate at which emerging disease becomes pandemic, there seems to be something mystical—something almost "paranormal"—about the utterly profound role of numbers and patterns in nature. From the microcosmic world of subatomic particles to the massive and violent creation/destruction dance of the cosmos, numbers are integral to our scientific understanding and perceptual reality.

Even our own consciousness appears to be intimately linked to numbers and patterns. After all, as above, so below. As without, so within.

In this book, the authors desire to take you, the reader, on an amazing and exhilarating journey into an area of the unknown where few have explored. Due to the fact that we are constantly being bombarded with numbers and patterns, have we become immune or indifferent to them? Do we take these special signs for granted?

Many of the concepts and hypotheses that we will discuss are, in fact, theory, speculation, and conjecture. However, taken in totality, it is food for thought that will hopefully lead you to an even greater understanding of who we are, how we came to be, and what our ultimate purpose may be. Intriguingly, but perhaps not surprisingly, numbers play a key role in determining all three.

We guarantee you that when all is said and done, and the book has been read from cover to cover, you will likely never think of numbers the same way again.

And you shouldn't, because as Pythagoras said, "All is number."

All is number.

—Pythagoras

CHAPTER 1:1

Wake-Up Calls From Beyond

> *There is divinity in odd numbers,*
> *either in nativity, chance, or death.*
> —William Shakespeare

The first couple of times it happened, Mary (not her real name) thought it little more than just sheer coincidence. For the past several months at exactly the same time—11:11p.m.—Mary awoke to experience what some would call a paralysis episode.

During these frightening incidents, Mary felt herself physically bound to her bed—almost as if there was an unseen force holding her down against her will. Try as she might, she was unable to open her eyes or move. Thankfully, this feeling of utter helplessness would shortly subside, although the first time it happened it was all she could do not to scream once the paralysis ended and she was freed from its terrifying grip.

The next few times it happened, Mary surrendered and allowed the experience to run its course, while wondering what it might mean. What was it trying to tell her? Finally, the seventh time she awakened to 11:11 on her alarm clock, she managed to open her eyes during the paralysis episode, and saw a dark, shadowy figure standing at the foot of her bed. Somehow intuitively sensing it was not there to harm her, Mary asked it to identify itself. The figure was silent for a moment, and then Mary clearly heard a deep, male voice inside her head simply say, "Your guardian spirit."

Mary never saw that spirit again, but the experience remained a part of her life from then on, prompting her to feel watched over, guided, and even inspired through some tough challenges she would face. Whenever she saw 11:11 from that point on, whether on a clock face, or just the number 11 on a park bench ad or billboard, she would know, in her heart, she was cared for.

Intriguing scenarios similar to Mary's experience are being reported throughout the world. People of all cultures, beliefs, and attitudes are waking up at the same time each night, or noticing a nearby clock at exactly the same moment each day, far too many times for it to be simply coincidence. For many, these "wake-up prompts" lead to unusual, often mystical or paranormal experiences. Many have reported the appearance of an angelic being, a spirit guide that readily imparts some personal wisdom or insight. Others have recounted the vision of a loved one who has passed from this world. For some, these seemingly prescient experiences can be life changing.

11:11

One of the most popular and widely reported time prompts seems to occur predominately at 11:11 a.m. or p.m. It has been theorized by some that this time prompt may be associated with a type of transformational portal or doorway that opens during this period, a "thinning" of the veil between worlds, if you will. This hypothesis posits that contact with a completely separate level of awareness, consciousness, or reality may be somehow accessed during these times.

To those who have actually experienced the 11:11 phenomenon, they believe the numbers are saying something else: "Pay attention!"

The vast majority of phenomenological instances, however, don't seem to involve anything at all beyond the annoyingly repetitive synchronicity. We, the authors, put the word out about this subject matter to a wide variety of our sources. We invited people to send us their anecdotes of time prompts, as well as their experiences with synchronistic or repeating numbers. Within a very short span of time, the responses started to pour in. People from all walks of life seem to have had these occurrences and wanted to tell their stories. Their experiences transcend all educational, socioeconomic, and religious boundaries. One commonality is that all expressed a desire to better understand why this was happening.

"I wake up every night at the same time, sometimes 11:11 p.m., sometimes 1:11 a.m., 2:22 a.m., 3:33 a.m.," a geophysicist told us. When asked if anything unusual occurred, he said no, but that the very circumstances intrigued him. Was the brain triggering this, or some outside source?

Others reported the exact same circumstances, even down to looking at clocks throughout the day and noticing the time to be 11:11 a.m., 1:11 p.m., and on and on. Each time they looked, they became "aware" of the synchronistic pattern, but did not really understand what was behind it. Is it sheer coincidence? Is the brain acting as an inner alarm clock, or prompt?

One woman told us, "I have this problem and it really IS becoming a problem…I don't even wear a watch anymore; I'm always looking at the clock at 11:11 a.m./p.m. and 1:11 a.m./p.m. I'll even wake up just to look at the clock at 1:11 a.m.…It's getting worse, too. Last night I woke up at 1:11 a.m., 2:22 a.m., and 3:33 a.m.!" Similar to this woman, many people reported an apparent increase in these prompts, not to mention their confusion and outright annoyance about them.

Another woman named Paige reported:

Since you brought time prompts to my attention, I have been noticing how much I always glance at the clock at 13 past the hour. I know a lot of people are superstitious when it comes to 13, but I never really have been. Instead, I'm the type who has researched why that became an unlucky number and after my research, I actually feel it is ridiculous to have triskaidekaphobia.

My notice of its reoccurring on clocks (daily—several times) and in other places, such as it being the preferred volume setting in my car to one of the sections I am always assigned to at work has to do with my grandfather (the same one I believe visited me after his death). One of his favorite stories was about 13 being his lucky number because he was drafted into the navy to serve in WWII on the 13th (of January— I believe). I always told him that was ridiculous, most people would not see the day they were drafted to go off to war as their lucky day, but he did. He claimed that it changed his life for the better because it offered new opportunities that he would not have had otherwise. Considering the rush of bad luck I feel I've had lately with my some of my decisions, I often wonder if maybe he's trying to send me a message that I'm on the right track, but this has been going on for years. I guess now I just wonder if there is something more to it.

Another person named Cinde had much to say about these prompts.

First of all, I try very hard NOT to follow man's time. To me, clocks and the structure of time were created by man to control man, and I simply do not want to be controlled by anyone. I do have to follow it for work, however. The rest of the time, I try to simply go by natural time. No clock required.

I work the second shift. So I'm up pretty late. And because of this stupid phenomenon, I don't sleep well at night. I tend to wake up at 11:11 p.m. (on my night's off), followed by 1:11 a.m. Sometimes, but not always, it will continue with 2:22, 3:33, and so on. But that is rare.

As a result of not sleeping well, I tend to snooze in the mornings, relaxing, cat napping, and watching TV until I FEEL it's time to get up. When do I get this "feeling"? 11:11 a.m. I'll get up, do what I have to do, and hang around until it's time to get ready for work. I have an alarm set for 1:30, since I have to leave by 2. But it never fails, I will look at the clock early, and it's usually 1:11.

When I'm at work, and the third shift comes in to take over, and I turn the machine over to them at 11:11 p.m. Every night, same time. Just works out that way. By the time I get home, and settled in for the night, it's 1:11 a.m. when I look at the clock. Then the cycle starts over again. At this point, I think it has become a habit to look at the clock at these times, but it's not just the clocks I have trouble with. And there doesn't seem to be a reason for it. The number 11 pops up quite a bit in my life. I was born on the 11th. The house I grew up in was numbered 1101. When I lived in Florida, my mailbox was number 11, even though my address was 5508. My license plate has two 11s in it. (I can't wait to see what I get when I change to my Kansas plates!) When I moved out here, I made a deliberate effort to get an apartment that did NOT have any 11s in the address. I live on 118th street, which is a bit of a stretch for this theory, but there it is. The weirdest part about my new address is, after I signed the lease, I drove around to look at my new apartment, along with the location and view. I was startled to see that each building was numbered. Although they were numbered with the address of the building (9607, 9608, and so on) each building had another number assigned to it. Guess which building I'm in? Yup, number 11.

The more people we spoke with, the more we came to realize that these stories all seem to share common, recurring traits. Is there a scientifically objective reason why the time prompt phenomenon seems so incredibly common? From a statistical standpoint, it would seem patently obvious that there was some type of connective correlation.

One man found it more than sheer coincidence that he was born on November 7th (11/7) and his sister was born nine years later on July 11th (7/11), as if they were "twins born nine years apart." Another woman marveled at the fact that she was hospitalized three times throughout the course of three years, and each time was put in Room 209, which adds up to 11.

A gentleman from India on one public Internet forum reported a series of surprising extended encounters with the number 11 in one day. First, his medical expenses from a minor accident totaled $11,111. The number of his hospital room was 1111. The date of the accident itself was November 11th (11/11). The man even reported going to a bookstore later that day and finding mention of the 11:11 phenomenon by accident! Another man, on a public 11:11 message forum reported that "today was such a great day. I saw 11:11 and moments after a VW bug with personal plates reading "nmaste9" just made me grin from ear to ear...."

Another member lamented, "Last night when I switched the TV off, I glanced at the clock: 10:10. As I snuggled into bed ready to sleep, I glanced at the bedtime clock: 11:11. I slept though the 6 a.m. alarm this morning—the time I awoke? 06:06. When I went to rewind a videotape this morning, containing a number of programs taped from the night before, I happened to notice the cumulated time on the digital display: 4:44:44. I did some photocopying on my morning tea break—the amount left on my photocopy card when I finished? $8.88. And I happened to glance at my computer clock as I started typing this piece: 11:11."

On another online message board, one person reported "Everyday of my life it seems I see, 1:11, 2:11, 3:11, 4:11, 5:11, 6:11, 7:11, 8:11, 9:11, 10:11, 11:11, 12:11. I was born on 4/11/89; I've been seeing 11:11 for quite some time now and I know there is no way it can be a coincidence; I have so many unusual 11:11 stories...." One of the more intriguing reports: "One of my sightings that really stands out is walking past two boys wearing bright red football shirts. As I turned around to look back at them (don't know why I did) they both had number 11 on their backs! "

Over at AngelScribe.com, readers post their stories of encounters with invisible angels at such times as 11:11, 2:22, and so on.

"Last night as I pulled into my driveway, I looked down at my mileage and it read 11,111.1! Weird! Than (sic) I woke up this morning at 2:22 a.m.! This is just getting too weird! Those angels are working their magic!"

■

"In the summer of 1978 I began seeing 1111. I also see 111, 222, 333, and so on. Sometimes I'll wake in the middle of the night at exactly 1:11. These numbers have appeared on boxes, license plates, house numbers, friends addresses, phone numbers, totals at the grocery store."

■

"Hi, I was playing slingo...looked at the score...it was 11100 and the time was 11:01. Those angels—I saw them everywhere today!"

■

"I woke up at 11:11 last night! I had only been asleep a short time! This morning I was outside with my granddaughter and she said she wanted to go in! Weird, she never wants to go in! LOL...so we went in and sat in the rocking chair and turned a video on...I noticed that the time on the VCR and cable box was 11:11! I love the little reminders...makes my day go so much better!"

Time Prompts

Are these all just simple coincidences? After all, numbers can and do repeat, and even take on patterns. They cannot help but do so, especially those digits under 20, which are such an integral element of our lives. Driver's licenses, phone numbers, house numbers, special anniversary dates, birthdates, ages.... As we shall see in a later chapter, there are simple reasons why numbers "do what they do." However, with that being said, in the case of some time prompt reports, there definitely seems to be more to the story than just odd luck or random happenstance.

We found this simple and rational explanation for time prompts on a public Website forum.

The concept of an easily recognized number pattern (for example, 1234) is already explained in the Website. All I have to add about this is a Psychology 101 jargon, called "chunking." Basically, our brain could only hold "x" number of items in our short-term memory; from the idiot to the genius, it's about five to nine items respectively, which is not a whole lot. So, to increase our brain capacity for storing things, we tend to use this mechanism called "chunking"—which basically means putting like items together. The perfect everyday example is our phone numbering system; a typical phone number (in Canada) with area code, if we remember it, would make us look like geniuses! For example, a hypothetical phone number, 6134789890, by itself would exceed our five to nine items of maximum capacity, because there are 10 digits all together. Of course, any idiot can remember a phone number once in a while, especially if it's from some hot chick or guy! The reason is because we "chunk" the numbers by area code and then by three digits dash four digits together. So, visually we see 613-478-9890. In essence, the total number of items we are remembering is only three items. Similar explanations can be applied to things such as acronyms (that is, CIA, FBI, FEMA, and so on) to help people remember useless things, such as government agencies. The digits 12:34 or 11:11 displayed on a digital clock is instinctively chunked as one item, while more randomized times such as 11:56 or 3:48 and so on have no real obvious pattern, so it is not being chunked by our brain, which makes it about three to four items. Obviously, the fewer the items the easier it is to remember.

Although the brain does seem to possess the ability to create and recognize patterns, we still have to wonder why so many people report the *same* numbers and sequences over and over again. "Chunking" certainly applies to our everyday brain functions and our ability to organize thoughts and patterns; remember numbers, addresses, and amounts; and do many other useful things we need to do. But it still does not take into account the sheer numbers of people chunking the same numbers over and over again.

Not everyone's experiences can be ascribed to harmless episodes. Angelic beings or transformational epiphanies are but one piece of the puzzle. There have been numerous reports of wake-up codes and time prompts involving people seeing or sensing sinister or demonic entities. These figures were not only terrifyingly real to them, but also appeared within the seeming safety of their own homes. Individuals have also experienced frightening sleep paralysis, appalling or shocking images, and even seemingly precognitive visions of a horrific event that has not yet occurred. One such a post on GreatDreams.com spoke of 11:11 as "a warning."

Every time I saw 11:11, something bad ALWAYS happened to me! After a while I became scared...now, well, I'm just used to it and at least I can predict WHEN something is going to go wrong. Is it just a warning for me, or are the numbers causing me the bad luck? I haven't worked that much out yet. The last time I saw 11:11 was about a week ago. Most times, something bad happens within 24 hours.... The majority of the time it meant I was going to have a bad argument with my boyfriend (who's name has 11 letters).

Within the context of the 11:11 experience, you may be surprised to learn that not every interest group focuses on the new age concepts of enlightenment, transformation, and the shift of conscious awareness. One Yahoo forum, perhaps appropriately titled "End Times 11:11," spotlights the Judeo-Christian concept of the apocalypse and the Second Coming, in terms of the 11:11 phenomenon. The Western religious belief system tends to see these time prompts in a little more sinister light, due to the preexisting notion that supernatural events of ANY kind are not considered holy or divine, but rather the workings of darker entities out to fool or misguide humans.

There is even a Yahoo group for kids interested in 11:11! Not to be outdone, MSN offers its own active 11:11 forum, where many members await the year 2012 and post their experiences and theories regarding how the two phenomena may be inextricably linked. Interestingly, the more of these posts one reads, the more "similar" the experiences sound. Perhaps the experiencer is the only one privy to the depth or meaning of the event?

We found it difficult to find actual salient examples of people having major, life-altering experiences during or resulting from a time prompt event. Certainly, many of these people did sense the presence of something good, or maybe even not so good, such as angels, guardian spirits, or even demons. But there is little if anything to suggest that these connections, and experiences, were anything other than subjective interpretation—the human imagination searching for meaning outside of itself. Some who do experience these prompts will argue that life-altering experiences are not the ultimate goal anyway. Rather, these time prompts are just little prods and urges to compel us to wake up and take notice of the bigger picture.

Time

From a young age, we are taught that our world is dictated by the constructs of time. Our parents probably instilled within all of us the importance of being "on time," as well as recognizing the importance of time management.

Digital clocks and watches tell us the time of day or night quickly and conveniently. When one sees time in a visual manner, there can be no question as to its meaning. However, according to the thousands of people posting on online forums and meeting up at 11:11 gatherings, these clocks may also tell us the time on a completely different level of reality—a level of which we are neither cognizant nor receptive to on a normal basis.

Time itself is an illusion made up of numbers. The concept of time is an artificially created reality in which individual digits combine to tell us where we are located along the landscape of the fourth dimension. Perhaps the time prompt experience is strictly a latent biological one. Perhaps there truly is no ultimate goal.

But why do the same digits seem to be involved in these enigmatic wake-up calls? What does the number 11 signify? And why are so many other time prompts reported, such as 2:22, 3:33, 4:44, and so on? Does each time have its own special significance? Is the repetition significant in itself?

The Number 11...Coincidence?

Perhaps not surprisingly, the number 11 seems to be the most frequently reported. The number 11 is a double digit, considered a Master/Power Number in numerological belief systems. The number 11 is commonly thought to represent visionary ideals, intuition, idealism, revelation, and artistic and inventive genius. This sacred number also allegedly carries a balance of female/male energies and properties. The number 22, the result of 11 + 11, is a Master or Masonic number. Some metaphysicians suggest that 11 also may represent the twin strands of human DNA moving into a higher level of conscious awareness.

Even Aristotle is linked to the number 11. His worldview consisted of four spheres that lay beyond the planets, and seven planetary spheres. This combination is evident in the 11 layers of the Chartres labyrinth, which was designed into the floor of the Chartres Cathedral in France before the French Revolution. This maze-like design consists of 11 tracks, or folds, one must walk to reach the center. The number corresponds to this higher ideal of mystical union with a divine pattern, which Dr. Keith Critchlow, author of numerous books on geometry and a leading expert in sacred architecture, interpreted in the paper "Chartres Maze, A Model of the Universe" as "the way in and out of the planetary system" with Earth as the center point.

The Labyrinth at Chartres Cathedral has 11 folds that correspond with a higher worldview of the planetary system, and Earth's place within it.

Predictably, conspiracy theorists have had a virtual field day with their creative interpretations of current societal events. As might be expected, observable numeric patterns play a significant role in their reasoning and deductive cleverness. Whether or not you believe in numerology (which we will explore more thoroughly in a future chapter), modern history includes certain numeric patterns, which appear to have unusual significance. And where there is coincidental smoke, there is someone determined to find the cause, and fan the flames.

Look at the back of a $100 dollar bill; you may never have noticed it before, but if you count the windows on the smaller buildings (not including doors) to the right and left of the main part of Independence Hall, it adds up to 11 and 11. Is this part of some grand conspiracy to ingrain this mysterious number in our brains? A message from some secret society? Or could it be just plain dumb luck?

Coincidence or not, the windows on either side add up to 11, a most mysterious number that seems to hold some meaning for many people. Image courtesy of U.S. Federal Reserve

September 11th

The dramatic events of September 11, 2001 will forever be ingrained in the hearts and minds of our nation. Before our country even had time to fully process the extent of what happened, almost immediately, the rumor mill cranked up full force. Whether you believe the official but tenuous government version, or espouse one of the multitudes of alternative scenarios, the number 11 seems to occur with astonishing frequency. Some of the more profound "coincidences" regarding the event:

- 9/11/01—September 11th terrorist attacks on New York City.

- Mohammed's birth is celebrated on the 11th day of the ninth month.

- September 11th is the 254th day of the year: 2 + 5 + 4 = 11.

- After September 11th, there are 111 days left to the end of the year.

- The number of stories in each World Trade Center building was 110 and 110. Remember that zero "0" is not a number, so we have 11:11.

- There were 21,800 windows total. 2 + 1 + 8 + 0 + 0 = 11.

- The third building to fall (#7) had 47 stories. 4 + 7=11.

- The first plane to impact the towers was Flight 11.

- The phone number for American Airlines is 1-800-245-0999 (1 + 8 + 0 + 0 + 2 + 4 + 5 + 0 + 9 + 9 + 9 = 4 + 7 = 11).

- The State of New York was the 11th State added to the Union.

- New York City has 11 letters.

- Flight 11 had 92 people on board. 9 + 2 = 11.

- Flight 11 had 11 crew members.

- Flight 77 had 65 people on board. 6 + 5 = 11.

- The Flight 11 call letters were AA11: A = 1, A = 1, AA = 11.

- The suspected base of the terrorists is Afghanistan, which is 11 letters.

- Osama bin Laden's birthplace is Saudi Arabia, which is 11 letters.

- On September 7, 2002, NYC medical examiners announced the revised official death toll from the World Trade Center attacks was 2,801 (2 + 8 + 0 + 1 = 11).

Uri Geller, the well-known psychic, had a lot to say about the number 11 immediately after the terrorist's cowardly attacks on 9/11. He posted many of his assumptions on his Website. Some are as follows:

- The date of the attack—9/11. 9 + 1 + 1 = 11.

- *119 is the area code to Iraq/Iran (1 + 1 + 9 = 11).

- The Twin Towers side by side looked like the number 11.

- Names that have 11 letters: Air Force One, George W. Bush, Bill Clinton, Saudi Arabia, and Colin Powell.

- Afghanistan—11 letters.

- The Pentagon—11 letters.

Adding Up 11:11

Geller's Website is filled with mysteries about the number 11, namely 11:11. "If you multiply 1111 by 1111 you get 1234321, representing a pyramid, and the number 11 is a sacred number of the pyramid with the proportions of the great pyramid being of the ratio 7:11. 11 is also a number harmonious with pi. Therefore, it seems that the number 11 is of central importance in understanding the mathematical infrastructure of the universe." This same pyramid effect can be seen if you multiply 111,111,111 by 111,111,111; you get 12,345,678,987,654,321. Geller also asks us to take note of the fact that many famous people have 11 letters in their names (including one of the authors of this book!): Fidel Castro, Genghis Khan, Leon Trotsky, Harry Truman, Keanu Reeves, and so on."

Geller goes on to state that 11 and the appearances of 11:11 in people's lives may be all about learning to think outside of the box. "11:11 does not allow you to forget about the larger questions because it is always popping back into your reality, acting as a catalyst to distract our consciousness away from the sublime and onto something far more challenging."

Intuitive Solara, author of *11:11—Inside the Doorway*, agrees, stating that the endless reoccurrences of times that include the digits 0 and 1 represent a "positive connection and a gateway to the mysteries of the universe and beyond." But then, why would something so positive be associated with the worst act of terrorism on U.S. shores in our lifetimes? Are we simply applying any explanation we can find to the repetition of a particular number, whether it all makes sense or not?

Not all believe Geller's magic. Such pessimists as those at Skepdic.com note that so many more elements surrounding the events of 9/11 do not add up to that mysterious number. As they point out on their Website:

- There were 19 hijackers (1 + 9 = 10).

- One plane was a 767 (7 + 6 + 7 = 20).

- One plane was a 757 (7 + 5 + 7 = 19).

- Pennsylvania and Washington, D.C., both have 12 letters.

- None of the following have 11 letters: Osama Bin Laden, Pentagon, Taliban, World Trade Center, Iraq, Iran, Pakistan, jihad, and the names of eight of the other hijackers.

Perhaps Geller and others are guilty of what has been termed "confirmation bias" or selective thinking—coincidences that fall into the Law of Truly Large Numbers, which we will discuss more in depth in a later chapter. One could easily speculate that on any given day, at any specific time, there will be plenty of coincidental occurrences. Imagine the number of these occurrences spread out throughout the course of many decades, centuries, or millennia!

So, why do so many people continue to report strange events associated with 11:11? One must keep in mind that it is not just clocks displaying these mysterious digits. People have reported seeing them appear on phone number read-outs, license plates, and any other known source of numeric display. It seems almost evident that the wake-up call is intended for a mass audience; a mass "awakening" on a truly global scale.

According to the Website 1111spiritguardians.com, people have also reported bizarre physical anomalies during these time prompts. Such unexplained phenomena as lights turning on and off when they pass by, doorbells ringing when there is no one there, and traffic lights changing at will. The theory supported here involves the Akashic Construct, a theoretical level of reality in which people can purportedly make contact with their personal spirit guides and experience interactions with them (sometimes rather mischievous interactions!). Interestingly, this theory seems to coincide with the supposed Akashic Records prophesized by healer and visionary Edgar Cayce. Cayce claimed that he was able to mentally access these records of "life information" to procure necessary medical information during client readings. If true, this also suggests a possible connection to the Zero Point Field (ZPF). Within the framework of quantum and theoretical physics, the ZPF is a self-regenerating field of energy that is believed to contain within it all matter—formed and unformed. Although the Zero Point Field still lies within the realm of speculation and conjecture, scientists and scholars continue to debate its veracity.

Midwayers

One popular theory points to the mischief of 1,111 angels or spirit guardians called "Midwayers." These angels supposedly have the special job of assisting people as they progress through life. One man, George Barnard, has declared himself to be their original human member. Mr. Barnard claims to have been working with these celestial guides for nearly 60 years. His experiences are documented in *From the Desk of George Barnard*, and have created a loyal following of Midwayers. His supporters look to the year 2012 as the wake-up end date, to which these prompts seem to be alerting us and moving us toward. Many people on the popular 11:11 Web forums do indeed seem to have visitations, or imagined ones at the very least, from what they deem guardians or ascended beings out to help them, guide them, and direct their very steps.

According to the Website, the Midwayers seem to interpret different time prompts to mean different things:

- 11:10 means "we want to talk with you" and that a lesson will be imparted.

- 11:11 means "Hello" from a Midwayer.

- 11:12 means data has been "uploaded," and will surface when needed in the conscious mind.

Barnard has offered some suggestions as to why he believes that certain people receive prompts and others do not. On his Website, he states that perhaps some people are more intrinsically "tuned" or receptive to the prompts. Another supposition that Barnard has presented is that a person's unique skills or abilities appeal to the guides and can be utilized for higher purposes.

The aforementioned implications seem to give meaning to the "reminder calls," as George Barnard so eloquently labeled them. Furthermore, it may also indicate which levels of Midwayers are making contact. Barnard and others have stated their belief that we are all genetically capable of contact with these celestial beings. Integral to this belief is the idea that, at some point, data that will help us through the coming transformation will be somehow "loaded" into our conscious mind.

The 2012 Connection

Barnard's predictions may possibly be directly linked to the coming year of 2012, when many people expect either an end of times, or a new beginning. The Mayan Calendar, upon which the end date of December 21st, 2012, is derived, suggests that something significant is going to occur at 11:11 a.m. on that very same date. Many theories have been presented regarding 2012, however, until the date actually occurs, they are all speculative. Will human life as we know it cease to exist? Will we experience some type of cosmic portal? Will there be a profound global shift in human consciousness?

As many would anticipate, in the year preceding 2012, there likely will be a tremendous surge of interest and attention paid to the evolution of consciousness—as if people are gearing up for the "final showdown" of 12/21/2012. (Which also adds up to 11!) For some, January 1, 2011 (1/1/11) and November 11 of the same year (11/11/11) are key points of acceleration toward the great year. Big parties are already being planned, so be sure to mark your calendars!

Another interesting 2012 connection, albeit this one to the year 2013, comes from an AOL Members site called "Seeing is Believing." The site's author concludes that the 11:11 prompts are actually related to the timing of the end of the zodiacal Age of Pisces and entering the Age of Aquarius. The formula is quite confusing and hard to follow, and involves dividing, adding, and multiplying specific numbers to represent minutes, hours, and years to arrive at the final end date, but it is one of many examples of people using creative means to link 11:11 to the Mayan Calendar end date.

Using the symbolism of Pisces as fish, as well as its link to Jesus, the "fisher of men," the author supposed that the Age of Pisces began with Jesus' birth—Year 0. I realize that there is no Year 0 and that it begins in Year 1; however, my reasoning is that Jesus was 0 (not 1) when he was born and did not turn 1 until a full year later on his 1st birthday. So take the Age of Pisces being 2,160 years and convert that into a clock format as follows:

- 12 hours = 2,160 years.

- 1 hour = 2,160 / 12 = 180 years.

- 1:00 = 180 AD; 2:00 = 360 AD; 3:00 = 520 AD, and so on.

- 11:00 = 1980. Continuing with this train of thought, if 11:00 began in 1980, when is 11:11?

- 1 hour = 180 years.

- 1 minute = 180 years / 60 = 3 years.

- 11 minute = 3 years × 11 = 33 years.

- 1980 + 33 years = 2013.

- 11:00 = 1980.

- 11:11 = 2013.

Again, a confusing, yet enigmatic connection to the coming end of the Mayan Calendar. Are we indeed in the 11th hour?

Interestingly, George Barnard does not buy into the 11:11/2012 connection. He argues that if there were truly a connection, then people would be getting a 20:12 time prompt. That is a fair supposition, however, the time predicted for the ascension to occur is widely considered to be 11:11 a.m. GMT. Barnard believes that the "spiritual uplift" that seems to be occurring now on our planet is acting as a communications beacon. This autonomous signal has been steadfastly calling for literally billions of celestial beings to come to our assistance (but that out of tribute to the original 1,111, they continue to use the 11:11 wake-up prompts) and that "well over a million folks are being given these 11:11 prompts." Perhaps these will be the chosen ones to lead the rest of the population into a new age of existence? This is certainly not a new idea, as the New Age movement has had the long-standing belief that alien guides are here to bring us out of the apocalyptic pit of human destiny—a destiny at which we seem to be plunging toward rapidly.

Doorways

11:11 has also been associated with the concept of Light Workers. These are a supposed group of individuals who all share the gift of physical and spiritual healing, and who, on some forums, seem to believe that the time has come (thus the time prompts) for Light Workers of every background to raise their own consciousness, increase their healings, and bring even more light to the world. This is similar to the theory proposed by Solara, whose book *11:11: Inside the Doorway* suggests that 11:11 sightings not only occur during times of heightened awareness, but are intended to have a powerful effect upon us by "activating" our cellular memory banks and reminding us of something long forgotten.

Solara writes "11:11 is a pre-encoded trigger placed within our cellular memory banks prior to our decent into matter, which, when activated, signifies that our time of completion is near. The 11:11 is hereby being activated." She goes on to explain the origins of 11:11 and its purveyors, the many lucky souls who have been awakened from the first Doorway of the 11:11 activation, which she claims occurred on December 31, 1986, followed by the Harmonic Convergence of 1987, the Earth Link of 1988, and the last big Activation of Earth Day, 1990. Apparently, the big opening of the Doorway started on January 11, 1992, and is set to close 20 years from that date. She states, "The Doorway of the 11:11 opens once and closes once. Only One may pass through. This One is our Unified Presence, the Many as One. The 11:11 opened on January 11, 1992, and closes on December 31, 2011."

During this time, presently incarnate beings called "Star-Borne" (who supposedly originate somewhere beyond Earth) will begin to serve in the ongoing "transmutation of matter" and assist the planet and humanity through this period of activated "remembering." We, Solara states, will go through the Eleven Energy Gates, which are "stepping-up stations to new plateaus of awareness."

The book describes a very detailed vision of this process, during which we will all receive our "sealed orders," encoded within our cellular memory until the time of revelation is upon us. As these orders are unsealed, we will all remember whom we are and where we came from, and thus move toward what Solara believes is the true "Oneness" of reality.

DNA

One of the most widely suggested methods of how this great collective ascension might occur involves the coding of human DNA itself. As scientists have discovered, our genetic memory is encoded within our DNA. Similar to the numeric codes we live by in our daily lives, our DNA is programmed to trigger evolutionary developments that determine our physical makeup.

Geneticists have often wondered about the significant amount of "junk DNA," lurking within us, which appears to have no obvious purpose. According to molecular biologists, 95 to 98 percent of our DNA contains largely unknown functionality. Although presently unidentified, there may actually be a significant latent purpose. Scientists have found that the sequence of nucleotides in the DNA is not random—it bears a striking resemblance to the structure of human language! Recent experiments conducted by Russian scientist Dr. Peter Gariaev, who is a pioneering researcher of fractal genetics, indicates that some important aspects of gene regulation may actually be mediated at a quantum level: "It appears that the languages we were looking for, are, in fact, hidden in the 98 percent 'junk' DNA contained in our own genetic apparatus. The basic principle of these languages is similar to the language of holographic images based on principles of laser radiations of the genetic structures which operate together as a quasi-intelligent system, as it is particularly important to realize that our genetic devices actually perform real processes which supplement the triplet model of the genetic code." This raises some fascinating and intriguing possibilities, which we examine in much more detail in Chapter 10:10.

Peter Gersten, Esq., former director of Citizens Against UFO Secrecy (CAUS) wrote in "My Leap of Faith," his essay contribution to *2013: The End of Days or A New Beginning* about his idea of the 11:11 trigger.

> I believe that physical reality is an illusion—part of an intelligently designed cosmic computer program manifested by digital codes. Sacred geometry, frequency, and vibration define our existence. Our genetic memory is triggered by these digital codes at specific points in

our lives. They awaken the mind to the change and evolution of consciousness. 11:11 is such a code and a metaphor for the various cycles that manifest and re-manifest physical reality as if following a cosmic blueprint. The mystical 11:11 is also renowned for its symbolism—one aspect involving a *cosmic portal*. Most synchronistic is the fact that 11:11 is the exact time of the 2012 Winter Solstice. Could 21 12 2012 be a cosmic computer file with 11:11 being the cosmic equivalent of exe?

If the 11:11 time prompt is going to wake us up, perhaps it will be on a genetic or quantum level. The trigger of the specific time appearing over and over again could be activating the language of this "junk DNA." Perhaps this "gene language" is the key to a higher level of evolutionary development dormant within the human species, and waiting for the proper "key" or event to unlock it.

Could, as some theorists suggest, our DNA also hold the answer to the 11:11 mystery? Might this be why people who experience the 11:11 prompts also report more synchronistic events?

On the popular metaphysical Website Crystalinks.com, 11:11 time prompts are thought of as a digital code. "Physical reality is a consciousness program created by digital codes. Numbers, numeric codes, define our existence. Human DNA, our genetic memory, is encoded to be triggered by digital codes at specific times and frequencies." The author goes on to explain that these codes will awaken the mind to the evolution of consciousness. The idea of consciousness as a program suggests a link to Information Theory (IT), which proposes that the Universe behaves like a giant computer.

Although this hypothesis may seem outlandish, it has garnered a surprising amount of support in the academic, scientific, and New Age circles. We will discuss the IT theory in a later chapter. Although computers operate in bits and bytes, our DNA may be utilizing time prompts and numeric codes as information, which is somehow converted to the "language of the body," which then activates changes in the body and spirit.

Again, many associate this activation with the year 2012, pointing to the Mayan and other Mesoamerican calendars as proof that a great transformation was indeed predicted—nay—expected at this very point in time. Some say that the number 11 metaphorically suggests the spiraling twin strands of DNA ascending into higher consciousness. Others point to the number as a sign of balance, when yin and yang, feminine and masculine energies, will work in harmony as this activation occurs.

11:11

Though as Uri Geller states, if this is something we can look at as being positive, we should. "I believe that people who have constant contact with the 11:11 phenomena have some type of positive mission to accomplish. It is still a mystery to me what it is that we all have to do or why we are all being gathered and connected together, but it is very real and tangible. I feel that it is immensely positive, almost like there is a thinking entity sending us these physical and visual signs from the universe."

The Pineal Gland

Junk DNA may not be the only activating agent in the human body associated with 11:11 and time prompts. Equally as mysterious, the pineal gland may also play a role in the awakening of a higher level of being. This structure is an endocrinal gland located deep within the center of the brain. The pineal gland has long been associated with metaphysical and even supernatural concepts, a sort of "magic" organ that acted as a third eye and elevated our experience above the five senses.

Many scientists once believed this to be a "dormant" gland whose purpose was still a mystery, and was spoken of as the enigmatic Third Eye by many mystical and spiritual traditions. According to lore, this was the window to the soul and the inner vision that parallels the actual eyes as tools of exterior vision. Associated with the crown chakra and the yogic third eye, the pineal gland or "pineal eye" has long been heralded by New Agers and metaphysicians alike as "the most powerful and highest source of ethereal energy available to

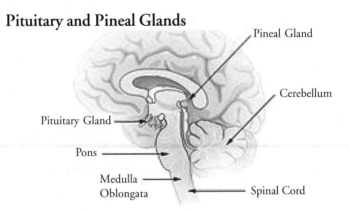

The tiny pineal gland has specific known biological purposes, but still suggests a mysterious and unknown deeper purpose. Image courtesy of Wikipedia.

humans...the pineal gland has always been important in initiating supernatural powers. Development of psychic talents has been closely associated with this organ of higher vision. The third eye can see beyond the physical," as several Websites devoted to the gland collectively state.

Approximately the size of a pea, and weighing no more than 0.1 gram, the pineal gland is shaped like a tiny pinecone and sits behind and just above the pituitary gland, behind the eyes in the vertebrate brain. Once referred to as the "seat of the soul" by Descartes, who suggested it was the link between intellect and the body, this gland actually has a biological purpose, controlling the biorhythms of the body and regulating thirst, sexual drive, metabolism, and the biological processes of aging. It has an eye-like structure and it functions as a light receptor, it controls melatonin and the wake/sleep seasonal functions and patterns, and it was once described as a "vestigial remnant" of a much larger organ. The gland starts out large in children and begins to shrink during puberty. Calcification of the gland in adults is common and leads to visible aging.

More esoteric belief suggests that when the pineal gland is awakened or activated, as during a time prompt or 11:11 experience, there is the feeling of pressure at the base of the brain. This pressure is described as the effect of connecting to higher resonances or frequencies than normally experienced. Thus, the belief by many is that perhaps the time prompts are leading us to the period of awakening in this higher reality, once often associated with increased paranormal activity and psychic abilities. The coming year 2012, with its connection to the end date of the Mayan Long Count Calendar, has been connected with the awakening of the pineal gland in large numbers of humans, causing a huge shift in awareness, consciousness, and perception. "As human beings continue to evolve further out of matter, on the journey from spirit to matter back to spirit, the pineal gland will continue to rise from its state of age-long dormancy, bringing back to humanity astral capacities and spiritual abilities," states the Website Crystalinks.

Whether the pineal gland truly contains these capabilities, as well as being the seat of intuition and inner guidance, is still up for debate. Similar to our alleged junk DNA, once thought to have no purpose, we are now discovering that every part of our body has a purpose, or had one during our evolutionary progress. If this gland is lying dormant, waiting to be awakened en masse, we might indeed see a complete shift in consciousness on a wide scale, leading to what many believe will be the dawning of a new age, possibly the Age of Aquarius and inner enlightenment. If this change occurs, then the outer material world, the one we see with our good, old-fashioned eyes, may suddenly take a back seat to the vision we have of our world with the inner eye.

Finding Proof

Unfortunately, for many who experience the 11:11 time prompts, and those of us researching them, there is little in the way of precise facts to rely on. We primarily have the subjective experiences of those who see these prompts, and whatever accompanying events that occur at the same time. There is no scientific proof, and little in the way of scientific methodology designed to test out these prompts. One would literally have to be present with someone each and every time a prompt occurred, measure their brain and the environmental effects present, and then do it over and over again with thousands of others to see any kind of solid pattern that can "stand up in court." Reproducibility and control are paramount concepts of scientific method, and both would be nearly impossible to maintain in these conditions.

The problem with ALL of the previously mentioned theories is that they are exactly that—theories. By its very definition a theory is an unproved assumption or belief. At the current point of our comprehension, they are just not provable, nor do they hold any scientific merit or legitimacy. Although the lack of scientific value may not matter to those of a more New Age or spiritual belief system, we as authors must ask "is it the event that makes the meaning, or the meaning that makes the event?"

Certainly, time prompts do occur, experienced every day by those alert enough to look at their clocks at just the right time. No one can deny this, just as no one can deny that all over the world, people report experiences with ghosts, UFOs, psychic abilities, and a host of other non-proven, yet pervasive, experiences. Perhaps alertness is the primary key factor. When one is more consciously aware of their environment and surroundings, they are bound to notice a few strange coincidences. Those who pay attention get to see things others might miss out on, just by the sheer fact that they were not focusing their conscious awareness in the right place at the right time.

A perfect example would be purchasing a new car. Ever since you dyed your hair that iridescent shade of pink and bucked mainstream fashion back in high school, you have always thought of yourself as an individual. Following that mindset, it is only natural that your vehicle be indicative of that personality trait. After much deliberation, you finally decide and set your sights on a purple Nissan SUV. You eagerly go to the dealership, and, to your amazement, they have one in stock! After signing the papers, you drive it home...and on the way see at least 50 other purple SUVs. Where the heck did they come from, you wonder? Is it possible that they were always there, but you had never had cause to notice them before? Becoming aware of time anomalies often triggers more of them simply because your level of awareness is raised, and you tend to notice things that you might normally ignore.

A causal link between the year 2012, on the other hand, and the Universal Time of 11:11 a.m. is something that we can prove, simply by waiting for that date to arrive and observing what does, or does not, happen. But for the rest of the "millions" experiencing time prompts, perhaps the significance is not an event that will one day change everything; maybe the significance is far more subtle. Perhaps the lesson to be learned is that we need to wake up to our own lives—pay more attention, and live our dreams regardless of the time on the clock face. Those of a religious bent often proclaim "God works in mysterious ways." Perhaps there is more to this 11:11 story than just fun or annoying coincidences.

It is our sincere hope that when you get through reading this book, you will have a newfound appreciation for numbers, and how they appear to work in strange and mysterious ways. As we shall see, there is far more to numbers than just plain math.

■

The whole is more than the sum of its parts.
—Aristotle (384 BC–322 BC)

CHAPTER

2:2

A World of Numbers

> *The knowledge of numbers is one of the chief distinctions between us and the brutes.*
> —Lady Mary Wortley Montagu

Look around the immediate vicinity. What do you see? Cell phone? Credit card? Remote control? Clock? It is almost a sure bet that something that involves numbers is within your immediate reach. Numbers play an integral role in virtually every aspect of modern existence. Akin to language, the presence of numbers in our daily lives is something that we often simply take for granted. Yet, similar to language itself, numbers are a form of communication on which we have come to rely. Could you imagine a world without numbers?

It would be a veritable impossibility to even attempt to cover the sheer volume of history behind the evolution of various number systems. As a result, we hope to provide you with a basic understanding of where our beloved digits came from, and how they mutated throughout the millennia. This background is necessary to understand just how intertwined with human evolution numbers truly are.

The Beginning of Numbers

From the dawn of time, humankind realized that it needed a way to measure things, to count things, to understand the quantity of things. In the beginning, man desired the need to simply track ownership. From this basic need, numbers were born, and have been utilized in such a manner ever since. Later, the economics of trade and barter necessitated the need for more advanced enumeration systems. Only as time went on, and we as a species evolved, did the basics of numbers evolve into a complicated system of negative, rational, irrational, real, transcendental, complex, computable, and abstract digits, integers, and numeric sequences. Many of these boggle the mind even as they balance the books.

Although there is no authoritative proof of when the utilization of numbers actually began, it is not too hard to imagine the possibility that perhaps the first need for numbers came during an escalating confrontation between two prehistoric Neanderthals. For this particular scenario, let's call these two ancient gentlemen Og and Ug. Og, always the adventurer, found eight apples while exploring, and, being quite hungry, planned to eat them all. But Ug, his erstwhile hunting and gathering partner, was also famished, and demanded his equal share (he had given Og half the berries he had found the day before?). So, Og, being the consummate friend, proceeds to dole out three apples to Ug. Ug senses something is amiss, and has Og put the apples down on the ground, whereby he proceeds to add one more apple to his own pile. Thus, the first act of counting and measuring was born (and a potential caveman smackdown prevented to boot).

Whether or not the aforementioned scenario actually occurred, the first known use of numbers as objects for purposes of counting is said to date back to approximately 30,000 to 40,000 BC, according to scholar Georges Ifrah, author of *The Universal History of Numbers*, when bones and artifacts with distinct "tally marks" have been dated. Prehistoric humans may also have used their basic understanding of numbers to help them track the stars through the sky, divide day and night into time frames, keep tabs on flocks of birds and herds of animals, and even track the growth of their children. Eventually, the crudeness of tally marks upon bone and stone was replaced with far more complex representations, but Ifrah states that tally sticks, as crude as they might seem, were still in use until fairly recently by Native American labor workers.

Ifrah calls tally marks "one-for-one correspondence," which "allows the simplest of minds to compare two collections of beings or things, of the same kind or not, without calling on the ability to count in numbers." For millennia, primitive peoples used this one-for-one correspondence with the things they had available at the time, such as bone and rock. This manner of mapping items requires no real knowledge of mathematics, just the ability to track beings or items and keep a record, which came in handy, Ifrah suggests, for shepherds in charge of how many sheep they took out grazing in the morning as opposed to how many sheep they returned home with that night.

The first known written numbering system, according to Ifrah's book, came to us from the fourth millennium BC in Elam. It was here that the pebble-method of accounting was discovered and used by accountants using "molded, unbaked clay tokens in the place of ordinary or natural pebbles." Each token had a different value representing a unit of one or higher, and even tokens of different shapes represented a specific value, that is, a small pellet might be 10, and a larger rock might be 100.

It is the subject of debate among anthropologists, historians, and mathematicians as to whether disparate cultures developed their own number systems, or the ideas of using numbers was somehow "seeded" from a handful of more technologically advanced cultures, which then spread. Most agree that our own numeric system is based upon the Hindu-Arabic system. The majority of experts also agree that cardinal numbers (1,2,3...) then led to ordinals (1st, 2nd, 3rd, and so on), and may have been the result of using fingers and digits to place objects in a specific order. And you always thought it was a joke about using both hands and feet to count!

Other than the typical crude bone and stone numbers of our cave-dwelling ancestors, the development of numbers seems to have closely paralleled the development of culture, language, and higher knowledge. The oldest of cultures represented numbers with the repeated use of pictorial images to represent a particular object. A good example might be the symbolic representation of three tablets being the alliteration for the word "tablet" repeated three times. Nowhere was this more obvious than in the Egyptian culture, which employed three types of number systems: the hieroglyphic, the hieratic, and the demotic.

Egyptian Numbering Systems

The hieroglyphic is the most widely recognized system, and was often written on stone. Hieroglyphics were not specifically focused on "numbers," as it was a much more formal mode of language. The hieratic, or temple writing, was more commonly used by priests, and was written on papyrus. The demotic system emerged from the hieratic and became the commonplace system of textual writing. Egyptian numbers were written right to left and the numbers 1 through 9 were represented with vertical lines or strokes. Higher numbers were represented by more symbolic shapes, such as the coil of rope for 100, and the man with upraised arms for 1,000,000 (this makes sense, for who would NOT raise up their arms upon receipt of 1,000,000 objects!).

Sumerian Numbers

The ancient Sumerians and Babylonians adopted the use of symbols to represent numeric groupings. The Sumerians, using the base-60, or sexagesimal, system, actually only had two numbers to deal with, 1 and 10, and all other digits combined the two symbols accordingly. Early Babylonians, using both the base-10 and base-60 systems, developed a series of vertical strokes and triangular shapes to indicate both low and high numbers. Amounts were represented by a corresponding increase or decrease in the number of lines and triangles. Interestingly enough, these simple systems rarely included the concept of zero, which we will discuss later.

Mayan Numbers

Other cultures, such as the Maya, used various types of horizontal strokes and dots to represent number groupings. Both the Maya and Aztecs operated on the vigesimal system of base-20, which is unlike the denary (base-10) system that is in use today. Their numbers combined sticks, bars, and dots, and unlike previous numeric systems, even included a shell-like symbol to represent the concept of "zero."

The Maya used lines and dots to create their number system. Image courtesy of Wikipedia.

Chinese Numbers

Their system shares some common patterns with Chinese numbers, which utilized a "rod system" and was derived from the ancient use of sticks of wood on counting boards. The concept of zero was indicated by a square, and higher numbers were written in monogram form. Vertical lines were added to the tops and bottoms of the sticks to represent increased numeric values. Also known as "math sticks," this ancient method of counting has been traced back 7,000 years to the Yangshao culture, according to a November 1993 article in the *UNESCO Courier* by Du Shi-ran titled "The Math Sticks of Early China—Chinese Calculation Using Counting Rods."

Earthenware shards excavated in the Henan and Shanxi Chinese Provinces show inscribed marks that are a combination of vertical lines. This early arrangement is believed to be the most ancient numeric system to have emerged from China. Early Chinese mathematicians used counting rods, which were sticks made of bamboo called "chou." These sticks were arranged into configurations, which were used to perform calculations. This became known as "chou suan," or "calculating with chou."

A more modern Chinese numeric system involved the use of "oracle bones" by the Shang people, upon which some 5,000 Chinese characters were inscribed as a way of tracking the number of birds and animals that were both hunted and sacrificed. These systems evolved throughout the millennia, and eventually became the present-day Chinese characters. From a historical perspective, these modern characters still maintain close ties with their early beginnings due to their close resemblance with those of the Han Dynasty, which existed between 206 BC and 220 AD.

Aztecs

According to new research by mathematician Maria del Carmen Jorge y Jorge of the National Autonomous University of Mexico, the Aztecs, on the other side of the world, also used combinations of hearts, arrows, hands, bones, and arms in their system of measurement. Working with geographer Barbara Williams, del Carmen Jorge y Jorge examined the Codex Vergara, an ancient Aztec land-surveying book, and discovered unequivocal correlations between land plot lengths and the combinations of images. The researchers also found a very surprising correlation: 60 percent of the fields matched the basic surveying calculations used today, and many of the fields were sloped and terraced, indicating a remarkable understanding of agricultural methodology.

The Aztec's agricultural and engineering successes prove that even this type of crude measurement provided an acceptable level of accuracy.

The ancient Romans, Greeks, and Hebrews used alphabetic systems that included a letter of their alphabet corresponding to a number. The 22 letters of the Hebrew alphabet represent the numbers 1 to 400, with numbers above that represented by composition. For example, the number 500 would be represented by the corresponding letters for 400 and 100.

Hebrew Numbers

Hebrew numbers correspond with a letter from the Hebrew alphabet.

1	א	10	י	100	ק
2	ב	20	כ	200	ר
3	ג	30	ל	300	ש
4	ד	40	מ	400	ת
5	ה	50	נ	500	תק
6	ו	60	ס	600	תר
7	ז	70	ע	700	תש
8	ח	80	פ	800	תת
9	ט	90	צ	900	תתק

Number	Hebrew Letter
1	*Aleph*
2	*Bet*
3	*Gimel*
4	*Dalet*
5	*Hei*
6	*Vav*
7	*Zayin*
8	*Het*
9	*Tet*
10	*Yud*
20	*Kaf*
30	*Lamed*
40	*Mem*
50	*Nun*
60	*Samech*
70	*Ayin*
80	*Pei*
90	*Tsadi*
100	*Kuf*
200	*Resh*
300	*Shin*
400	*Tav*
500	*Tav Kuf* or *Chaf Sofit*
600	*Tav Resh* or *Mem Sofit*
700	*Tav Shin* or *Nun Sofit*
800	*Tav Tav* or *Pei Sofit*
900	*Tav Tav Kuf* or *Tsadi Sofit*

Roman Numerals

Similarly, the Greeks and Romans also used an alphabetic number system. The Greeks actually had two systems. Their first system, which was in place through the first century BC used initial letters that corresponded to each number, again combining them with the letter for the digit 5 to create larger numbers. Dots indicated numbers in the thousands, and a bar was placed to the left of the numbers to indicate thousands. The Greek system, known as "Isopsephy" (which roughly translates to "equal pebble"), referred to the earlier practice of using pebbles to create patterns for learning basic math and geometrics. This early method is related to the Hebrew Gematria and has links to Masonic number symbolism, which is in use today.

Roman numerals may have been based upon the number 5, used specific letters to indicate the digits 1 through 10, and higher numbers from 50, 100, 500, to 1,000. Instead of "adding on" to existing number/letters, the Romans chose to do things a little bit differently by incorporating the "subtractive principle." An example would be the number 9, which is 10, or X, preceded by a 1, or I, equaling IX, rather than a 5 with four 1s after it.

Current Times

Today, we use a hybrid number system referred to as the Indian-Arabic. It is one of three main families of symbol sets that utilize the Hindu-Arabic Numeral System. According to Wikipedia, this system is defined as a "positional decimal system," and dates back to the ninth century. This arrangement is designed "for positional notation in a decimal system," using decimal points to indicate the separation of placement of 1s from the 10ths place. There are only two other families using this positional numeral system: the eastern Arabic numerals used in Egypt, and the Indian numerals used in India.

Our well-loved digits 0 through 9 were initially developed in India from earlier Brahmi numerals, between the second century BC and the sixth century AD. Although we generally refer to this system as Arabic (because it was the Arabs who taught these numbers to the Europeans in the Middle Ages) some historians suggest that the numbers 0 through 9 were actually first used in parts of West Asia. Their hypothesis is that this system quickly spread into Europe in the 10th century AD via the work of Arabic astronomers and mathematicians. The very first inscription found to use the number 0 came from the western Arabic world as well, around 870 AD, but Indian documents on copper plates also show the use of 0 as far back as the sixth century AD.

Once the exclusive purvey of mathematicians, the Indian-Arabic system is now the most widely used and recognized in the world. Two mathematicians, the Persian Al-Khwarizmi and his Arabic colleague Al-Kindi, are credited with the spread of the Indian-Arabic system throughout the Middle East and into the West via their books *On the Calculation with Hindu Numerals* and *On The Use of the Indian Numerals,* respectively. Both tomes, written between 825 and 830 AD, were the later foundation for 10th century Middle Eastern mathematicians who expanded the original system to include fractions.

Is It All About Angles?

Have you ever thought about why 1 means "one" and 2 means "two"? The Roman numerals are easy to understand, but what was the logic behind the phonetician numbers? It's all about angles! If one writes the numbers 1 through 10 on a piece of paper in their older forms, one quickly sees why.

- I have marked the angles with "o"s.
- Number 1 has one angle.
- Number 2 has two angles.
- And so on. Zero has no angles.

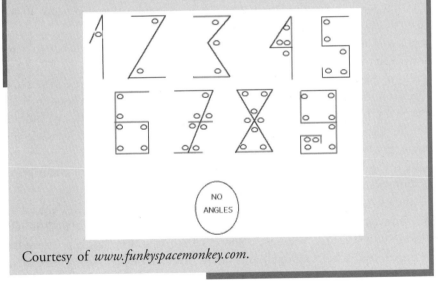

Courtesy of *www.funkyspacemonkey.com.*

Into the Modern World

Intriguingly, it was an Italian mathematician named Fibonacci (whom we shall discuss more extensively in Chapter 3:3) who also heavily promoted the Arabic numbers. In his book *Liber Abaci*, written in 1202 AD, he served to help spread the usage and understanding of the Arabic numerals (although he still referred to them as Indian), which were arranged right to left in order of increasing numeric value. The Europeans readily accepted this new system from the East, and the invention of the printing press no doubt led to its increased adoption and use. As evidence of its success one need only look to the many inscriptions dating back to the 15th century featuring the numbers on clock faces, tombs, and doorways of churches and towers.

Today, we readily associate this ancient number system with the Latin alphabet, and we now refer to numbers as either a binary or a decimal numeral, depending upon the context in which it is used. The basic simple idea of using fingers, objects, and pictures to show measurements, amounts, and quantities has now exploded into a brain-jarring complex mathematic empire of real, complex, and mythical numbers—and everything in between.

Base Systems

Starting with base systems, we find that there is indeed a way to measure everything, from the amount of information a computer can process, to how many yak can cross a ravine in three weeks.

Digital computers use the binary, or base-2, system in general, to represent two states of transistor voltage, either high or low, one or zero. The binary system is often equated with states of "on" or "off." In comparison, many ancient cultures utilized the base-5 system (quinary) most likely because that is how many fingers they had on each hand! But the Yuki, a Native American tribe in Northern California, took that idea one step further, developing a base-8 system that included the spaces between fingers, yet only included digits up to 8. This novel idea is certainly unique among the various system permutations.

By far, the most popular system in the world is the base-10 decimal system. Widely used today, its origin is also allegedly linked to the total number of human fingers. Yes, the next obvious system would be base-20, as we have 20 fingers and toes combined, and many Pre-Columbian Mesoamerican cultures such as the Maya used this vigesimal system. Imagine linking this with the Yuki's utilization of the space between fingers. Between fingers and toes that could theoretically have provided up to base-40!

Another system, the base-12, also gained popularity. The duodecimal and dozenal base-12 systems are used in multiplication and division, and led to the popularity of the "dozen" quantitative measurement. Also, 12 is a common unit of measurement in the United Kingdom. There are 12 inches in a foot, and day and night are divided into 12-hour chunks of time. On a more epicurean note, not only was the famous "Philly Cheese Steak" originally created as a 12-inch delicacy, but most pizza joints standard size pie is 12 inches.

The base-60, or sexagesimal, system is also a familiar one as it is used in our measurement of time. As we all know, there are 60 seconds in a minute, and 60 minutes in an hour. This system was used by many Mesopotamian cultures, including the Sumerians, and may have originated by combining the base-10 and base-12 systems. Proof of this is utilized in the Chinese calendar, which uses a base-60 system to denote years, yet gives two "symbols" to each year, one base-10 and one base-12 (the base-12 corresponding with the 12 animals of the Chinese Zodiac).

Although we have mentioned only a few systems, you may be delighted to know that there are base systems associated with dozens of other numbers. Thankfully, we have little use or familiarity with them in our daily lives. Could you imagine the information overload we might face?

Just as a variety of base systems were developed to fit specific needs, mathematicians also developed varying types of numbers. Fortunately, for the average person, the "real" basic digits (1 to 10), as well as a modicum of addition, subtraction, multiplication, and division skills will suffice for the vast majority of everyday needs. But for those truly obsessed with the magnetic power of numeric possibility, or those in scientific and other fields that actually require more than just the basics, settling just for the real digits, would be, well, unreal.

Zero

Starting with the most obvious, the concept of zero, one might imagine that a mathematician was sitting around one day, looking at his crude counting apparatus, adding and dividing and combining. His young daughter came in and said "Hey, pops, what if you put them all on this end, then you don't got nothing on that end." And thus, zero was born. Other than that supposition, about the only thing we do know about the origin of zero is that it seems to have appeared in various cultures around the same time.

The word *zero* comes from the Italian *zefiro* via the Arabic *afira*, meaning "it was empty" or "nothing." This was used originally in the translation of the Sanskrit *nya*, meaning "void" or "empty" (think also "null"). In the second millennium BC, the Babylonians were indicating a positional value for zero in their numeral system. Indian scholars such as Pingala were using the Sanskrit word for zero (*nya*) as far back as the second century BC.

Even the ancient Greeks waxed poetic about the existence of zero. In fact, it became a topic of philosophical discussion, and religious scholars joined the debate during the medieval period. Scholars questioned the concept of "nil." How could there be such a thing as nothing? Yet already, most numeric systems were indeed making a special place for zero, either as a true number used alone, or, as a placeholder to create a specific context. Once the Hindu decimal system we use today spread from western Arabia into Europe, the concept of zero or nil spread along with it.

A true zero was also utilized in the Roman numeral system, sometime around 523 AD, with the word *nulla* meaning "nothing" and leading to the widespread use of the word by most medieval mathematicians. Another very early documented use of true zero dates back to 628 AD in the *Brahmasphutasiddhanta*, later spreading into China and the Middle Eastern Islamic world. But in 1229 AD, the Roman Catholic Church banned the use of zero, stating it was a Godless number because division by zero resulted in infinity. Thankfully, a medieval monk and abacus counter named Raoul de Laon reintroduced the concept of zero into western Europe, despite pressure from Italian bankers and abacus users who objected to the "empty" number on their books! Zero soon became a sort of underground symbol used by merchants and smugglers who used the number in their "account keeping."

Infinity

At the other end of the spectrum, the idea of a never-ending number, or "infinity," had its earliest recorded mention in the *Isha Upanishad* of the Indian *YajurVeda* circa the third century BC. The reference "If you remove a part from infinity or add a part to infinity, still what remains is infinity" is the first known written idea of the infinite. The Indian mathematical text *Surya Prajnapti* categorized numbers into three sets: enumerable, innumerable, and the infinite. This set system was quite complex for its time, and was later adapted by the Jain sect, who believed that even infinity had various subdivisions: infinite in length, infinite in volume, infinite in area, and perpetual infinity (dimensional). The mind boggles at the infinite possibilities.

The symbol which is commonly associated with infinity may have its origins rooted in the Latin *lemniscus* meaning, "ribbon." Anthropologists and historians suggest that this symbol may have originated with the Tibetan rock carvings of the ouroboros, or "world snake," which is also associated with infinity and a never-ending circle.

The one person who has been most readily associated with the origin of the infinity symbol is John Wallis (1616–1703). Wallis was an English mathematician who is also partially credited with the creation of calculus. As a ...portant contributions, Wallis also has an asteroid named after ...oid 31982 Johnwallis.

...ular suggestion as to the origin of infinity comes from time ...ieve that the symbol is a derivation of the hourglass turned ...resenting "unlimited time" that remains in stasis—never seem- ...end.

...ng to everything, numbers run the gamut. In between these ...e following have emerged:

- Natural Numbers—The integers we use every day, from zero to 1, 2, 3, 4, and onward. These are our counting numbers, therefore, our natural numbers, represented by N.

- Negative Numbers—Integers less than zero, opposites of positive numbers (anything over a zero!), and are usually written using a "minus" symbol, as in –7. Therefore, the opposite of 7 is –7. We use the Z to indicate negative integers.

- Real Numbers—All measuring numbers, usually written using decimal points to indicate position.

- Rational Numbers—Numbers that can be expressed as a fraction, with the numerator (which is the top of the fraction, for the mathematically challenged!), a natural integer, and the denominator (bottom of fraction), a natural number other than zero. All rational numbers are also considered real numbers (which means that it can be written in decimal form as well as fraction form). Confused yet?

■ Irrational Numbers—Opposite of rational numbers. Pi is also an irrational number that we will look at in a later chapter. Irrational numbers are not crazy, they are just not rational.

■ Complex Numbers—A set of numbers that are represented as C and allow a negative number to have a square root. The origin of complex numbers dates back to Heron of Alexandria in the first century AD. Complex numbers occur when you put a real number and an imaginary number together. Don't attempt this at home without adult supervision.

■ Computable Numbers—Also known as recursive numbers or "computable reals," these are real numbers that can be "computed to within any desired precision by a finite, terminating algorithm." Suffice to say, you don't need to know these to balance your checkbook.

■ Palindromic Numbers—Palindromes are numbers with digits that read the same backward as forward. 23432 is a palindromic number. They are used in recreational mathematics where palindromic numbers with special properties are sought. A "palindromic prime" is a palindromic prime number. For some odd reason, whenever I (Larry) hear this term, I automatically think of Battlestar Galactica or Star Trek.

■ Superreal Numbers—Take real numbers and extend them by adding either infinitesimally small numbers, or infinitely large numbers. Why do this? Only a mathematician knows for sure.

■ Imaginary Numbers—Numbers we give the special letter I symbol to in an example to represent an unknown or imagined property. They can also be defined as "a number whose square is a negative real number." Still following us?

■ Prime Numbers—A prime number (or a prime) is "a natural number greater than 1, which has exactly two distinct natural number divisors: 1 and itself. An infinitude of prime numbers exists, as demonstrated by Euclid around 300 BC. The first 30 prime numbers are: 2, 3, 5, 7, 11, 13, 17, 19, 23, 29, 31, 37, 41, 43, 47, 53, 59, 61, 67, 71, 73, 79, 83, 89, 97, 101, 103, 107, 109, and 113, according to Wikipedia. Prime numbers are a part of "number theory," the branch of mathematics that studies natural numbers.

■ Mythical Numbers—Numbers that don't really exist except for in the minds of man and myth. Mythical numbers are often accepted as fully factual, yet have no exact origin. Max Singer of the Hudson Institute coined the term in 1971. An example of this would be the popular claim that humans only use 10 to 12 percent of their brains. Most of us know the truth—they use far less! Another mythical number is 20—for the 20 times most grandmothers suggest you chew your food before swallowing (in order to aid digestion).

■ Indefinitive/Fictitious Numbers—Numbers of a "ginormous" size used for comical effect or exaggeration. Examples would be: zillion, jillion, gazillion, and umpteen. These terms serve to take numbers far beyond the point of, say, hundreds of billions, but come short of just reaching infinity. Most are simply unfathomable to the brain to actually envision, so why we use them is simply a matter of using silly language to describe that which is just too darned big to write down on paper (how many zeros would be in a gazillion anyway?).

These, as well as others, which we will not touch upon due to their extreme complexity, all serve a distinct purpose for the many branches of mathematics developed to solve the problems of reality. Simple division. Algebra. Calculus. Geometry. Trigonometry. Were these constructs designed to torture and confuse us? Perhaps, but, more importantly, they all play significant roles in measuring and quantifying everything around us. As we shall soon see, even our own bodies are not immune from their influences. Although this book is in no way going to expound on the history of math itself, and its many branches (that's what high school and college was for), the fact is that "math" does serve as a foundation for most of the things we take for granted.

But, just in case, let us introduce you to some real mysteries involving numbers—ancient mysteries with a modern edge.

CHAPTER 3:3

Sacred Sequences and Cosmic Codes

Numbers are peculiar animals. They can unlock secrets, split atoms, reveal the inner workings of people and machines or draw patterns of outstanding complexity and beauty.
—Dame Anita Roddick, *Numbers*

When buildings talk, it is never with a single voice.
—Alain de Botton, *The Architecture of Happiness*

Throughout time immemorial, numeric sequences, patterns, and codes have proven useful to humans. As a significant part of our daily lives, they have also become an integral part of the mystery, mystique, and magic of the human experience.

Many forms of music, cosmology, art, architecture, and nature incorporate patterns and sequences, which, while appearing to be haphazard on the surface, deeper examination reveals commonalities simply too deliberate to be random or accidental. Nowhere else is this more significant than in the mysterious and enigmatic world of sacred geometry.

Sacred geometry constitutes the foundation of the design of sacred architecture and art. Geometrical and mathematical ratios, harmonics, and proportion are found in music, light, cosmology, and natural structure, and these ratios have, at their respective foundations, a divine origin. Among the uses of sacred geometrical proportions are the building of structures such as temples, mosques, megaliths, monuments, and churches; the location and placement of sacred spaces such as altars, temenoi, and tabernacles; meeting places such as sacred groves, village greens, and holy wells; as well as the creation of religious art, iconography, and symbolism.

Again, the underlying premise behind sacred geometry is that there is a divine influence and connection between objects and their physical placement and measurements. It is believed by some that this divine influence can, if studied and dissected, lead to a transformative understanding of a greater reality at play in the Universe. Of course, at the heart of this concept we find numbers—glorious and magnificent numbers.

Mathematician Heinrich Hertz is quoted as saying "We cannot escape the feeling that these mathematical formulae have an independent existence and an intelligence of their own, that they are wiser than we are, wiser even than their discoveries, that we get more out of them than was originally put into them." For those who designed architecture, created art, and formed structures around the mystery of numbers, that intelligence came from a heavenly source.

Pythagoras

We might say that the worship of numbers began with the famed Greek mathematician Pythagoras. Pythagoras lived from approximately 572 BC to 490 BC, and was the founder of a monastic religious movement called, not surprisingly, Pythagoreanism. This group espoused the mysticism of math and philosophy. Pythagoras, known as "the father of numbers," is said to have made major contributions to many areas of study, yet few scholars can pinpoint definitive proof, suggesting that perhaps some of his greatest ideas and accomplishments may not have been his own! Perhaps our friend Pythagoras's behavior was a model for the famous copycat band of the 1980s, Milli Vanilli.

Nevertheless, the followers of this man of wisdom (who called themselves "Pythagoreans") spent their days living under strict cultural rules and conduct, eating no meat and disowning all personal possessions. In many ways a school, the inner circle of this organization, called the "Mathematikoi," and the outer circle, the "Akousmatikoi," under Pythagoras's influence, studied religion and mathematics under the cloak of secrecy. Eventually, the inner and outer circles clashed and split off, leaving Pythagoras's own wife, Theano, in charge of those closest to the teacher himself.

In addition to his interest in math and the magic of numbers, Pythagoras was fascinated with music theory and harmonics. One of his most intriguing theories regards the "the harmony of the spheres." His belief was that the movement of the planets and stars corresponded with mathematical equations as well as musical notes, thus producing a "symphony of the spheres."

Many of his other beliefs, such as reincarnation, the transmigration of souls, and life after death heavily influenced other deep thinkers of his time. At one point, Pythagoras even went so far as to suggest that the very essence of being, or reality, is number, and that knowledge of one's own essence must come from a deeper understanding of number and the study of mathematics.

Plato

Pythagoras was a recognized influence upon another famous individual—the classical Greek philosopher Plato (428/427 BC to 348/347 BC). Plato, who was a student of Socrates, and teacher of Aristotle, was one of the most critical forces behind the philosophical foundations of Western culture. Plato, also a mathematician, was founder of the Academy in Athens, which was believed to have been the first institution of higher learning in the Western world. Plato's own studies into music and harmonics suggest that he was influenced by a third generation Pythagorean named Archytas, who contributed a great deal to geometry.

Mysterium Magnum

Some scholars have linked the ancient secretive society of Pythagoreans to more modern secret orders such as the Rosicrucians, Knights Templar, and Masons. These groups have rich histories rife with the teachings of sacred geometry and mystical mathematics. Often incorporating the concept of the "Mysterium Magnum" (Latin for "great mystery") and usually associated with alchemy and mysticism, they were (and continue to be) a cause for frequent speculation, rumor mongering, and scholarly debate.

The Mysterium Magnum, also called the "Great Design," denoted a universal source energy from which all of the Classical Elements emerged. This concept bears striking similarities to both the Zero Point Field of quantum physics as well as the Akashic Records of renowned clairvoyant and healer

Edgar Cayce. Indeed, the patterns and proportions ascribed to geometrically inspired objects were thought to be inspired by heavenly forces, and by all accounts, would seem to suggest a Great Designer.

Golden Ratio

Not surprisingly, the natural world offers a plethora of examples of divine and intelligent patterns ripe for analysis. Many of these patterns are even present in the structure of living organisms! Two of the most stunning examples are the Golden Ratio and the Fibonacci spiral, both of which imply a higher order of measurement behind what many of us take for granted, such as our own bodies…or a seashell.

The Golden Ratio, also known as the Divine Ratio, the Golden Ration, and Golden Mean, is an irrational number of approximately 1.618033988749. One might ask why that specific ratio would be any more "divine" than any other. Perhaps only the Great Designer knows for sure, but this ratio is found throughout the natural, scientific, and man-made worlds as the highest expression of balance, symmetry, and aesthetics. This fundamental formula can be described as "the ratio whereby the ratio of the whole to the larger section equals the ratio of the larger section to the smaller section."

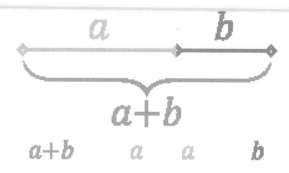

The Golden Ratio, or Golden Mean.

Referred to as "phi," this ratio is present in many sacred icons such as the measurements of the Great Pyramid of Giza, the structure of a five-pointed star, a Pentagram (a sacred object to followers of Plato and Pythagoras), and even in the outline of the Acropolis near Athens, Greece (which takes the shape of a Golden Rectangle). Most notably, as represented by Leonardo da Vinci's famous Vitruvian Man, the Golden Ratio is present in the structure of the human body, with outstretched arms and legs showing the Golden Ratio at work.

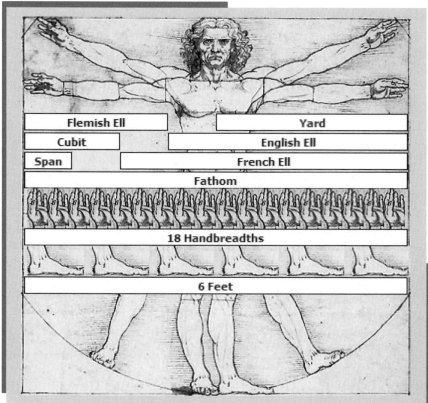

This derivation of the Vitruvian Man by Leonardo da Vinci depicts nine historical units of measurement: the yard, the span, the cubit, the Flemish ell, the English ell, the French ell, the fathom, the hand, and the foot. The Vitruvian Man was drawn to scale, so the units depicted are displayed with their proper historical ratios. Image courtesy of Wikipedia Commons.

According to da Vinci's notes, the following ratios were present in the male human figure:

■ a palm is the width of four fingers.

■ a foot is the width of four palms (that is, 12 inches).

■ a cubit is the width of six palms.

■ a man's height is 4 cubits (and thus 24 palms).

- *a pace is 4 cubits.*

- *the length of a man's outspread arms is equal to his height.*

- *the distance from the hairline to the bottom of the chin is one-tenth of a man's height.*

- *the distance from the top of the head to the bottom of the chin is one-eighth of a man's height.*

- *the maximum width of the shoulders is a quarter of a man's height.*

- *the distance from the elbow to the tip of the hand is one-fifth of a man's height.*

- *the distance from the elbow to the armpit is one-eighth of a man's height.*

- *the length of the hand is one-tenth of a man's height.*

- *the distance from the bottom of the chin to the nose is one-third of the length of the head.*

- *the distance from the hairline to the eyebrows is one-third of the length of the face.*
  Courtesy of Wikipedia.

da Vinci's Creations

The Vitruvian Man got its name from the ancient Roman architect, Vitruvius, whose "De Architectura" has been credited as being the inspiration for da Vinci's use of the Golden Ratio in his scientific and artistic endeavors. The drawing itself was found around 1487 AD as a part of da Vinci's many written journals that were filled with notes and diagrams of his intellectual and philosophical musings. Da Vinci was apparently so enamored of the Golden Ratio that he included it in his famous *The Last Supper* painting. The overall composition of the painting contains three vertical Golden Rectangles, and one decagon (a Golden Ratio shape) in the figure of Jesus.

The famous Last Supper mural depicts the Golden Ratio in art.

The Last Supper is a 15th-century mural painting da Vinci created for his patron Duke Ludovico Sforza and his duchess Beatrice d'Este. The painting measures 460 by 880 centimeters (15 feet by 29 feet) and is found in the back halls of the dining hall at Santa Maria delle Grazie in Milan, Italy. In addition to the Golden Rectangles and decagon, the painting makes references to the number 3, which most likely represents the Trinity, in the groupings of the Apostles, the number of windows behind Jesus, and Jesus' own triangular shape in the image.

Da Vinci also used the Golden Rectangle for the face of his Mona Lisa, giving her the kind of profile that women today generally pay thousands of dollars to plastic surgeons for (maybe that's why she's smirking!). According to measurements, the Golden Ratio is present in the ratio of the width of her forehead compared to the length of the top of her head to her chin.

Impressionist painter George Seurat, creator of the drawing technique of pointillism, often used the Golden Section in his works, believing, as da Vinci did, that this heavenly ratio had an aesthetic value and beauty to which the human eye was naturally drawn. Other geometric ratios, although not necessarily designed for aesthetic value, can be found in Celtic and Indian art, as well as in the design of labyrinths (Eulerian paths, similar to mazes) and mandalas, where symmetry and measurement were intended to create a spiritual resonance between object and observer. Much to the joy of "circle watchers"—

individuals who study the phenomenon of crop circles—there have been suggestions that they encompass similar types of geometric ratios. Although crop circles remain a highly debated topic, their meaning and symbolism continue to evade our understanding. Perhaps they may be identifiable on a subconscious level?

Fibonacci

One of the most important and well-known Golden Ratios comes from the discovery of an Italian with a whole lot of names. Leonardo of Pisa was born in 1170 AD and went by the names Leonardo Pisano, Leonardo Bonacci, Leonardo Fibonacci, and finally just Fibonacci. Could you imagine what his driver's license would look like today? His name comes from "filius Bonacci," or "son of Bonaccio," a nickname that was originally given to his father. No matter which name he goes by, Fibonacci is responsible for the spread of the Hindu-Arabic numeral system into Europe, as well as the number sequence now named after him.

Fibonacci, the man behind the sequence.

In his 13th century book, *Book of Calculation*, or *Liber Abaci*, this brilliant and creative mathematician used the knowledge he had gleaned regarding the mathematical systems used in the Middle Eastern countries during his travels throughout Northern Africa. With that knowledge, he went on to further the development of a previously discovered sequence of numbers (Indian mathematicians were using the sequence as early as the sixth century AD) that are now called the Fibonacci sequence. For anyone who has read the novel, or seen the blockbuster movie, *The Da Vinci Code*, you should be aware of the meaning and importance that it was given. For those who are not aware of this, the

Fibonacci sequence is a series of numbers designed in such a manner that each number after the first two numbers is the sum of the previous two numbers:

0, 1, 1, 2, 3, 5, 8, 13, 21, 34, 55, 89, 144, and so on...

In *Liber Abaci*, Fibonacci used this sequence as an example of the growth rate of a hypothetical rabbit population by using a number that showed the generation-by-generation increase. Beyond rabbits, this sequence is also found throughout nature as an inherent structural pattern in which the higher the numbers in the sequence, the closer the two consecutive numbers divided by each other will approach the Golden Ratio of 1:1.618. In the natural world, we see the Fibonacci sequence at work in many instances, such as the branching rate of plants. In several distinct species of flora, not only do the branch levels follow the pattern, but also, the spacing of the leaves match the number sequence! Some of the flower species that follow this pattern are buttercups, delphiniums, sunflowers, asters, and lilies.

A great many examples of "floral sequencing" can be found on the comprehensive Website *http://library.thinkquest.org*. One representation involves the passiflora incarnate. On the back of this flower there are three "sepals," the non-petal part of flower, that protect the bud and make up the outermost layer. This layer is then followed by five outer green petals. Finally, there is an inner layer of five more paler green petals. On the front of the flower there are five greenish T-shaped stamens in the center, followed by three "deep brown carpels and style branches."

Other examples of the Golden Ratio (or Golden Mean) in nature include the manner by which lightning branches out, the way a tree spans its branches for maximum sunlight exposure, the way rivers branch, and even the proportions of the bodies and wingspans of birds and flying insects. Snowflakes and crystals also show distinct geometric patterns of formation, as does the coded "language" of our DNA.

Nature definitely seems to have received more than its fair share of Fibonacci sequences. The Chambered Nautilus (*Nautilus pompilius*), which is a marine creature of the cephalopod family, grows at a rate that matches the Fibonacci sequence. This creature has the honor of being partly responsible for the naming of yet another Fibonacci permutation—the Fibonacci spiral. This spiral configuration allows the growth of the shelled creature to be accommodated in a logarithmic spiral, without changing its actual shape as it grows. Honeybees also construct hexagon-shaped cells to hold their honey stores, which have prompted many scientists to suggest that the Fibonacci patterns may actually be a logical outcome of natural principles, rather than the mysterious "signature of the Gods" that many Sacred Geometrists have labeled them.

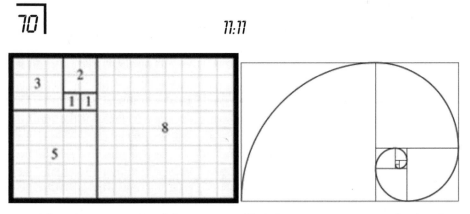

The Fibonacci spiral and the pattern in block form. Images courtesy of Wikipedia.

Other Sequences

According to Pythagoras, it was numeric sequences such as this, or numbers that expressed ratios, that were of far greater importance than the simple singular units we most often use in our day-to-day lives. Pythagoreans looked at these mysterious sequences as proof that there was an underlying layer of reality beneath that which we experienced, and that it was powered by numbers and the connections between them.

Even when expanded to a more macrocosmic level, there appears to be ample evidence of sacred patterns at play. The belief that the cosmos contained a geometric underlying reality is not new, and persists today with modern science and cosmology. It is believed that Johannes Kepler, the German astronomer and mathematician, is responsible for promoting a worldview that combines the sacred with the geometric. Known best for his laws of planetary motion, Kepler, once an assistant to the brilliant astronomer Tycho Brahe, often combined his knowledge of astronomy and astrology while also incorporating aspects of religious, spiritual, and philosophical arguments into his studies. During Brahe's time, this was deeply frowned upon; however, it did not discourage his zeal. He truly believed that there was an intelligent and divinely created plan to the Universe that could be accessed through reason. This theory, which he termed "celestial physics," may have been a supplemental line of study to Aristotle's earlier *Metaphysics* and *On the Heavens*.

Kepler

Kepler, whose love of astronomy began early in childhood, was at one time a theology student and attended seminary, yet had an intense interest in astrology. Although the two disciplines may seem to be in opposition, surprisingly, there are many similarities. Kepler was so skilled in astrology that he was often called upon by his fellow students to do readings for them. Due in part to the melding of his understanding of theological and astrological principles, Kepler later formulated his treatise of a divinely inspired geometrical reality to the Universe. This theory later became known as the Kepler platonic solid model. Once the basic framework was established, the view took the form of a sectioned model that showed the layers of the universe in accordance with his Great Cosmic Mystery, or "Mysterium Cosmographicum." This idea deeply reflected his own excitement for the Copernican system and its potential to bridge both the physical and the spiritual realms. So certain was he of his beliefs, that he even published a more detailed follow-up to the "Mysterium" in 1621 to further elaborate upon his initial writing.

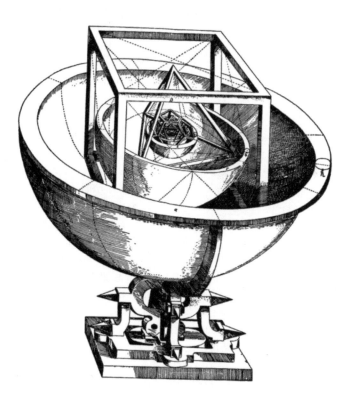

Kepler's belief system echoed the popular worldview of the time among those who believed that the nature of reality was geometrically structured. This worldview combined the complexities of the best scientific modalities of the time involving space, matter, and time with religious symbolism and metaphysical

The Kepler Model represents a worldview of sections or pieces of a pattern or puzzle that fit to make a whole reality. Image courtesy of Wikimedia.

concepts thrown in for good measure. According to this, all of existence fit to-gether in a pattern, akin to a giant cosmic jigsaw puzzle, and the creator of this puzzle was the Great Designer. The Great Designer was an omnipotent entity whose laws operated on a higher order, yet manifested in the simplest of things, such as the petals of a flower.

Sacred Numbers

In his book *Sacred Number and the Origins of Civilization*, author Richard Heath states that the four mathematical arts of arithmetic, geometry, musical harmony, and astronomy comprised the "Quadrivium." These four elements were considered essential elements in the building of megalithic monuments. The idea behind this, again, was that "the field of number provided the foun-dation for all these numerical sciences. From this foundation a full numerical worldview would have been possible—one that found its fullest expression within the design, location, and structure of ancient monuments." But before we venture into a discussion of sacred structures, we first need to look more closely at the finer intricacies involved in determining the sacred from the mundane.

Even the realm of music does not escape the inclusion of intricate, number-based patterns. Harmonics are, at their source, nothing more than simple math-ematical sequences of sound, notes, and chords that create resonance. Once again, the relationship between geometry, mathematics, and music can be at-tributed to Pythagoras. It was he who, through experimentation, discovered that strings that were stopped at certain points along their length would pro-duce certain notes or octaves, and that certain ratios produced intervals that, as Pythagoras believed, had certain powers of healing. Followers of Pythagoras believed that musical harmony produced physical and spiritual harmony. Phy-sician Hans Jenny, while being somewhat skeptical of the healing powers of music, was a firm believer in the connection between geometric figures and wave interactions. Jenny's research in this field led to the development of cymatics, in which he elaborated upon ancient knowledge provided by Pythagoras and the ancient Egyptians.

In his book *The Spiritual Technology of Ancient Egypt*, noted author and researcher Edward Malkowski examines how the Pythagorean Science of Num-bers developed to show the relationship between numbers and, as Aristotle claimed, "the first principles of all things." Malkowski concludes that "At the heart of Pythagoras' science of numbers was the belief that all relationships could be reduced to number associations, and that all things are in fact number." This science of number was discovered through the science, or art, of music. Harmony, another concept rife with mystical allusions, maintains a close relationship to resonance and vibration. This established correlation was thought to be quite simply the basis of the hidden order of the immediate, perceivable world, and behind it all were the numbers. It seems that we just can't escape their grip!

Numbers in Music

In addition to his comprehensive historical research, Malkowski also delves into the philosophy of numbers as researched by 20th-century French philosopher R.A. Schwaller de Lubicz. Lubicz's early book *A Study in Numbers* was published in 1917, and examined numbers as not only symbols of expression, but as the purist manner to "convey a cosmogony." Schwaller believed that quantity was critical, but that only when quantity and quality were equal could true harmony be achieved. This homeostatic state would result in an observable, or real, phenomenon. Even consciousness could be described as "a result of the relationship between quantities and the absolute state, where we can conceive of absoluteness only in relation to quantity."

Schwaller also believed that two cosmos existed in one singular universe; one being the absolute, macrocosmic, the other the harmonic microcosmic. He also described this as "quality fragmented and organized into quantity," and Malkowski makes the connection between this worldview and physics, where "there are the immediate and quantum worlds—two very different worlds that exist simultaneously." Schwaller's ideas were certainly ahead of their time, and Malkowski describes his philosophical treatise on numbers as such (obviously mirroring Pythagoras's "All is number" mentality!):

- One: The Monad—The concept of absolute, the unity of all things, the unchanging "all" from which all other numbers are produced. Also known as Chaos, Axis, Tower, Styx, Atlas, and the Throne of Jupiter.

- Two: The Duad—Duality and polarity, the most fundamental aspect of all natural phenomena (not to mention the foundation for Western religious belief in good/evil, light/darkness).

- Three: The Triad—Our first odd number, and the sacred composition of the monad and duad (think Holy Trinity), the function of which is to create equilibrium between the monad and duad.

- **Four: The Tetrad**—The "primogenial number," the first born of the combined principles of the three numbers before it. The basis for all nature in that the tetrad is the sum of 1, 2, 3, and 4 = 10, the decad. The number of God. The four elements. The four directions.

- **Five: The Pentad**—The union between the first even (2) and odd (3) numbers. Symbolized a fifth element known as "ether," and symbolic of nature as the Pentacle or five-pointed star. Pentagrams are considered deeply sacred symbols. Also symbolized the manifest Universe.

- **Six: The Hexad**—The formation of matter into the cosmos, space, and time. Six directions of extension (up, down, left, right, forward, and backward), and the union of the two sexes as in the interlaced triangles of the Star of David or King Solomon's Seal. Male and female, matter, and spirit.

- **Seven: The Heptad**—The mystical nature of Man. The marriage of the threefold nature of mankind (body, mind, and spirit), and the four elements of matter. Also, the combination of the higher principle of the trinity upon the lower four "mortal" principles.

- **Eight: The Ogdoad**—Renewal and self-replication. A new unity based upon the fact that eight is divided into two 4s, then into two 2s, and then into two 1s.

- **Nine: The Ennead**—The first square of the first odd number 3. Spiritual and mental achievement, the limit of all numbers for all other numbers come from the first nine, yet can create an infinite amount of new numbers.

- **Ten: The Decad**—comprising all arithmetic and harmonic proportions. The number that perfects all others. Within 10, all nature exists, the root source of eternal nature.

These 10 numbers form the basis of the Pythagoreans' philosophy, represented in the "tetractys," four rows of 10 dots where, according to Malkowski, "the three higher numbers represent the invisible, metaphysical world, and the lower seven refer to physical phenomena." The bottom level consisted of the four elements of earth, water, air, and fire; the center row was the Three Principles of the Moon, Sun, and Sulfur; and the top two rows, contained by a triangle, were the Two Seeds of the Moon and Sun, topped by the One Fruit of Stone. Each row represented a different experience or reality, "a gradation from more collective to more individual experiences." The One Fruit, or Stone, at the top of the tetractys represented the "Unus Mundus," or the Self, and is the totality of the universe, or the World Soul.

The Pythagorean cosmology consisted of the two worlds of the Supreme and the Superior, and the lower Inferior World of form, which has three levels similar to the Trinity as a basis of reality. Yet, only in the Inferior World could quantity exist, and be measured, and that is the world we live in, where the sacred science of geometry longs to bridge the gap between the lower and upper worlds, as well as the individual souls to the World Soul.

In his book *The Dimensions of Paradise: Sacred Geometry, Ancient Science and the Heavenly Order on Earth*, author and researcher John Michell examines the role of music and proportion in bridging this gap, as well as the strong influence of music on the theories of both Plato and Pythagoras. He begins by looking at Plato's theory of education, which posits that "children must be exposed from their earliest days to the influence of harmonious proportions in everything around them, so that they will grow up with a sense of proportion and the ability to distinguish between the good and the meretricious."

Musical intervals, Michell states, can be expressed as ratios between numbers, thus creating a sort of "numerical canon" that is the composition behind the world soul. From this canon, musical scales evolved. "By forbidding 'noise' as non canonical music," Michell continues, "Plato and his ancient forebears intended to preserve the soul from disruptive influences, nurture it on those sounds that are conducive to its natural development, and thus produce the type of citizens who will appreciate and maintain a society constituted in imitation of the cosmos." A tall order for its citizens, Platonists believed that they had an obligation to work with the harmonies of such divinely inspired proportion to be better people, thus creating a better Universe. Imagine a leader today asking our youth to do the same. Would some forms of modern music, that is, rap, punk, and thrash metal, constitute an "imitation of the cosmos"?

As Michell points out, Plato strongly believed that the secrets of the Universe were to be found not by setting one's eyes up to the heavens, but by examining in detail the "precise proportion of number." In addition to the harmonies it inspired, this proportion could only truly be understood through numerical analysis, which Michell's book delves into a bit more deeply than we shall here. Basically, behind the harmonies and chords and scales that were thought to be of a positive, or divine, nature, there were numbers and sequences of numbers that combined to make up notes and half-notes, intervals and octaves, fourths and fifths, and everything in between.

Harmonic proportion, one of the three recognized types of proportions (arithmetic and geometric being the others), were deeply understood by Pythagoreans. Their knowledge carried on a sacred science, which began in civilizations from far more ancient times. As Michell states, "Timaeus" is identified as the earliest account of the three proportion types as part of Pythagorean music theory, "where Plato describes the numerical creation of the physical universe and the soul that binds and animates it."

Plato believed that the world soul was created out of a range of four octaves. Furthermore, he said that there was a specific number code that served as the root of all natural and philosophical reality (which we will examine in a later chapter). Ironically, through time, scholars have continued to disagree as to what that exact number code is. Michell and others suggest that the first 12 numbers are the basic foundation of creation. These numbers, though, were adapted through time to the units of measurement that a musician playing a wind or string instrument would produce as sound, depending upon the length of pipe or string utilized. Anyone who has ever studied modern music theory, or even tried to learn to read music, knows that precision and measurement play important roles in the nature and quality of the sounds produced. Even the human ear can discern a lovely chord from a distinctly brain-shattering cacophony. Based upon some examples of modern "music," it might be argued that today's youth have lost this ability!

According to Heath's *Sacred Number and the Origins of Civilization*, musical harmony is comprised of the most fundamental of numbers, 1 through 6, and that "musical ratios are the irreducible elements without any common factors taken out." His book extensively describes the harmonic ratios and octaves created by the numbers 1 through 12, and why these special combinations and ratios form the foundation of musical structure, a structure with a parallel in the very resonances of the earth, stars, and planets that make up the cosmos. These ratios may even govern and influence the resonances that we, as humans, vibrate in accordance with.

To get an actual breakdown of the various ratios and harmonics, we strongly suggest reading Heath's book. In it, he explores details too numerous and elaborate to mention here. Heath pays particular attention to the importance of certain prime numbers. "A very important principle emerges within the field of number as it evolves what is, to us, harmony. As stated, the prime numbers two, three and five are responsible for the principle of harmony; this means that all the higher primes are fated to occupy the voids left by the field of harmony." Even the prime numbers 7 and 11 have a critical role in the formation of "primary creation," because, as Heath points out, the ratio between the

Earth's mean radius and its meridian is 22/7, or two times 11/7, thus giving the two numbers a special place in the hearts and minds of ancient civilizations who linked musical harmony with that of the planets and stars.

Metrology

This serves as the foundational platform for the scientific disciple known as "metrology," which Heath describes as "similarly structured to find the units that maintain simplicity of relationship between different dimensions of built or implied circles." He ascribes this same simplicity as the manner by which ancients transmitted knowledge via the building and study of monuments and temples that were built in accordance with this worldview—think of Stonehenge and its circular shape. Heath calls this association of number and harmony, which was seemingly known and utilized by the ancients, the "metrological application," and its impact can clearly be seen in the architecture of old.

Heath, Michell, and John Neal, also an expert in the area of metrology, all come to similar conclusions about the importance of harmonics in relation to the physical shape of the earth. Neal and Michell discovered "grid constants" that reveal, as Heath puts it "that the shape of the Earth is related to the harmonic products of the first 25 numbers, seen from the perspective of harmony, and employing only those prime numbers below 12." Michell and Neal's grid constants found a relationship between variations in ancient measurements, approximations to pi used in ancient times, and the ratios found at the end of the series from 1 to 25 with 2, 3, 5, 7, and 11 as "harmonically generative" primes.

The genesis of Metrology may have begun with the simple measurement of the English foot and its many ancient variations, all of which related to the size and shape of our planet. However, as Heath points out, the ancients measured things within a "created scheme or order." Today, we measure things as they are actually found in approximation to reality. What you see is what you get. This may tell us why sacred geometry is considered a "science" of the past, but one that still holds great mystery and intrigue today, when our true understanding of reality is based entirely on what we experience right in front of us, and rarely on what is occurring beneath the surface, or beyond the veil.

Much of the worldview upon which sacred geometry is based can be traced back to concepts forged by the likes of Lao Tsu, author of the *Tao Te Ching*, and even to Socrates, mentor of Plato. Both agreed that the whole of creation was divided into three parts (also a basis for the Trinity of Catholicism, as we shall discuss in a future chapter): creation as entirety was the first part; the division of the whole was the second part; and, finally, the interconnectedness between the whole and the parts was part three. From this foundation, all other numbers and number fields supposedly sprang forth. Nowhere is this more obvious than in the yin and yang symbol of Tao, which shows the whole of the circle, the division into white and black halves, and the interconnectedness of the contrary smaller circles within.

This belief in the sacredness of all of creation's foundational structure was clearly evident, and quite obvious in architectural objects. Of all the elements comprising sacred geometry, architecture—whether the building of a crude stone megalith or a precise and intricately detailed chapel—stood as the most profound manner by which man could somehow emulate the divine patterns of the heavens—right here on Earth. Even today, these sacred structures elicit a deep and lasting impression upon those who view them.

In the classic *Philebus* (often called "The Philebus"), one of the last Socratic dialogues of Plato (who was Socrates's student), Socrates talks of the connection between beauty and form:

I do not mean by beauty of form such beauty as that of animals or pictures, which many would suppose to be my meaning, but, says the argument, understand me to mean straight lines and circles, and the plane or solid figures which are formed out of them by turning-lathes and rulers and measures of angles; for these I affirm to be not only relatively beautiful, like other things, but they are eternally and absolutely beautiful, and they have peculiar pleasure, quite unlike the pleasures of scratching.

The dialogue's central question concerns the relative value of pleasure and understanding, as well as producing a model for thinking about how complex structures are developed. Called "philosophical geometry," this concept also served as the basis for the sacred geometry we study today.

Platonic Solids

We may wish to start the discussion of form and beauty with Plato again, and the five perfect three-dimensional shapes that came to be known as the Platonic Solids.

Tetrahedron—4 faces, 4 vertices, 6 edges

Hexahedron (cube)—6 faces, 8 vertices, 12 edges

Octahedron—8 faces, 6 vertices, 12 edges

Dodecahedron—12 faces, 20 vertices, 30 edges

Icosahedron—20 faces, 12 vertices, 30 edges

A Platonic Solid is basically a convex regular polyhedron; its name is derived from the total number of its faces. The beauty of Platonic Solids lies in their symmetry and angles. Because of this, they have long been regarded as sacred. Although some scholars argue that the octahedron and icosahedron may have been the discovery of Plato's contemporary, Theaetetus, who also may be responsible for determining that there are no other convex regular polyhedra, it was in fact Plato who associated four of the solids with the four classical elements of earth (hexahedron), water (icosahedron), air (octahedron), and fire (tetrahedron).

A convex polyhedron can only be a Platonic solid if:

1.   All its faces are congruent convex regular polygons.
2.   None of its faces intersect except at their edges.
3.   The same number of faces meet at each of its vertices.

In the mid-1980s, University of Chicago professor Robert J. Moon managed to prove that the entire periodic table of elements, of which the entire physical world is comprised, is based upon the five Platonic Solids. Moon also proposed a geometric ordering of the atomic nucleus, inspired by Johannes

Kepler's conception of the solar system, as described in Kepler's *Mysterium Cosmographicum*.

Interestingly, Kepler himself tried to apply the five Platonic Solids to the five known non-Earth planets at the time—Mercury, Venus, Mars, Jupiter, and Saturn—but was unable to make the connection work. His model of the solar system, pictured earlier in this chapter, was his attempt at a physical correspondence—the innermost layer was the octahedron, the next layer was the icosahedron, the next layer was the dodecahedron, the next was the tetrahedron, and finally the last was the hexahedron, or cube. But all it served to do was inspire his new discovery of the Kepler solids, and the understanding that planetary orbits are not circles. Both of these attempts served as the foundation for his famous Laws of Planetary Motion and an excellent example of failure leading to greater success!

Proportional harmony, Platonic Solids, and sacred constants all come together most visibly in the architecture of Ancient Egypt, India, the area once known as Mesoamerica, Easter Island, and even rural England and Wales, places often described as magical and mystical by all who have had the pleasure of walking among their temples, pyramids, megaliths, and monuments. The designers of sacred sites looked to both earth and sky to determine locations, alignments, and even purposes. Nothing was ever built without a purpose, whether that purpose was to better understand our place in the cosmos, or create a new type of energy or level of consciousness, as has been suggested as the true purpose of the Great Pyramid of Giza.

Sacred Architecture

Other sacred sites were meant to invite worship, but even they were built with a divine connection to location in mind. The history of sacred architecture is paralleled by the history of religious architecture, symbolism, and use of motif, with some buildings purposely rendered huge and public, while others were small, private places intended for more personal modes of mediation and reflection. Architect Normal L. Koonce suggested that sacred architecture served to "make transparent the boundary between matter and mind, flesh and the spirit," and this intention is apparent throughout the ancient world. In his inspiring and beautiful book *The Architecture of Happiness*, Alain de Botton states, "Belief in the significance of architecture is premised on the notion that we are, for better or for worse, different people in different places—and on the conviction that it is architecture's task to render vivid to us who we might ideally be."

Although it might seem blasphemous, the idea that humankind might somehow be equal to the Gods (or, at the very least, able to access their wisdom and guidance) serves as the structural foundation for sacred geometry.

Not surprisingly, dozens of books have been written about the lineage and age of the Great Pyramid of Giza, the means of construction for the Pyramid, and even its overall purpose. Some of the more creative theories definitely seem to stretch the limits of believability. In fact, the somewhat derogatory term "Pyramidiot" has been penned to describe opponents to the hard-line, fixed paradigms.

Although extremely fascinating, unfortunately, we do not have the time nor space to get into these discussions in this book (see our Bibliography for our suggestions on books that delve deeply into this subject matter). What we must examine here, however, is the use of number and numeric sequence in the actual design of this remarkable and enigmatic sacred structure, suggesting that ultimately the numbers themselves may point to the purpose and meaning behind the Pyramid. As John Michell states in *The Dimensions of Paradise*, "The pyramid, of course, was no mere mathematical model, but an example of the cosmic temple whose traditional function was to procure fusion between upper and lower elements."

Just for starters, here are but a small sampling of the enigmatic number mysteries that the Pyramid contains:

- The ratio of the diameter of the middle of the earth is 11, and the distance between the center of the earth and the center of the moon as 7 is the exact ratio built into the Great Pyramid of Giza (Heath).

- The height times the base length, in English feet, is the length of the degree of latitude for the Pyramid at Giza at 30 degrees North (Neal).

- The cubic capacity of the Ark of the Covenant (71,282 cubic inches) is incredibly similar to the cubic capacity of the stone vessel knows as "Pharaoh Cheops' Sarcophagus" in the King's Chamber (71,290 cubic inches), which has led some researchers to suggest that the Ark was once encased in the Sarcophagus.

- The builders of the Pyramid were apparently aware of the Pythagorean theorem, of the relationship among the sides of a 3:4:5 (right) triangle, and they had knowledge of the concept of pi (Malkowski).

■ The accuracy and precision of the construction prompted engineering expert Christopher Dunn to proclaim in his 1998 book *The Giza Power Plant*, after closely examining the Pyramid for two decades, that "The Great Pyramid is the largest, most precisely built, and most accurately aligned building ever constructed in the world."

■ The angle of the slopes of the sides is a ratio of 10:9, thus for every 10-foot ascent up the slope of the Pyramid, you rise an altitude of 9 feet. Multiply the altitude of the Pyramid by 10 raised to the 9th power, and you get 91,840,000 miles—the distance from the earth to the sun.

■ A pyramid inch is .001 inch larger than an English inch. There are 24 pyramid inches in a cubit, and there are 365.24 cubits in the square base of the Pyramid. There are also 365.24 days in a calendar year.

According to Marshall Payn, author of "The Case for Advanced Technology in the Great Pyramid," in the book *Forbidden History*, the Great Pyramid's builders most likely looked to the stars and astronomy for their precise measurements in construction. Even slight inaccuracies could not be dismissed, Payn suggests, pointing to the minute differences in some measurements of the Pyramid's height in feet that closely match the polar radius of the earth when incorporated into a formula, whereby the base perimeter is equal to one half of a degree of equatorial longitude. The result proved to be off by only a difference of 27 miles, yielding an accuracy of 99.3 percent for the ancient Egyptian builders. Even with the advent of modern-day GPS, that accuracy level is considered negligible, and certainly incredible considering the circumstances!

Payn also points to the importance of the number 43,200, which mythologist and scholar Joseph Campbell traced to the original myths of various ancient cultures (he even traced it to Neolithic times). This figure is even more remarkable when we learn that Khufu's Pyramid scale is 2 × 60 × 360, which equals 43,200.

Aside from the astounding preciseness of measurement that created the dimensions of the Pyramid, we must focus on the meaning behind many of the actual measurements involved, because, ultimately, it all points to the relationship between earth and cosmos, man and the divine, matter and spirit. Who cares if the base of the Pyramid measured this or that? Only when we see the relationship of form to the higher principles can we fully appreciate the intricacies of the numbers behind the measurements.

The Great Pyramid is in no way an exclusive sacred portal of sorts between earth and heaven. Even the Temple of Luxor speaks of sacred geometric proportions. Again, we turn to R.A. Schwaller de Lubicz, who superimposed a human skeleton over a drawing of the Temple to show how sacred geometric proportions were at play. As outlined in his seminal book, *The Temple of Man*, Schwaller posits that the Golden Section was widely used in the construction of the Temple of Luxor. He believed very strongly that this temple was built to actually contain and encode a system of knowledge within its architectural symbolism.

This "science of correspondences," also attributed to 18th-century Emanuel Swedenborg, a Swedish scientist, philosopher, Christian mystic, and theologian, was deeply understood by the ancients, but has effectively been considered a lost art and science today. Swedenborg believed that "the most ancient people, who were celestial men, thought from correspondence itself, as the angels do," and wrote extensively in his book, *Heaven and Hell*, about the correspondence and connection between the natural world and the spiritual world.

One such place that elicits an ethereal, spiritual feeling is the Stonehenge-Avebury Complex. Everyone has heard of Stonehenge, the circle of massive stones in England's Wiltshire County, built throughout a period of 3,000 years (the standing stones as early as 2000 BC, the bank and ditch approximately 3100 BC) that supposedly encode astronomical and cosmological knowledge in their placement and purpose.

You may be interested to know that Stonehenge, though, is not Britain's largest, or even most important, monument. To the direct north is the largest "henge" monument in the country: Avebury. Interestingly, Avebury was built upon what is known as the "Michael Line." The Michael Line is an invisible geographic line that connects sanctuaries dedicated to St. Michael (more on this later). Henge monuments are traditionally defined as "circular banked enclosures with an internal ditch," according to Wikipedia, and archaeologists have long recognized them as a classic form of sacred earthwork. Despite its bank being inside its ditch, Stonehenge is grouped into such monuments for its "standing stone circle" formation.

Avebury, along with Stonehenge and other key sacred locations, form a triangle in the landscape that, according to John Michell, suggest a ground-based model of the "three key radii of Earth." The key unit is 1,728 feet, equaling 72 Roman feet, and one-forth the radius of nearby Silbury Hill, another point in the landscape triangle. Michell also compares Stonehenge's ground plan with that of the city of "New Jerusalem," described in Saint John's book of

Revelation, and with the mystical 12 hides (measurements of land) of Glastonbury, defined as the area of land able to support a farmer and his family, and equal to 1,440 acres. Stonehenge, when overlaid upon a diagram of the city of New Jerusalem (as envisioned by Saint John) can be seen as a square 7,920 feet wide, and an inner circle of 14,400 cubits around. The dimensions, Michell states, are on a scale of 1:100. "The outer circle," he posits, "has the same perimeter as the square, 316.8 feet. Stonehenge is thus founded on the classic image of sacred geometry, the squared circle representing the reconciliation of opposites, which is the common feature of temples and foundation myths the world over."

St. Mary's Chapel at Glastonbury also features a similar measurement, with the perimeter of its square measuring 316.8 feet with a diameter of 79.2 feet. Michell's book also shows the diameter of an inner circle representing earth at 7,920 miles; the perimeter of the outer circle and square as 31,680 miles. These numbers, as we shall learn later, hold a special sacred spot in the "pattern of the heavens."

The ancient "heavenly city" of New Jerusalem of Saint John the Divine in the book of Revelation is suggested by Michell as the "eternal standard" by which all other sacred structures should be measured, judged, and even copied. "In the symbolism of all religions, a geometric construction representing the heavenly city or map of paradise has a central place," Michell writes. "It occurs in sacred art as a mandala, a concentric arrangement of circles, squares and polygons depicting in essence the entire universe." These sacred places were thought to be a fixed constant in a constantly changing world, a representation of that which never changes. Many have speculated that these arrangements also served to exert a calming, ordering influence on civilization.

In Revelation, Saint John actually describes the measurements by which this heavenly city would be constructed. "And the city lieth foursquare and the length is as large as the breadth; and he measured the city with the reed, 12,000 furlongs. The length and the breadth and the height of it are equal...and he measured the wall thereof, an hundred and 40 and 4 cubits...." Michell did the math, so to speak, arriving at specific measurements that took the form of a cube with 12 sides each, 12,000 furlongs, six faces, 144 million square furlongs, and a wall of 144 cubits. He does point out the discrepancy in scales used, as a furlong is 660 feet and a cubit 1 1/2 feet. But "the basic plan of the New Jerusalem is a square of 12 furlongs containing a circle of 14,4000 cubits." In feet, the diameter of the New Jerusalem circle within the square is 7,920 feet. The earth's diameter in the square is 7,920 miles. The circumferences of both the New Jerusalem and the earth measure 24,883.2 feet and miles, respectively, and the perimeter of the outer square are 31,680 feet and 31,680 miles, respectively.

No matter the numbers, the whole idea was to match the measurement of what was being constructed upon the earth with the earth itself, as if in homage. Perhaps it was also an attempt to reign in the power of the earth's harmonics and resonance by creating a microcosmic "earth" as a city. The idea behind the city of New Jerusalem was obviously an attempt to bridge the gap between "as above, so below." This pattern became the blueprint for other sacred sites, many of which, such as Stonehenge and Avebury, were spaced equidistant along a very magical line.

Ley Lines

The St. Michael Line that joins Avebury, one of the largest Neolithic henge monuments in Europe dating back as far as 5,000 BC, to Stonehenge and other noted sacred sites is called a "ley line," a straight alignment that measures across England from Cornwall to East Anglia. Discovered by John Michell, the St. Michael Line is said to be the most widely known ley line in the world, linking several "holy" sites devoted to St. Michael. With St. Michael's Mount at the southern tip, the line dissects through the Hurlers stone circle, Glastonbury (site of the Tor megalith), Avebury, and the Wandlebury Stone Ring to Hopton in the north.

Ley lines, leys, or Magic Lines are purported alignments of sacred sites, usually ancient in origin, that connect across a landscape in either a straight or curved line. Ley lines often link marker sites along several miles, and it has been thought that they might possibly follow the paths of prehistoric trading routes.

The so-called "discoverer" of ley lines is considered to be the English businessman Alfred Watkins, who allegedly found evidence of these alignments in June of 1921 while studying a map. He noticed that various points of historical interest followed a line that traversed across hilltops and created a pattern of lines across a vast landscape. Watkins described a ley line as having "a set of points, chosen from a given set of landmark points, all of which lie within at least an arc of 1/4 degree." He wrote about ley lines in his 1922 book, *Early British Trackways*, and later in his 1924 book, *The Old Straight Track*, in which he urged readers to "imagine a fairy chain stretched from mountain peak to mountain peak, as far as the eye could reach." This chain linked mounds, circular earthwork, and "high places" of the earth at various spaced locales.

Watkins associated the lines with the Roman messenger god Mercury (Greek Hermes), the God of communication, boundaries, and guide to travelers. Watkins also felt there was a Druidic connection to the ley lines, and later wrote a book entitled the *Ley Hunter's Manual* in the late 1920s. However, it was Dion Fortune, the occultist and author of *The Goat-Foot God* who originated the claim that ley lines held a special power that linked ancient holy sites.

Later, the New Age crowd ascribed a sense of cosmic energy to ley lines, determining that the lines followed a specific grid or pattern in the earth itself. Dowsers and psychics alike claimed to be able to "read" and locate ley lines, which also became linked to the Atlantean mythology courtesy of author John Michell's book, *The View Over Atlantis*.

Allegedly, there are ley lines running across the landscapes of western North America (many linked to Native American sites), the southeastern United States, the Glastonbury-Avalon line in the United Kingdom, the Glasgow lines of Scotland, and the south of France linking various holy sites linked to the Mary Magdalene legend. Wales and Ireland also have their share of ley lines, magical sites, and hot spots of mythical interest. The Nazca lines in South America are considered ley patterns, and these mysterious lines are even said to connect the ancient pyramids of Mexico.

In the 20th century, interest in and research of ley lines has reached epic proportions. It seems that everyone has a theory! Some of the theories and ideas are "out there"; however, until we have solid, definitive proof, nothing should be discounted. One example is the New Age thinker's belief that ley lines are UFO landing strips or guides for extraterrestrial travelers. Until extraterrestrial contact occurs, and the "little green men" announce that ley lines are, in fact, landing guides or runways, what proof do we have that they are wrong?

Of course, not everyone believes in the mystical concepts ascribed to ley lines. According to Skepdic.com, "There is no evidence for this belief save the usual subjective certainty based on uncontrolled observations by untutored devotees. Nevertheless, advocates claim that Uluruthe alleged energy is connected to changes in magnetic fields. None of this has been scientifically verified."

Are ley lines simply random? The famous skeptic Randi further states that the Stonehenge structure (and, in fact, almost any structure or random location) can be shown to lie at the intersection of at least a pair of ley lines.

Those of the lines that are actually straight (most are not) can be shown to fall within expected chance occurrence on a map of a heavily populated area, especially when features no longer in existence can be included.

A similar notion was developed by the ancient Chinese far before the English came up with it. The Chinese called their lines "dragon tracks," and they used them for weather forecasting. They were somewhat less successful in that field than today's average TV meteorologist.

Regardless of the lack of scientific evidence either for or against ley lines, a new, emerging area of archeology called "geodesy" has formed, which incorporates geological surveying as a factor. This modality suggests that these lines are nothing more than humankind's attempts to mark surveying lines, property and boundary markers, as well as the most commonly traveled trade and migration routes.

Watkins himself never attributed any metaphysical or supernatural meaning to ley lines, however, the belief persists today that lines of energy that resonate in the same electromagnetic vibrational frequency as the earth itself mark the landscape and speak of an ancient knowledge far superior to our own. No matter what the origin of these lines, it is really the sites to which they point that continue to intrigue those interested in hidden knowledge and the power and symbolism of numbers.

One of the most interesting end points of ley lines is the famous Rosslyn Chapel, itself a remarkable display of sacred geometry and the use of symbol, harmonics, and numbers to convey a sense of otherworldliness and a divine connection.

Rosslyn Chapel is a 15th-century chapel designed by William Sinclair of the St. Clair family of Scottish noble's descended from the Norman knights, and some claim, linked to the Knights Templar. Originally known as the Collegiate Chapel of St. Matthew, Rosslyn has gained notoriety from the recent best-selling book and movie *The Da Vinci Code* by Dan Brown, which served to further inextricably link it to the legend of the Holy Grail. Many historians and esotericists even insist the Grail legend itself ends at Rosslyn, where ensconced deep within its walls may lie a secret that only music itself can unlock.

The Chapel's construction began in 1440 and lasted for approximately 40 years. Throughout its history, Rosslyn Chapel has been associated with mystery and intrigue as well as the occult and hidden knowledge. Such Collegiate Chapels were intended to be both spiritual and educational places of power and knowledge, but as suggested in a three-volume study by Father Richard Augustine Hay, Rosslyn held even deeper mysteries. Hay was the principle authority of the Chapel and St. Clair family. He wrote that Rosslyn was unlike any other house of God's service, and that it was a "most curious work, that which it might be done with greater glory and splendour." Sir William is said to have engaged the services of the best masons and workmen available in Europe at the time to build this magnificent structure. Throughout its history, the chapel has maintained an association with the legendary Knights Templar. According to theologians, that association continues even today.

Many authors and Rosslyn researchers suggest that the west wall of the Chapel was intended by design to be a model of Jerusalem's Wailing Wall. In addition, mystical symbols carved into the stone ceiling were reportedly discovered in 2005, which appear to be a musical score. John Mitchell undertook this genius accomplishment, finding codes hidden in 213 cubes in the ceiling. The cubes, when combined, formed a series of patterns that resulted in a one-hour musical accompaniment for 13 medieval prayers!

When the composer also discovered that the stones at the foot of 12 pillars formed a classic 15th-century cadence (three chords at the end of a musical piece), he suggested that the music sounded like a "nursery rhyme," a child-like tune that would have been more fitting of a man like William Sinclair. A man who may have been a great architect, but a lousy musician! Mitchell is himself the son of Thomas Mitchell, who spent more than two decades trying to unravel the musical code on the Chapel ceiling. Stuart's recording of the mysterious musical notes is called "The Rosslyn Motet," and it is his hope, among other researchers, that when played on medieval instruments, it creates a resonant frequency throughout the chapel similar to a Cymatic or Chladni pattern, which form when a sustained note vibrates a sheet of metal covered in a powder. The frequency creates a pattern in the powder, and different musical notes produce different patterns such as rhombuses, flowers, diamonds, hexagons, and other shapes...all of which were found on the Rosslyn ceiling cubes!

Many scholars insist that these musical tones and corresponding patterns on the ceiling cubes are far more than just coincidence, and that one day we may be able to unlock a medieval secret by repeatedly playing the proper frequencies. So far, the musical mystery remains just that.

Perhaps William Sinclair was familiar with sacred geometry and harmonics, and utilized them in the building of this magical, mystical chapel. These esoteric, yet science-based mysteries, combined with the many links of Rosslyn to the Masons, Knights Templar, and other secret societies serve to ensure that Rosslyn remains a popular tourist spot and place of intrigue. Two of the chapel's pillars are believed by Masons to refer to the pillars of Boaz and Joachim, and there are pictorial references on wall carvings to the Key of Hiram, as well as to certain plant species that are found only in America—and which would not be officially discovered for some 100 years or more.

Some legends state that a huge treasure of amazing proportions, perhaps the Holy Grail itself, lies hidden in the sealed chambers below the Chapel's basement floor. It has been said that within the Chapel, three giant medieval chests are filled with shocking contents that might change our entire religious history. Others believe the secret lies within the stone walls themselves, ripe with symbolism and hidden meaning. Perhaps one day, the correct series of musical notes may reveal to us the secrets of Rosslyn.

Other sacred sites whisper of ancient knowledge available to those who can discern their symbols, their signs, and their secret patterns of numbers and sequences. Although it is unfortunate that we seem to have lost much of the knowledge or motivation to design sacred architecture, take solace in the fact that perhaps one day it will be rediscovered, and will usher in a new generation of understanding and awareness. In the next chapter, we will take a look at why certain numbers play such a huge role in occult and religious beliefs and traditions, and even in more modern capacities as fairy tales, often masked as signs and symbols that represent more than meets the eye.

CHAPTER

4:4

Signs and Symbols

In a symbol there is concealment and yet revelation: here therefore, by silence and by speech acting together, comes a double significance. In the symbol peroper; what we can call a symbol, there is ever, more or less distinctly and directly, some embodiment and revelation of the Infinite; the Infinite is made to blend itself with the Finite, to stand visible, and as it were, attainable there. By symbols, accordingly, is man guided and commanded, made happy, made wretched.

—Thomas Carlyle

"Stop." "No right turn." "Yield." Fortunately for our insurance carriers, most of us are familiar with the various signs and symbols utilized in modern transportation. Although sometimes aggravating, they serve a valuable and important purpose. Throughout millennia, mankind has developed and assigned signs and symbols as representative depictions of nearly everything of significance. For example, when you think of the big golden arches, what first comes to mind?

Symbols

The word *symbol* has its roots in the Greek term *symbolon*, which means "contract, token, insignia, and a means of identification."

Symbols are objects, pictures, or other visual representations of ideas, concepts, or abstractions. For example, in the United States, Canada, Australia, and Great Britain, a red octagon is a symbol for "STOP." And here in the United States and now abroad, a pair of golden arches signifies a burger. Signs and symbols have allowed us to use readily identifiable monikers and icons as representations of the original item.

Signs, symbols, and glyphs have been used for religious and occult purposes from the very beginning of time. Early rock and cave art depictions present a fascinating view into the minds of our prehistoric ancestors. Many theories abound regarding the purpose of these creative signs—some have ascribed them to ceremonial purposes, while others believe that they were utilized as a means to transmit information. Whatever the true explanation, they remain a mysterious and enigmatic part of the human experience.

Religion

Religious use of symbology has likewise been commonly employed throughout history. On a daily basis we are confronted with a virtual cacophony of sacred religious icons such as the Christian cross, the Jewish Star of David, the Islamic crescent, the Buddhist Wheel of Dharma, and so on. With the modern societal belief in cultural and religious diversity, suburbia has an increasing number of billboards and street corners dedicated to churches, synagogues, mosques, and other places of holy worship.

Numbers

Even our favorite topic of numbers is not immune from the influence of signs and symbols. Math iconography has generally been used to express mathematical statements in an easily understood, plain language. Lancelet Hogben, the famous English statistician and writer said:

Every meaningful mathematical statement can also be expressed in plain language. Many plain-language statements of mathematical expressions would fill several pages, while to express them in mathematical notation might take as little as one line. One of the ways to achieve this remarkable compression is to use symbols to stand for statements, instructions and so on.

Many of the world's most mysterious and sacred places also employ signs, symbols, and numerology as representative icons. From the ancient to the modern world, such wonders as the Great Pyramid of Giza, Stonehenge, Easter Island, Machu Picchu, the Taj Mahal, and even the Rosslyn Chapel all contain within their very structures symbols purposely inscribed to reveal a higher, secret knowledge to those who are willing to look for them. And more times than not, that knowledge has a connection with numbers.

We even have a symbol for numbers themselves: #

The relationship between the symbols and numbers is inescapable.

The Triad

Numbers, whether in plain digit form or represented as arcane symbols, have had a profound influence on religion the world over. One of the most well-known symbols is that of "three"—referred to as a triad.

A triad, a group of three, may refer to:

■ Greek philosophy: The Pythagorean symbol for the number 3.

■ Music: A set of three notes, most commonly forming a diatonic tertian chord.

■ Relationship: A term for a relationship between three people.

■ Religious: Three deities commonly associated together; three deities forming a group with common associations; three deities thought of as three phases of one deity; or three entities thought of as aspects of one deity (for example, the "great goddess," or Triple Goddess: grandmother, mother, and daughter; crone, matron, and maiden; and, in Catholicism: father, son, spirit); triple deities.

■ Sociology: A term for a group of three people as a unit of study.

Most notably, the triad holds great importance in many religions, from the most ancient Pagan traditions to modern Tao and Christianity. The power of "three" is seemingly everywhere!

In fact, every major and minor religious system has a similar triadic concept that does one of two things: (1) describes the nature of reality, and (2) describes the path to enlightenment. Only semantics separate these worldwide concepts from what could be termed a "spiritual unified theory," which can be explored and embraced by people no matter what their claimed religion or belief system.

Cosmology

In the ancient Sumerian culture, cosmology was an integral and important part of daily life. Their cosmology centered around the *Enuma Elish*, which was an epic poem about the creation of the gods, as well as all other forms in existence. The *Elish* would later become a framework for many themes found in mystical Judaism and Islam. The story begins with Nammu, the primeval sea and Mother of all, who created heaven (*an*) and earth (*ki*). According to the story, when the hard metallic shell of the sky was separated and raised above earth by the God Enlil, a third layer of existence opened up, which has the great waters of Nammu. Thus we have one of the first images of a triadic structure of existence on record. From this triadic primordial mess, the substance of which had been in existence for all eternity, the gods themselves, emerged two-by-two, and the parade of creation began.

According to Gerald A. LaRue in *Ancient Myth and Modern Life*, this idea of a three-tiered structure found its way into ancient Greek, Egyptian, and even Hebrew creation myths.

In the Egyptian legend, heaven and earth were separated by water. In the Hebrew myth, it was air. Always the mysterious sort, the Babylonian's espoused the "Abyss." These and other similar ancient creation myths would eventually develop into more symbolic descriptions of the universe, such as the Shamanic belief in the Lower World, Middle World, and Upper World, and the much later Christian concept of heaven, hell, and purgatory. Now, if you were paying attention, and not still pondering Mr. Hogben's name, you may have noticed that all of those concepts were based on the triadic system of three.

Paganism and Shamanism

Ancient Paganism and Shamanism suggest that even within the realm of a genderless divinity, there were still three levels of existence of which humans would be forced to contend: the physical, mental, and spiritual. These three could be more easily termed as body, mind, and spirit. Again, the power of three!

Even Neo-Platonists understood this basic Hermetic Law: As Above, So Below. Earth-based religions understood the connection between man, nature, and the creative force behind it all. Using sacred rituals, herbs, chanting, and cadence, Shamans journeyed through the vast realms of the Lower World, where the basest primal existence occurred, the Middle World of day-to-day existence, and the Upper World where superior guidance and knowledge was available. At least 40,000 years before the dawn of Christianity, Shamanic peoples understood that the only way to wholeness and connection with the creative force was to be able to move easily between the Triple Worlds. They believed that in order to enter the realm of pure spirit, they needed the ability to transcend the limits of the physical body and mind.

Were these ideas the precursors of later concepts of God, Man, and Holy Spirit? Were they forerunners of the concept of Id, Ego, and Superego as introduced by Freud and later reconstructed to indicate the subconscious, conscious, and super conscious? And what about the Buddhist concept of Personhood, Mindfulness, and Nirvana? Or the metaphysical suggestion of Self, Conscious Awareness, and Higher Self? Even the much more recent concept of Right Brain/Intuitive, Left Brain/Analytical, and Third Eye/Spiritual may have its underpinnings in these ideas.

Egyptian Beliefs

The ancient myths and stories of creation, including the Egyptian tale of the Reigning Queen as Mother of God, the Reigning Pharaoh as Sun God or Father immanent in the flesh among men, and the Heir Apparent (Prince) as the Son both of God and God to be, all speak of a triadic structure upon which man could understand not only the way the world around him was made, but the way he, himself was made and meant to express his being. This idea of expression would repeat itself throughout history, from Queen, Pharaoh, and Prince/Son; to Buddha, Dharma, Sangha; to God, Christ, and Adam; to Father, Son, and Holy Spirit; to today's popular notion of Me, Myself, and I.

Christianity

Perhaps the most obvious physical Trinity occurs in Christianity, where the Father, Son, and Holy Spirit are first described as actual beings. The Father is God, the Son is the Christ, also called Son of God and Son of Man, and the

Holy Spirit is often described in the New Testament as a "presence, which descended upon" whomever was the lucky chosen. But even the Christian church in its earliest configuration had issues with the simplistic, physical-oriented Trinity. If Jesus was the Son, yet also the Word (*Logos*) made flesh, was he, too, God? Was Christ made of the same nature as God? And who or what was the Holy Spirit?

When the early church bishops gathered at the Council of Nicaea in the year 325 AD, they actually resolved (although there were a few dissenters) this questioning by creating the Apostle's Creed. This historic meeting decided that from that point on, it would be officially stated that the Creator and the Redeemer were one and the same. At this point, the Trinity became less a physical reality and more a spiritual symbol representing a path to divine union, with God as the Father Almighty, the Son of God as Lord Jesus Christ, and the Holy Spirit as the binding agent, so to speak.

Yet even as Christianity developed, and as Gnostic and Mystical Christianity began to grow, the somewhat physical concept of One God, One Son (Jesus), and some mysterious third "entity" named the Holy Spirit began to expand into something more symbolic, and less material. This was likely due in part to the natural evolution of human thought and spiritual unfoldment. Most of the original concepts of a Trinity began just as human thought did: simplistic, physical-oriented, and based upon what could be seen and immediately understood within the physical and material realms. But the more that man developed, and the more his consciousness expanded, the farther away from a physical nature the Trinity concept seemed to move.

This and other similar thoughts would be echoed in the ancient Eastern wisdom schools as well. The Bhagavad-Gita, long considered the exemplary text of the Hindu culture, states in its Eighteenth Teaching:

There is no being on earth
or among the gods in heaven
free from the triad of qualities
that are born of nature.

In his introduction to Barbara Stoler Miller's translation, *The Bhagavad-Gita*, Huston Smith states that, "To uncover the nature of the self, the Gita approaches it from three directions that triangulate the self…. One of these concerns its makeup, its attributes or qualities. A second distinguishes different spiritual attitudes that serve as starting points for the journey to God…the third system of classification turns on differences in what grabs people's interests in the world." All three attributes, as per Huston, create a model of the human self and the psychological and spiritual nature.

Even the various aspects of Krishna's material nature are described as triadic and are analyzed in terms of the three fundamental qualities of lucidity (*sattva*), passion (*rajas*), and dark inertia (*tamas*). These three natural qualities are what constitute, in Hindu thought, the nature of man. Note here the similarities to the Id, Ego, and Superego concept of Freud! Was Freud's famous theory possibly based upon the Hindu teachings?

Looking closely, one can even see a parallel here with the later Christian concept of heaven, hell, and purgatory. Krishna tells Arjuna in the *Gita's Fourteenth Teaching*:

Men who are lucid go upward;

men of passion stay in between;

men of dark inertia,

caught in vile ways, sink low.

The triadic nature of Hindu faith is also made up of these three elements, inherent in the embodied self, and this trinity of lucidity, passion, and dark inertia presents itself throughout the Gita as a symbol of the three levels of man's nature, both physical and spiritual.

Chinese Belief

In the *Tao Te Ching*, the centerpiece of all Chinese religion and philosophy, we see a close parallel between the Tao teaching of *te* (individual soul), *Tao* (universal or cosmic soul), and *chi* (universal energy), and the older Hindu Vedic concept of *atman* (individual soul), *Brahman* (universal soul), and *Moksha* (liberation). *Tao* and *Brahman* both represent Cosmic Unity, or the Father. The individual soul as represented by *te* and *atman* can also be called the Son. And as for the Holy Spirit, we offer *chi* energy present in all things, or for the Vedic Hindus, a pure liberation or freedom of the soul. The Tao teachings of the Yan Hui, one of Confucius's disciples, also include the idea that the human being and cosmos share three life-forces: spirit (*shen*), breath (*qi*), and vital essence (*jing*), also known as the "Three Pure Ones." This personification of the triadic nature of being is echoed in every tradition from the East, with only slight variations in presentation and semantics.

Chinese Buddhism presents the trinity concept as present throughout spiritual teachings as the Three Jewels: Buddha, *Dharma*, and *Sangha*, or the God-Head, his teachings, and his community (also referred to as The Teacher, His Teaching, and the freedom the teachings inspire). These three jewels symbolized the actions to be taken to achieve union with the Divine, and was a common concept throughout Eastern thought; it was even paralleled in the Jain religion with the trinity of *samyag-darsana* (correct perception of insight), *samyag-jnana* (correct knowledge), and *samyag-caritra* (correct conduct).

Thich Nhat Hanh emphasizes the need for a budding Buddha to live from the teachings of the Three Jewels, and urges those seeking enlightenment to understand that "every moment is an opportunity to breathe life into the Buddha, the *Dharma*, and the *Sangha*. Every moment is an opportunity to manifest the Father, Son, and Holy Spirit." Thus, the concept of Buddha as a physical deity, *Dharma* as a physical reality of right action, and *Sangha* as a physical community or the "body of man" is transformed into symbols of inner transformation, where the inner God uses inner right thought and action to achieve a community of spirit. This is what Hanh means when he emphasizes that we can "touch the living Buddha and the living Christ" within each of us.

In Robert Thurman's translation of the *Tibetan Book of the Dead* we see a triad appear in the Tibetan Buddhist concept of Three Bodies of Buddhahood: (1) Truth Body, associated with the ultimate reality; (2) Beatific Body, the subjective and transcendent wisdom aspect; and (3) Incarnational Emanation Body, the physical manifestation. In this we see a powerfully obvious match-up with the Christian Trinity of the ultimate Father God, the subjective Holy Spirit that permits transcendence, and the Son who is the physical manifestation that embodies the other two.

Thurman draws a beautiful correspondence between the Buddha bodies and the processes of life (Emanation Body), death (Truth Body), and the Between (Beatific Body). For many Christians of the Western World, these correspondences can also be applied to heaven (Death), earth (Life), and purgatory (what lies between), with Death being the ultimate permanent union with the Divine (and appearing to be somewhat more "superior" than life, at least to the Buddhists!).

Hanh also constantly refers to the parallels between the Buddhist foundational practice of the Three Jewels of Buddha, *Dharma*, and *Sangha*, and the Trinity of the Christian church. The common symbolism is not lost on Hanh, who suggests that just as taking refuge in the Three Jewels is at the foundation of every Buddhist practice, taking refuge in the Trinity is at the foundation of every Christian practice.

Other Ways of the Trinity

Meanwhile, Gnostic Christian texts would bring the feminine face of God into the fray. Author and scholar Elaine Pagels recounts a passage from the Apocryphon of John, which tells of a mystical vision of the Trinity he experienced while grieving for the Crucified Christ: "...and I was afraid, and I saw in the light...a likeness with multiple forms, and the likeness had three forms." John questions the vision and receives this answer: "I am the one who is with you always. I am the Father; I am the Mother; I am the Son."

Pagels explains that this version of the Trinity is based upon the Hebrew term for spirit, *ruah*, which is a feminine word, thus concluding that the feminine "person" conjoined with the Father and Son must be the Mother. Another feminine Trinity symbol appears in the Gospel according to Philip, which describes the Holy Spirit as Mother and Virgin, consort to the Heavenly Father. Philip believes this is the true account for the Virgin Birth symbolism of Christology, "Christ, therefore, was born from a virgin," meaning from the Holy Spirit, not from a virgin woman named Mary.

Pagels also suggests that Wisdom (Sophia) could have also served as the feminine aspect of the Trinity. Sophia, wisdom, translates a Hebrew feminine term, *hokhmah*, and refers to the saying in Proverbs, "God made the world in Wisdom."

Another powerful Gnostic text that suggests a feminine aspect of the Trinity is the poem *Thunder, Perfect Mind*, which most scholars agree was written by a woman (although the author is uknown). "I am the first and the last...I am the whore, and the holy one...I am the wife and the virgin...I am godless, and I am one whose God is great." This parallels another text, the Trimorphic Protennoia (Triple-formed Primal Thought), discovered from the famed Nag Hammadi site. This text proclaims the three feminine powers of Thought, Intelligence, and Foresight, and opens with the stunning lines, "I am the Thought that dwells in the Light...she who exists before the All... I am the Invisible One within the All...."

Sefirot

Jewish mystics who studied the Kabbalah (also spelled Qabbala, Cabala, Cabalah, Cabbala, Cabbalah, Kabala, Kabalah, Qabala, and Qabalah) also understood the triadic symbolism of their Christian counterparts. It was the Hebrew God Yahweh, after all, that the early Christian Church was trying to define by adding the Trinitarian nature. In the Kabbalah, a more metaphysical understanding of the nature of God, the All, *Ein Sof*, takes form in the three major *sefirot*, or the qualities through which the Divine emanates and performs its actions. The first major emanation is *Keter*, called *Ayin*, Nothingness. From Keter a second point emanates, *Hokmah* (wisdom) also called *Yesh*, Being. This sefirah is the beginning of being-from-nothingness, the beginning of revelation and existence. The third point of emanation is *Binah*, Understanding, which is required to reveal that which exists. From these three sefirot emerge the six dimensions of providence, from the *Hesed* (Love) sefirah to the following.

Each group of sefirot is revealed in triads from a sefirah before it; for example, *Hesed* (Love) emanated from *Hokhmah* (Wisdom); *Gevurah* (Power) from *Binah* (Understanding); and *Tif'eret* (Beauty) from *Keter* (Nothingness). Kabbalists claim that it is improper to probe the essence of the first three sefirot because they constitute the Divine Mind, Wisdom, and Understanding. Note the parallel here with the early Greek Christian Orthodox church's claim that the true nature of the Divine was unexplainable, thus the need for a more symbolic interpretation of the Trinity.

Kabbalah

Kabbalists understood the *Ein Sof* as the Infinite, from which all else emanated, including humankind. In "The Chain of Being" from *The Essential Kabbalah* we are told "The entire chain is one. Down to the last link, everything is linked with everything else; so divine essence is below as well as above, in heaven and on earth. There is nothing else." And then, in *"Ein Sof and You"* we learn that "Each of us emerges from the *Ein Sof* and is included in it. We live through its dissemination." The *Ein Sof* is the Father of the Christian world. We are the Sons. And the dissemination of the *Ein Sof* is the Holy Spirit that moves in and through us.

As Rabbi Eliezar ben Judah of Worms, Jewish mystic and philosopher, proclaimed in "The Song of Unity" in Gershom Sholem's *Major Trends in Jewish Mysticism*:

Everything is in Thee and Thou art in everything: Thou fillest everything and dost encompass it: when everything was created Thou was in everything; before everything was created, Thou was everything.

Another concept of Kabbalah is the Supernal Triad. According to the Universal Kabbalah Network (*www.universalkabalah.net*):

> The Supernal Triad is very much like the Celtic trinity knot; there are three aspects, yet they are all interwoven such that the three are one and the energy flow between them is unbroken. While there are three aspects, they occur simultaneously with Kether being the initial spark, Chokmah being the flame that extends out, and Binah like the holder that contains the flame, allowing its light to emanate out but not its destructiveness.

This triadic concept of unity is very interesting, and, it would seem likely that it has served as the basis for diverse religious iconography. Again, from the Universal Kabbalah Network:

> The supernals are the "3 mothers" associated with the Hebrew Letters Shin (spirit/fire), Aleph (air), and Mem (water), which are also the 3 mother rays of Amon Ra: numbers, letters, and sounds that are used to write the name of God, from which all creation comes. The third ray, Binah (Mem), being the one from which all other rays and creational energies are birthed or emanated out from. We see this in the Kabbalah by the path that the lightning bolt or "flaming sword" takes as it carries the creational energies down from source to Malkuth. Binah is the last of the supernals that it enters before coming into the lower realms. Thus, Binah is the closest of the supernals to the world of form; hence it is the original archetypal form, whereas Chokmah is the original archetypal force. These roles of form and force can also be explained through the beginning stages of creation.

Unlike its sister religions of Judaism and Christianity, Islam considered the Trinity a blasphemous concept. To the followers of the Koran, trying to speculate on things theologically was referred to, somewhat condescendingly, as *Zanna*. This term translates roughly to "self-indulgent guesswork about things that cannot possibly be known," and perfectly describes their disdain for theological pondering.

The idea of a triadic nature of God was definitely not something Muslims accepted, or would even consider. To the Muslim, God, or Allah, was all, is all, and will always be all there is.

Muhammad the Prophet, who supposedly channeled the Koran in a series of trance states, considered the Koran the word of God directly translated to Arabic. According to the Koran, Allah, was indivisible All. This emphasis on total and complete oneness would turn the Islamic churches away from the Trinity doctrine being embraced in nearby Christian churches. According to author Karen Armstrong, a former Roman Catholic nun turned religious scholar, the Christian Incarnation of Christ was also blasphemous to the Islamic Church. Instead, the Koran spoke of an impersonal God who cannot be personified, but only glimpsed through signs of nature and contemplation of the Koran itself.

Islam

The Islamic Church, however, does believe in an experience of transcendence with the Ultimate Reality by utilizing the Koran as a spiritual discipline, and it is this context that we see a trinity concept. Muhammad, and any other Muslim devotee, surely could study the Koran and pray to Allah in a trance state, and experience this transcendence. This would suggest the man as the Son, the study of the Koran and prayer as the activating agents of the Holy Spirit, and Allah of course, as the Father. In this sense, do we see a Trinity evolve in the Islamic religion? Otherwise, the Koran more closely parallels an older Semitic concept of divine unity and refuses to accept that God can somehow "beget" a son. To the Muslim, there is no God but Allah and no human being (such as Christ or Buddha) that can be a "part" of the Divine Nature. But admittedly, Muslims could develop a "sense" of the transcendent presence by study of the Koran, prayer, and devotion.

Eventually, even Islam would develop a more philosophical branch of mystics known as the Sufis. Similar to many other spiritual sects, they used chanting and prayer to achieve a union with the Divine. Unlike earlier Muslim teachings, the Sufis suggested that the Divine could indeed be manifest in man. To the Sufis, much like the Kabbalists and Gnostic Christians, the distinction was made between the essence of God, and the God we glimpse in revelation and the creation around us. God is, and would always be, essentially unknowable. However, the essence could be experienced through prayer, meditation, or, as with the Mawlawiyyah order of Sufis known as the "whirling dervishes," through concentrated dance and spinning to create a transcendent state in which the boundaries of self dissolve into a union with the Divine. Thus, the worshipper uses a more metaphysical approach and becomes the Son who uses the trance-like spinning and dancing (or chanting, praying, bowing, and so on) as the means of inviting in the Holy Spirit. As part of this process, one's consciousness supposedly expands while breaking down ego boundaries to become one with the Father (Allah, Divine Essence).

Images of the triune nature of God and reality abound in religious traditions, from ancient Celtic paganism to Christianity. Top left: a triskele; top right: a trefoil; bottom left: a triquetra; and bottom right: a shield trinity. Images courtesy of Wikipedia Commons.

Fairy Tales

As we have seen, the number 3 holds a very profound place in religion. Believe it or not, it is also a critical number in, of all things, fairy tales.

Remember Goldilocks? Goldilocks crashed the home of the Three Bears. How about our friend the troll? The troll made trouble for the Three Billy Goats Gruff. The Three Blind Mice tried to escape an old lady's wrath. The Three Little Pigs learned about the effects of wind on housing materials. Fairy tales, long a staple of folkloric studies, prominently display a preference for certain numbers, namely the number 3. From the three notes to the Pied

Piper, to Cinderella and her two ugly stepsisters, to three wishes, three tasks, and three corners to go around, the prevalence of the number 3 in the stories, which in certain cultures conveyed knowledge, taught lessons, and entertained children all in one fell swoop, cannot be ignored. We can even see this pattern in the Arthurian tales of the quest for the Holy Grail, not to mention the story of the Three Wise Men of the Christian Bible.

Some experts believe this is because of the structure of story itself; every story has a beginning, middle, and end. Within this framework, the story unfolds, as a "hero's journey" of sorts, that involves, as Joseph Campbell once put it, an initiation, a quest, and a resolution. These three stages permit the magic of 3 to appear yet again!

But perhaps it is our Indo-European background that provides us with this triadic pattern. If so, was this designed expressly to challenge the usual dichotomies of good and evil, night and day, black and white, rich and poor, and so on? According to Herb Buckland in "The Number Three—Folklore-Fantasy-Fiction?" for Suite101.com, if we hold to the Out of Africa theory, it can be suggested that we are all third generational descendants, with Africans being the first line of descendancy, Asians the second, and the Indo-Europeans the third. These cultural explanations parallel the idea that even in the world of science, and our own bodies, we see the triadic pattern, as in our DNA, RNA, and proteins.

There may be a subtler, archetypal reason for the number 3 in fairy tales and stories. With each of the three challenges, the ante is upped, requiring more of our hero or heroine. With each bear or pig, there is a greater problem, and a better solution to solve the problem. Let us not forget our favorite ignoramuses—the three stooges. With each third wish, the chance for three more.... After all, we are the third planet from the sun.

Fairy tales and stories don't just stop at the number 3. Persian legends speak of seven caverns that aspirants must move along during their 70 years on earth. We tell tales of the seven seas. And who can forget the House of Seven Gables? Egyptian legend tells of the seven Hothors, fairy godmothers that bestow certain fate upon newborn babies. In the Talmud, we have seven stages of a man's life: the infant, the child, the boy, the young man, the married man, the parent, and the old man. Shakespeare wrote of the seven stages of a man's life in his play, *As You Like It*:

The Seven Ages of Man by William Shakespeare
All the world's a stage,
And all the men and women merely players:

They have their exits and their entrances;
And one man in his time plays many parts,
His acts being seven ages. At first the infant,
Mewling and puking in the nurse's arms.
Then the whining school-boy, with his satchel
And shining morning face, creeping like snail
Unwillingly to school. And then the lover,
Sighing like furnace, with a woeful ballad
Made to his mistress' eyebrow. Then a soldier,
Full of strange oaths, and bearded like the pard,
Jealous in honor, sudden and quick in quarrel,
Seeking the bubble reputation
Even in the cannon's mouth. And then the justice,
In fair round belly with good capon lined,
With eyes severe and beard of formal cut,
Full of wise saws and modern instances;
And so he plays his part. The sixth age shifts
Into the lean and slipper'd pantaloon,
With spectacles on nose and pouch on side,
His youthful hose, well saved, a world too wide
For his shrunk shank; and his big manly voice,
Turning again toward childish treble, pipes
And whistles in his sound. Last scene of all,
That ends this strange eventful history,
Is second childishness and mere oblivion,
Sans teeth, sans eyes, sans taste, sans every thing.
As You Like It, act 2, scene 7.

Psychologist Maria von Frans suggests that number patterns in fairy tales are clues, and may possibly be indicative of ancient patterns of destiny that mark a natural rhythm to events. This rhythmic pattern no doubt applies to our own lives and, as Dame Anita Roddick stated in *Numbers*, there might just be a numeric pattern or combination of patterns that "predict the futures we are hurtling towards." Thus, the use of numeric patterns in the stories by which we define ourselves, and the legends and myths and even religious beliefs we pass down from generation to generation makes sense. We are always predicting the outcome of our own stories, our own lives.

So there is a reason why the king has three daughters, the cock crows three times, the three little kittens keep losing their mittens, and the three ships sail into the harbor each morning at Christmastime; a reason that cannot be foreseen except in the murky mists of future time.

In addition to our friendly number 3, the numbers 1 and 2 also hold great significance in religious traditions (as well as in both mythology and folklore). The number 1 represents the ultimate unity, God, the Divine. This is the number that unites all others into wholeness. One need only think about the symbol of interlocking wedding rings to give the idea of two becoming one, or the Star of David, combining the masculine and feminine triangles in one extraordinarily sacred symbolic image. Even with the importance of this uniting icon, the number 2, representing duality, is present here as well. And the number 3, of such huge importance, cannot exist without these two numbers coming before it, merging to create a complete tri-fold identity. Similar to the yin and yang symbol, the two halves combine to produce the one, whole unit. In the next chapter, we will also look at other numbers of significance; however, when it comes to symbols and signs, few hold the kind of power over us as the first three, literally defining our reality as body, mind, and spirit; earth, water, and sky; birth, life, and death.

Two images representing the duality of male/female in Union. Images courtesy of Wikipedia

Vesica Piscis

One of the most mystical and powerful images of the concept of two becoming one is the Vesica Piscis, the union of two circles of the same radius whose intersecting point lies on the circumference of the other. The term *vesica piscis* means "the bladder of fish" in Latin and has definite religious connotations. Jesus Christ was associated with Pisces, the astrological symbol of two fish enjoined, as well as with the Age of Pisces we are now living in, a time of duality that would eventually lead into the more transformational and unified Age of Aquarius.

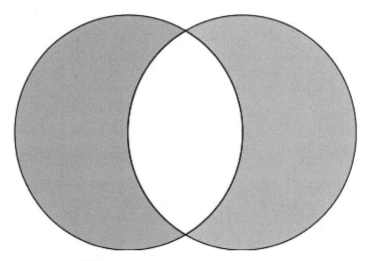

Image courtesy of Wikipedia.

The Vesica Piscis is one more example of an iconographic symbol that represents a numeric concept. Because the human mind, most notably the subconscious, responds more readily to images and symbols, the interlocking of two circles takes on a greater importance as a spiritual concept than any mathematical equation describing the same ever could.

5

In occult traditions, the number 5 takes on metaphysical importance, embodying the image of the human body, with limbs outspread, as in the famous Vitruvian Man of da Vinci fame. The Pentagram, a mystical prime number that combines the sum of 2 and 3, 1 and 4, has been sacred to Pagans for centuries. The number 5 is prevalent in the stories of the New Testament, with Christ receiving five main wounds to his body at Calvary, and feeding the 5,000 masses with five loaves of bread. Five represents humanity, and to both ancient Pagans and modern Wiccans, it represents air, fire, water, earth, and spirit—the stuff of which life is made.

Eliphas Levi's pentagram, said to encompass the magical formula of man within its numbers and symbols. Image courtesy of Wikipedia.

The ancient Chinese believed that there were five basic elements that formed the elemental basis for all things: wood, fire, earth, metal, and water. We have five senses, five digits on each hand and each foot. The Pentagram symbol was widely used in magickal practices, and is still considered a sacred occult symbol to those who believe it embodies mankind within its points. But inversely, the pentagram also has a more sinister representation due to its often falsely associated link to the satanic religion. The identification with the Pagan god Pan, or the mysterious horned Baphomet, surely did not add to the inverse

Pentagram's appeal to Christians, who proceeded to label the innocuous image as evil. Pan was a harmless woodland god promoting procreation and good times. Baphomet? The creation of occultist Eliphas Levi in his "Dogmas and Rituals of High Magic," in which he included an image he had drawn himself that he described as Baphomet and "The Sabbatic Goat," a winged humanoid goat with breasts and a torch on its head between its horns. Strangely, though, in Levi's original drawings, the Pentagram was not inverted. Yet Baphomet worship was linked to the Templars and even the Freemasons, which may have lent more ammunition to devout Christians looking to undermine secret societies with metaphysical teachings.

Even Heinrich Cornelius Agrippa added to the confusion by stating in Eliphas Levi's *Transcendental Magic, its Doctrine and Ritual*, "A reversed pentagram, with two points projecting upward, is a symbol of evil and attracts sinister forces because it overturns the proper order of things and demonstrates the triumph of matter over spirit. It is the goat of lust attacking the heavens with its horns, a sign execrated by initiates." Followers of the Church of Satan founder Anton LeVay kept the negativity going with their belief that the inverse pentagram described the denial of the trinity by placing the three points downward. This Satanic image would also gain momentum with the beliefs of occultism and black magickal traditions.

The Bolzani pentacle (left) is a depiction of Christ the man as a macrocosmic whole. The inverse pentagram of Eliphas Levi represents the Goat God Baphomet of occult tradition. Images courtesy of Wikipedia.

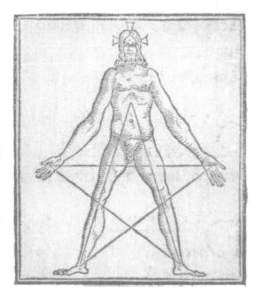

Regardless of one's personal beliefs or convictions, the power of numbers and symbols have shaped our beliefs to the point where everyone on earth recognizes the positive elements of a star, and the negative elements of that star turned on its tip.

Streetwise Numbers

Obviously, numbers and their use as a means of measuring a variety of things deemed important, both physical and spiritual, played a significant role in the cultural beliefs that are evident in stories and ideals passed down from generation to generation. Yet, even today, in a more modern cultural context do we see the symbolic use of numbers to represent "something else" at work, albeit in a more streetwise manner.

Take modern public safety professionals for example. Police officers, firefighters, and EMS personnel all use number codes to convey information about certain crimes, behaviors, status, even their own physical locations. Interestingly, street gangs have developed a number-related code of their own, as a means of communicating, as their law enforcement counterparts do, without really saying what they mean to say. It's a form of shorthand for the select few to understand, just as, perhaps, the numeric codes evident in legends, myths, and tales of old.

On both sides of the law, numbers speak a language all their own. The following is just a sampling.

Cop Talk	Gang Slang
1-1 Receiving Poorly	0-0 Shot gun
1-2 Receiving Well	006 Silence
1-3 Stop	013 Get him; assault him
1-4 OK	13 Meth or Marijuana
1-5 Relay	100 proof the real thing
1-6 Busy	187 Threat to murder
1-7 Out of Service	3R respect, reputation, revenge
1-8 In service	410 Folks in battle
1-9 Repeat	420 Time to light up (pot)
1-10 Out to lunch	88 Heil Hitler (Aryan Nation)
Code 1—Murder	5-0 Police

Cop Talk	Gang Talk
Code 2—Rape	50/50 Non-gang member
Code 3—Robbery	23/24 Inmate lockup
Code 4—Assault	24/7 On the street all hours
Code 5—Burglary	023 Watch your back
Code 6—Theft	025 What's your rank?
Code 7—Auto Theft	5150 Mental case

Numbers are such an integral part of our society, and have come to represent and symbolize so much. Ever since man first learned to measure and specify quantity, we have been on a progressively increasing path. It is only natural that numbers have taken on symbolic significance in image form—the form we humans best relate to and understand. Perhaps Sergeant Joe Friday's famous catch-phrase "Just the facts, ma'am" should have been "Just the numbers, ma'am."

CHAPTER 5:5

Mystery Numbers

The creator of the Universe works in mysterious ways. But he uses a base 10 counting system and likes round numbers.
—Scott Adams (American Cartoonist)

On a regular day, the average human experiences hundreds, if not thousands, of events—some big and bold, others trivial and forgetable, but all involving numbers. As we have made clear in previous chapters, for many, a particular number or numbers will show up time and time again. Often, this seeming coincidence infuses a deeper meaning, or a greater mystery into our normally mundane existence.

Mystery numbers suit up and show up a little more often than their neighbors. They get noticed. They stand out. We learned about the frequency of 11s in Chapter 1:1. In Chapters 3 and 4 we discussed the deeply symbolic nature of the first 10 digits, especially the number 3 in relation to the triadic view of reality. In addition, we explored the use of higher numeric sequences in sacred geometry, art, and science. Now we get down and dirty with a host of other numbers that seem to be trying to tell us something, this time without the need for symbol, rhetoric, or nuance. These are in-your-face numbers, strangely beautiful even as they astound with their magnitude and ability to awe us, frighten us, or even bring us incredibly good luck. Of course, there is no golden lining, and these previously wonderful numbers can also annoy, frustrate, and worry us to no end. Think of all the number sequences of which one must remain cognizant: social security numbers, driver's license numbers, account numbers, phone numbers, ATM pin codes, alarm codes.... The list is endless, and certainly a source of irritation and aggravation for many.

Similar to the lead characters in the popular book and movie *The Da Vinci Code*, we notice them, popping up in the least, and sometimes the most, likely of places, and akin to Tom Hanks, we shake our heads in confusion at their persistence. We cannot escape them.

Perhaps we should call them the "Pythagoras Code."

13

Because we authors are generally not superstitious creatures—well, except for the fact that Larry still knocks on wood—let's start with the most misunderstood number: 13. To some, this simple number that follows 12 strikes horror into the heart and fear into the darkest corners of the soul. Unlucky 13 means black cats and broken mirrors, shadows not to be crossed over, ladders not to be walked under, and cracks not to be stepped upon (lest you wanna break your momma's back). How on earth did 13 get such a bad rap anyway? The number is so bad it has even garnered itself its own phobia—"triskaidekaphobia." According to Wikipedia, "Triskaidekaphobia (from Greek tris=three, kai=and, deka=ten) is an irrational fear of the number 13; it is a superstition and related to a specific fear of Friday the 13th, called paraskevidekatriaphobia or friggatriskaidekaphobia."

Some hotels and buildings won't even label the floors between 12 and 14 the 13th floor (although only a moron would fall for that, right?). Others refuse to leave their homes on the 13th of each month, most notably on any Friday the 13th, when unspeakable horrors might occur. On some passenger aircraft, such as those of Continental Airlines, Air New Zealand, Alitalia, and Meridiana, you never have to worry about being assigned to that unlucky seat number because it is not available.

When it comes to explaining why we hate the number 13, there are many theories and beliefs. One, posited by landscape designer and architect Charles A Platt in 1925, suggests that 13 is the first number that a person is unable to count to using their eight fingers, two thumbs, and two feet. This rather far-fetched explanation is matched by suggestions that 13 is unlucky because it is the number of full moons in a year, or because it is a number unable to be paired or mated, or even because Judas Iscariot was the 13th person to sit down to dinner before he betrayed Jesus Christ.

Other explanations refer to the number before it, 12, as the number of wholeness or completeness, as indicated in the 12 Apostles of Christ, the 12 signs of the zodiac, and the 12 months in a year. The number 12 also adds up in single digits to 3, the trinity number, which, as we saw in the previous chapter, holds great influence and power in religious traditions and metaphysics alike. There were 12 knights in King Arthur's Round Table, 12 days of Yule, 12 disciples each to Buddha and Mithra, 12 descendants of Allah and 12 tribes of Israel, 12 paladins of Charlemagne, and 12 fruits of the spirit. There are 12 inches in a foot and 12 fruits on the Cosmic Tree.

No wonder poor 13 is the odd-man-out, the leftover, and the rebel.

In an August 2004 *National Geographic* article titled "Friday the 13th Phobia Rooted in Ancient History," John Roach and Donald Dossey, founder of the Stress Management Center and Phobia Institute in Asheville, North Carolina, and a folklore historian who authored *Holiday Folklore, Phobias and Fun*, said fear of Friday the 13th is rooted in ancient, separate bad-luck associations with the number 13 and the day Friday. The two unlucky entities ultimately combined to make one super bad unlucky day. Dossey traces the fear of 13 to a Norse myth about 12 gods having a dinner party at Valhalla, their heaven. In walked the uninvited 13th guest, the mischievous Loki. Once there, Loki arranged for Hoder, the blind god of darkness, to shoot Balder the Beautiful, the god of joy and gladness, with a mistletoe-tipped arrow.

"Balder died and the whole Earth got dark. The whole Earth mourned. It was a bad, unlucky day," said Dossey. From that moment on, Dossey states, the number 13 has been considered ominous and foreboding.

We authors prefer a simpler explanation to explain the horror behind the number 13: it is the number that indicates the age when a child becomes a teenager.

Despite its bad rap, especially on Fridays, in countries such as Sweden, Belgium, and Germany (Tuesdays in Greece and Spain), there are just as many indicators of the uniquely positive qualities of the number 13. It is the number of the 13 Attributes of Mercy of God in the Torah. Thirteen is the number of the original colonies that the United States was founded upon. It is the number of loaves in a baker's dozen (or donuts, if you prefer). It is also a prime number AND a Fibonacci number, thus proving that what is bad to some is good to others, and that even with numbers, it is all a matter of perspective and belief.

In the Kabbalah, the number 13 is the value of unity, Achad, which is Hebrew for "one." According to Rabbi Michael Berg, writing for About.com, "The number 13 holds great significance according to Kabbalah. The Hebrew words for 'love' (ahava), 'care' (de'aga), and 'one' (echad) all have the numerical value of 13. In addition, kabbalistically, the number 13 indicates the ability to rise above the influence of the 12 signs of the Zodiac (12 + 1 = 13), not being bound by the influences of the cosmos."

More down to earth is the influence of this number on something we all worship and adore: money.

The U.S. $1 bill has the following on the back:

- 13 steps on the pyramid.

- The motto above the pyramid has 13 letters (*annuit coeptis*).

- *E pluribus unum*, written on the ribbon in the eagle's beak, has 13 letters.

- 13 stars appear over the eagle's head.

- 13 stripes are on the shield.

- 13 war arrows are in the eagle's right talon.

- The olive branch in the eagle's left talon has 13 leaves.

So, if the fear of the number 13 is a part of your belief system, the authors ask that you send all dollar bills to us via our Website post office box address.

In their book, *The United Symbolism of America: Deciphering Hidden Meanings in America's Most Familiar Art, Architecture, and Logos*, authors Robert Hieronimus, PhD, and Laura Cortner come to the defense of number 13. They state that the misunderstanding of this innocent number is a recent phenomenon, appearing to be a "strange leftover from the superstitions of the Dark Ages." According to them, it began when the Church started its persecution of women and Pagan healers. "The number 13 is associated with the followers of the Goddess and the way this culture marked time, based on the annual menstruation cycle of the average woman." The authors contend that the word spread that the number 13 was evil, and the Pagan healers suffered by being burned at the stake as witches.

Yet, as the authors point out, these same "holy persecutors" failed to recognize the importance of the number 13 in their own Bible, a number mentioned even as far back as the book of Genesis. Before this negative connotation was attached, the number 13 was, according to Hieronimus and Cortner, "seen as a number of transformation, symbolizing renewal, rebirth, and regeneration. This interpretation may have resulted from the fact that 13 follows that nice, round, complete number of a dozen." They also point to the repeated use of the number by our nation's Founding Fathers, who must have understood its importance in the repeated symbolism of the Great Seal and the American Flag of our original colonies.

7

Superstition is one of the prime culprits to blame for negative values attributed to any number. The same goes for good values. Did you know that the number 7 is considered in many cultures to be the luckiest number of all?

In the Old and New Testament of the Bible, the number 7 shows up dozens of times: seven days warning for Noah before the flood; seven locks of hair on Samson's head; seven daughters of Jethro in Exodus; seven priests with seven trumpets on the seventh day in Joshua 6:4; seven devils possessing Mary Magdalene; seven sons of the priest Sceva in Acts 19:14.

In the book of Revelations, the vision of St. John the Divine, the number 7 appears repeatedly: seven churches; seven spirits; seven golden candlesticks; seven stars, angels, lamps, seals, horns, eyes, trumpets, thunders, crowns, plagues, vials, mountains, and kings. The number 7 obviously held a reverent position in the Judeo-Christian traditions. Other numbers do appear frequently in the Bible as well, but certainly not with the repetitive nature of 7. In occult symbology, the number 7 is considered deeply sacred, oft considered the number of the spirit of "all," or "the everything."

In the Jewish religion, the number 7 plays a significant role. According to Rabbi Yaakov Salomon, writing for Aish.com:

> The fact that the Torah begins with a verse containing 7 words and 28 letters (divisible by 7) is hardly remarkable. But when placed within the context of the overwhelming number of associations in Judaism with 7, a fascinating tapestry begins to unfurl. Kabbalah teaches that 7 represents wholeness and completion. After seven days, the world was complete. There are 6 directions in our world: north, south, east, west, up, and down. Add to that the place where you are, and you have a total of seven points of reference.

A few examples of the number 7 in the Jewish religion:

■ Shabbat is the seventh day of the week.

■ In Israel, there are seven days of Passover and Sukkot.

■ When a close relative dies, we sit Shiva for seven days.

■ Moses was born and died on the same day—the seventh of Adar.

■ The Menorah in the Temple had seven branches.

■ There are seven holidays in the Jewish year: Rosh Hashana, Yom Kippur, Sukkot, Chanukah, Purim, Passover, and Shavuot.

■ At every Jewish wedding, seven blessings are recited (Sheva Brachot).

■ Moses was the seventh generation after Abraham.

■ Each plague in Egypt lasted seven days.

■ God created seven levels of heaven. (Hence the expression, "I'm in seventh heaven!")

■ The Jewish calendar, largely lunar, has a cycle of intercalation that contains seven leap years during each 19-year period.

■ The Talmud lists seven female prophets: Sarah, Miriam, Deborah, Hannah, Avigail, Chuldah, and Esther.

The number 7 plays a significant role in religion and mythology

Christianity

■ *The seven sacraments in the Christian faith (though some traditions assign a different number).*

■ *The seven churches of Asia to which the book of Revelation is addressed.*

- *The seven joys of the Virgin Mary, of Roman Catholic, Anglican, and other traditions.*

- *The seven sorrows of the Virgin Mary, of Roman Catholic, Anglican, and other traditions.*

- *The seven corporal acts of mercy of Roman Catholic, Anglican, and other traditions.*

- *The seven last words (or seven last sayings) of Jesus on the cross.*

- *The seven virtues: chastity, temperance, charity, diligence, kindness, patience, and humility.*

- *The seven deadly sins: lust, gluttony, greed, sloth, wrath, envy, and pride.*

- *The seven terraces of Mount Purgatory (one per deadly sin).*

- *In the genealogy in the Gospel of Luke, Jesus is 77th in a direct line.*

- *The number of heads of the three beasts ($7 \times 10 \times 7 + 7 \times 10 \times 10 + 7 \times 10 = 1260$) of the Book of Revelation, and of some other monsters, such as the hydra and the number of seals.*

- *In the New Testament, the Gospel of Matthew 18:21, Jesus says to Peter to forgive 70 times seven times.*

- *There are seven suicides mentioned in the Bible.*

Islam

- *The ayat in surat al-Fatiha.*

- *The seven heavens in Islamic tradition.*

- *The seven Earths in Islamic tradition.*

- *The seven circumambulations (Tawaf) that are made around the Kaaba.*

- *The seven walks (Al-Safa and Al-Marwah) that is traveling back and forth seven times during the ritual pilgrimages of Hajj and Umrah.*

- The seven fires in hell, that is, the seven fires of hell.
- The seven doors to heaven and hell is also seven.

Hinduism

- The Sanskrit word sapta refers to the number seven.
- The Indian music has sapta swaras, meaning seven octats (sa re ga ma pa dha ni), which are basics of music, and are used in hundreds of Ragas.
- Celestial group of seven stars are named as Sapta Rishi based on the seven great saints.
- Seven Promises and Seven Rounds in Hindu Wedding and Seven Reincarnations.
- As per Hindu mythology, there are seven worlds in the universe, seven seas in the world, and seven Rishies (seven gurus) called sapta rishis.

Mythology

- In Khasi mythology, there are seven divine women who were left behind on earth and became the ancestresses of all humankind.
- The number of gateways traversed by Inanna during her descent into the underworld.
- The number of sleeping men in the Christian myth of the "Seven Sleepers."
- The seven sages in Sumerian mythology and various other mythologies.
- The number of sages in Hindu mythology; their wives are the goddesses referred to as the "Seven Mothers."
- The number of main islands of mythological Atlantis.
- In Guaraní mythology, the number of prominent legendary monsters.
- Japanese mythology talks of Shichifukujin (The Seven Gods of Fortune).

Others

- *The minor symbol number of yang from the Taoist yin and yang.*

- *The number of palms in an Egyptian Sacred Cubit.*

- *The number of ranks in Mithraism.*

- *The number seven is of particular significance within Cherokee cosmology.*

- *In Buddhism, Buddha walked seven steps at his birth.*

- *In Irish mythology, the epic hero Cúchulainn is associated with the number 7. He has seven fingers on each hand, seven toes on each foot, and seven pupils in each eye. In the Irish epic Táin Bó Cúailnge, Cúchulainn is 7 years old when he receives his first weapons and defeats the armies of the Ulaidh. His son Connla is 7 years old when he is slain by Cúchulainn in "The Death of Aife's Only Son."*

- *In British folk lore, every seven years the Fairy Queen pays a tithe to Hell (or possibly Hel) in the tale of Tam Lin.*

- *In the British folk tale of Thomas the Rhymer, he went to live in the faerie kingdom for seven years.*

Courtesy of Wikipedia.

Pythagoreans called 7 the perfect number, 3 and 4, the triangle and the square, the perfect figures. Philo of Alexandria, a contemporary of Christ, said that "Nature delights in the number 7," recognizing its significance in the number of notes in music, stars in the Great Bear, and stages of the life of a man. Seven is the number of external holes in the human head: two eyes, two nostrils, one mouth, and two ears. Seven is the smallest positive integer whose name in English is more than one syllable long. The United States Constitution, as drafted in Philadelphia in 1787, was composed of seven Articles. The United States declared independence in the seventh month of 1776.

There were traditionally seven wonders of the ancient world, though only the Great Pyramid of Egypt still stands today. There were seven seas, seven chakras, seven basic principles of bushido, and seven points on a sheriff's star (the heptagram, or seven-pointed star is a traditional symbol for warding off evil). Roll a 7 in Vegas and you are bound to go home with some cash in your pocket. Even one type of ladybug, considered a lucky friend to all gardeners, has seven spots.

Unlike the numbers 1, 2, and 3, it is not as easy to find the logic or reason behind the importance of the number 7, or why so many people hold it in such high regard. Even the Freemasons worshipped the number 7, so to speak. On a Scottish Mason's apron, there are seven tassels on each side. King Solomon took seven years to build his temple, which was dedicated to the glory of God in the seventh month in a festival that lasted seven days. There are seven liberal arts and sciences, which is a traditional Masonic concept. Masons require seven Brethren to make a Lodge perfect, and must have seven steps on the winding staircase. Even Albert G. Mackey's *Encyclopaedia of Freemasonry* devotes two full pages to the number 7.

But why? Why is 7 so special that it elicits such significance?

One of the only possible explanations we could find relates to the original belief by ancients that there were seven planets. Early cultures considered the celestial bodies to be deities, and to these seven celestial bodies were given tremendous power and influence over the lives of humans on earth. Once additional planets were discovered, most cultures had already embedded the number 7 into their belief systems, and continued the legacy of lucky number 7, infusing it into every area of life, including religion, myth, ritual, and celebration. Hieronimus and Cortner, in *The United Symbolism of America* speculate that 7 got its good rap because it is a fundamental geometrical shape, one achieved by drawing a triangle around a square "which was done to symbolize the sky over the earth, or by inscribing a triangle within a square, which was done to symbolize spirit within matter, the soul within man." They continue that 7 stands for "the complete period or cycle of time, such as seven days in a week, as well as the many other attributes previously mentioned."

23

Other numbers also hold unusual sway with humans, often appearing with frustrating frequency. One such example is the enigmatic number 23. Recently, it was the subject of a poorly received movie starring Jim Carrey, as a man plagued by the number. The "23 enigma" is the belief that all events revolve around the number 23, and that this number is implicated in every incident in a person's life in some form or another. But at least this time, we can trace the enigma to its source, namely several works of fiction via Robert Anton Wilson's *Illuminatus!* trilogy and to William S. Burroughs (who first recounted his own involvement with the number in a story about a mysterious

Captain Clark, whose ship and crew met with a terrible fate after 23 years, and the piloted flight #23 that was sent to find them). The number also plays a role in Discordian philosophy. Discordianism states that all events can be traced to the number 23 based upon the "ingenuity" of the interpreter. In other words, if you are clever enough, you can find a way to attach the number 23 to any significant event in your life. Imagine that—finally a number that we can all relate too! Does Kevin Bacon know about this?

The number 23 is certainly not alone. Take its closest relative for instance. The number 24.

The 24 Enigma?

- *There are 24 hours in a day.*

- *There are 24 ribs in the human body.*

- *24 is the smallest number to have eight different factors. (1, 2, 3, 4, 6, 8, 12).*

- *24 is the number of letters in both the modern and classical Greek alphabet.*

- *The 24th and last letter of the Greek alphabet is "Omega," meaning "the end."*

- *There are 24 "perfect" numbers. These are numbers that equal the sum of all its divisors except itself. (For instance, 6—the lowest of these numbers—is divisible by 1, 2, or 3, and 1 + 2 + 3 = 6.) The largest of the known "perfect" numbers has 12,003 digits.*

- *24 is the largest number divisible by all numbers less than its square root.*

- *24 is the number of cycles in the Chinese solar year.*

- *24 is the number of books in the Tanakh.*

- *24 is the total number of major and minor keys in Western tonal music, not counting enharmonic equivalents.*

- *The binary representation of 24 is 11,000.*

- *24 is the sum of twin prime numbers (11 + 13)."*

- *The earth travels 24,000 miles in 24 hours.*

666

We would be remiss in our duties if we did not explore one of the all-time most enigmatic numbers: 666. These three digits have long been the subject of great debate among religious scholars and amateurs alike. Again, we turn to the book of Revelation. In his vision on the Isle of Patmos, Saint John refers to a beast that bears the mysterious number 666. This is the alleged number of the Antichrist that will wreak havoc upon the earth until the return of Jesus himself and the day of final judgment.

But why three 6's? If number 7 is considered the number of perfection, then the number 6 symbolizes that which falls short of perfection. One only has to recall the story of the fall of the angel Lucifer, because of his vanity and imperfection, to realize that the number 6, tripled, is empowered with negativity. Many scholars have argued over the identity of this Antichrist, often referring to Hitler or Nero or even George W. Bush, yet always stretching their interpretation to fit the numbers.

According to Wikipedia:

- 666 were the winning lottery numbers in the 1980 Pennsylvania Lottery scandal, in which equipment was tampered to favor a 4 or 6 as each of the three individual random digits.

- 666 was the original name of the MacOS SevenDust computer virus that was discovered in 1998.

- In the Bible, 666 is the number of Adonikam's descendants who return to Jerusalem and Judah from the Babylonian exile.

- In the Bible, 666 is the number of gold talents that King Solomon collected in a single year.

- The number 666 is a frequent visual element of Aryan Brotherhood tattoos.

- The sum of all the numbers on a roulette wheel is 666.

- In *The Phantom of the Opera* (2004 film), the lot number for the chandelier was 666.

Beastly Number!

666 is an abundant number. It is the sum of the first 36 natural numbers (that is, 1 + 2 + 3... + 34 + 35 + 36 = 666), and thus a triangular number. Because 36 is both square and triangular, 666 is the sixth number of the form n2(n2 + 1) / 2 (triangular squares) and the eighth number of the form n(n + 1)(n2 + n + 2) / 8 (doubly triangular numbers).

666 is the sum of the squares of the first seven prime numbers. The harmonic mean of the decimal digits of 666 is an integer: 3/(1/6 + 1/6 + 1/6) = 6, making 666 the 54th number with this property. In base 10, 666 is a palindromic number, a repdigit, and a Smith number.

In the Eastern Orthodox Church, 666 is considered to be symbolic. Because 666 in Greek numerals stands for the Christ for man, because the man was created on the sixth day of Genesis, and the serpent represented what came between them.

The UPC barcodes found on most commercial products are characterized by guard bars at the beginning, middle, and end made up of two thin lines. Two thin lines also appear in the UPC encoding for the digit 6 (and no other digit), so to human eyes (but not to an electronic barcode reader) the guard bars appear to read 666. Some people interpret this as a fulfillment of the prophecy "Without this number an individual will not be able to buy or sell" (cited from the book of the Revelation 13:17).

The 2006 remake of the horror film The Omen *was released on June 6, 2006 (06/06/06) at 06:06:06 in the morning.*

The full name of former U.S. President Ronald Wilson Reagan contains six letters in each of his three names. This caused numerologists such as Gary D. Blevins to believe that Reagan was in fact the antichrist. Additionally, when Reagan moved to California following the end of his presidency, he asked that his house number be changed from 666 to 668.

In Chinese culture, 666 sounds a lot like the words things going smoothly. *It is considered one of the luckiest numbers in Chinese culture. It can be seen prominently in many shop windows across the country, and people there often pay extra to get a mobile phone number including this string of digits.*

It has not helped that occultists such as Aleister Crowley adopted the numbers as their own. Crowley often referred to himself as "the Beast" when he wasn't partaking in mind-altering drugs and libations:...or maybe he was imagining himself the personification of Saint John's wild and wicked revelatory dreams.

For some, the number 6 represents nothing more than man himself, with two arms, two legs, a torso, and a head. Six is also the trinity doubled.

If we are to label 666 as an "evil" number, then we must also ask the question: Was the original intention to be focused on the three digits themselves? Was it their sum of 18? Or, as in numerology, the sum of their sum—9?

Despite historical accounts and documents, we actually have no definitive proof of what the intention of those who spoke and wrote thousands of years ago really was...unless they spelled it out specifically. Unfortunately, the book of Revelation does no such thing.

We might be better off looking for the Antichrist by the nature of his character, not the number of his beastliness.

Yet all this points to the undeniable fact that numbers are, to humans, a true unsolved mystery. An enigma wrapped within a riddle. A topic worthy of a whole section of "X-Files" devoted to unlocking their secret chambers and uncovering their hidden treasures. Numbers are rarely random, except when we make them so. Most often, they seem to work in tandem, or at the very least, have a defined purpose.

Numeric anomalies exist everywhere, speaking of a higher intelligence adept at mathematical processing, one that often eludes us until we, well, crunch the numbers. The following pages hold some of the more unusual anomalies that we came across during our research.

Number anomalies abound. And you thought math was boring!

The number 37 will multiply into 111, 222, 333, 444, 555, 666, 777, 888, and 999.

$3 \times 37 = 111$

$6 \times 37 = 222$

$9 \times 37 = 333$

$12 \times 37 = 444$

$15 \times 37 = 555$

$18 \times 37 = 666$

$21 \times 37 = 777$

24 x 37 = 888

27 x 37 = 999

The number 2,520 can be divided by 1, 2, 3, 4, 5, 6, 7, 8, 9, and 10 without having a fraction leftover.

Except for 2 and 3, every prime number will eventually become divisible by 6 if you either add or subtract 1 from the number. For example, the number 17, plus 1, is divisible by 6. The number 19, minus 1, is also divisible by 6.

There are 24 known "perfect" numbers. These are numbers that equal the sum of all its divisors except itself. For instance, 6—the lowest of these numbers—is divisible by 1, 2, or 3 and 1 + 2 + 3 = 6. The largest of the known "perfect" numbers has 12,003 digits.

There is a way of writing 1 by using all 10 single-digit numbers at once:

148/296 + 35/70 = 1.

6,174—The Kernel of a Mystery Popped

The number 6,174 is a really mysterious number. At first glance, it might not seem so obvious. But as we are about to see, anyone who can subtract can uncover the mystery that makes 6,174 so special.

Kaprekar's operation

In 1949 the mathematician D.R. Kaprekar from Devlali, India, devised a process now known as *Kaprekar's operation*. First, choose a four-digit number where the digits are not all the same (that is not 1111, 2222). Then rearrange the digits to get the largest and smallest numbers these digits can make. Finally, subtract the smallest number from the largest to get a new number, and carry on repeating the operation for each new number.

It is a simple operation, but Kaprekar discovered that it led to a surprising result. Let's try it out, starting with the number 2005, the digits of a recent year. The maximum number we can make with these digits is 5200, and the minimum is 0025, or 25 (if one or more of the digits is zero, embed these in the left-hand side of the minimum number). The subtractions are:

5200 − 0025 = 5175
7551−1557 = 5994
9954 − 4599 = 5355
5553 − 3555 =1998
9981 − 1899 = 8082
8820 − 0288 = 8532
8532 − 2358 = 6174
7641 − 1467 = 6174

When we reach 6174 the operation repeats itself, returning 6174 every time. We call the number 6174 a *kernel* of this operation. So 6174 is a kernel for Kaprekar's operation, but is this as special as 6174 gets? Well, not only is 6174 the only kernel for the operation, it also has one more surprise up its sleeve. Let's try again starting with a different number, say 1789.

9871 − 1789 = 8082
8820 − 0288 = 8532
8532 − 2358 = 6174

We reached 6,174 again!

It works with other digit amounts, too. Here are the kernels for other digit groups.

Digits	Kernel
2	None
3	495
4	6174
5	None
6	549945, 631764
7	None
8	63317664, 97508421
9	554999445, 864197532
10	6333176664, 9753086421, 9975084201

From *http://plus.maths.org/issue38/features/nishiyama/*

The trouble with numbers, though, as we will see in a future chapter, is that evidence of their mysteries seemingly exists everywhere that you look. Take any number from 1 to 1,000, and by digging deep enough, you are bound to find all kinds of connections, repetitions, sequences, codes, and enigmatic anomalies. It might take you 6 degrees, it might take you 100 degrees, but, eventually, you will bring home the Bacon (as in Kevin). With a really good calculator, the sky (or pi), is the limit.

Any number is bound to be associated with some events in the course of a lifetime, with accidents and deaths, celebrations and happenstances, with moments in history important to nations and the world. Because our lives are so intrinsically linked to numbers, we cannot avoid these synchronistic associations. And because we are humans, we then attach even further meaning to the synchronicity itself. Eventually, we lean on numbers almost as much as we lean on words, simply because our brains are trained to do so, and because it gives us a sense that some higher intelligence is at play in the Cosmos—one that likes to tease, taunt, and tantalize us with signs and patterns.

In the next chapter, we will learn about an actual "science," or maybe we should call it an "art" that uses numbers to predict the future and determine the fate of individual and collective destinies alike.

Is nothing random?

CHAPTER

6:6

Name, Rank, and Serial Number

When you have mastered numbers, you will in fact no longer be reading numbers, anymore than you read words when reading books. You will be reading meanings.
—W.E.B. DuBois

God is ever a geometer.
—Greek Pythagorean motto

There are those who believe that numbers have the power to shape our lives, our relationships, and our destinies. This belief is so prevalent that the study of numerology was established.

Numerology consists of systems, traditions, or beliefs that posit a mystical or esoteric relationship between numbers and physical objects. Numerology and numerological divination were popular among early mathematicians, such as Pythagoras, but are now regarded as pseudomathematics by most modern scientists.

According to accepted scientific tenets, it would not be entirely accurate to call numerology a science. Rather, it can best be described as a belief system founded on the concept that the "number behind a name" can literally dictate a person's fate and fortune. Similar to astrology, numerology is based upon the idea that everything, even the names we were given by our parents at birth, has a profound meaning and purpose in the realization and unfoldment of our individual paths. From the jobs we choose to the places we live, to the mates we give our hearts to, people throughout the centuries have studied their astrological and numerological charts and signs in hopes of gleaning prescient information that might enable them to make better informed life choices.

The study of numbers as a means of divination is believed by many historians to have its initial roots in Pythagorean mathematics. Once again, Pythagoras is a key player in the development of what we consider the merging of numbers and letters as a means of describing and determining character, motivation, and purpose. Though the actual roots are probably far older, for numerology does appear in the ancient Hebrew Kabbalah, it was the Pythagoreans who perfected the "art" to the point where it gained widespread acceptance as a method of divination, similar to astrology, which blends birth times and locations with celestial influences.

Other influences on the evolution of numerology come from early Christian mysticism, Gnosticism, and the Vedas, as well as from Chinese and Egyptian ancient esoteric traditions. St. Augustine of Hippo is quoted to have written, "Numbers are the Universal language offered by the deity to humans as confirmation of the truth" and he shared Pythagoras's conviction that numbers were behind everything in life. Obviously, after the Council of Nicea in 325 AD, the early Christian authority figures all but banned the practice as a form of "magic" and divination, along with astrology and other Pagan beliefs and traditions.

As the power of the Church rose to great heights during the Dark Ages, so too did the more shadowy "occult" traditions that were practiced by millions behind closed doors. This included the study of numerology, which further evolved as an esoteric "science" in just about every culture, including the Chinese, who created their own entire numerological system. Even the Tarot, passed down through the Middle Ages, was often associated with numerology. By matching the 22 major arcana to birth name letters and birth dates, the connection between numerology and tarot was understandably linked.

Moving ahead to the 1920s, it was most notably the work of fortuneteller Count Louis Hamon, writing as Cheiro, which truly popularized the art. Cheiro, author of *The Book of Numbers*, is responsible for the development of the "fadic" system of numbers. The fadic method added together all of the digits of a person's birth date to glean their final number of destiny. Books by L. Dow Balliett published in the early 1900s, and those in the 1930s by Florence Campbell, also served to revive this "pseudoscience" of number divination.

As a time of newfound enlightenment and spiritual discovery, the New Age movement of the late 1960s and early 1970s led to an increased awareness of numerology, combined with growing curiosity of such anomalies as time prompts, Y2K, 2012, the Bible Code, and other number-based mysteries. This interest seems to have vaulted this occult tradition into the mainstream. Talk to anyone nowadays and chances are they know their "destiny number" or "summation number," the sum number of the letters of their birth name, which, as numerologists tell us, offers an intricate glimpse into our past, present, and future.

Though many of today's numerologists have expanded the basics into a whole range of potential readings, including birth name, life paths, destiny numbers, Soul Purpose numbers, Love Matches, and more, the most familiar way to use the numbers behind your personality is simply to take your full name given at birth, and find the corresponding digits, then add those for the total, or "summation number." But even that technique has variations. For example, let's take the names of the authors of this book:

The first technique simply adds up the digits in your name, and then comes to the summation.

Marie Dauphine Savino—$19 = 1 + 9 = 10 = 1 + 0 = 1$. Marie is a 1.

Laurence William Flaxman—$22 = 2 + 2 = 4$. Larry is a 4.

The second technique gives a corresponding number to the letter according to its placement in the alphabet:

Marie Dauphine Savino	**Laurence William Flaxman**
M= 13	L = 12
A = 1	A = 1
R = 18	U = 21
I = 9	R = 18
E = 5	E = 5
D = 4	N = 14
A = 1	C = 3
U = 21	E = 5
P = 16	W = 23
H = 8	I = 9
I = 9	L = 12
N = 14	L = 12
E = 5	I = 9

S = 19	A = 1
A = 1	M = 13
V = 22	F = 6
I = 9	L = 12
N = 14	A = 1
O = 15	X = 24
	M = 13
	A = 1
	N = 14

Marie total: 204 = 2 + 4 = 6

Larry total: 229 = 2 + 2 + 9 = 13 = 1 + 3 = 4

Thus, there would be a different final summation number for Marie, which means a different life path, purpose, and destiny depending on who would be doing her reading. Yet Larry's came out the same. Does that mean Marie has a split personality she knows nothing about?

DIY Numerology

Find the numbers that match your birth name letters, and add them up to see what digit dominates your destiny.

A 1	G 7	M 13	S 19
B 2	H 8	N 14	T 20
C 3	I 9	O 15	U 21
D 4	J 10	P 16	V 22
E 5	K 11	Q 17	W 23
F 6	L 12	R 18	X 24
Y 25	Z 26		

Other techniques claim to utilize your common name, as in Marie D. Jones and Larry Flaxman. Others yet incorporate a host of other determining factors. For example, your full name at the time of reading, your confirmation name, nickname, or the name your spouse calls you when he or she is angry with you (most of which are likely too obscene to mention here!) Many modern numerologists also incorporate birth time and/or date into their readings.

Scientists see this wide range of potentials as part of the problem with taking numerology seriously. If there is no solid agreement as to which name, date, or birth time to use, how could anyone possibly be certain of the singular outcome of a reading as proof of destiny? It certainly does not lend credence to the art, or pseudoscience of numerology, but, nonetheless, people swear by its outcomes, no matter how one gets to those outcomes.

Birth Names

The most widely used, oldest, and perhaps the most seriously studied forms of numerology uses the birth name, for that is the name you were given at the moment of your entry into this life. As with astrology, which posits that the positioning of stars and planets influences our fate, numerology also posits that there is incredible influence on a person from the chosen name they are given. Perhaps the parents are infused with a subconscious inspiration that matches letter and number, and comes out simply as the urge to name one's child Jane, Elizabeth, Michael, or Gertrude. It might truly be an interesting exercise to examine some of the more ridiculous and "weird" names, which are currently en vogue, and to see the patterns that emerge through time in chosen careers, love matches, and overall personality traits.

Once the Destiny Number, or Master Number as it is often referred to, is determined, there are variations on what personality traits—both positive and negative, one most associates with those numbers.

For example, let's pick on Marie. She is both a 1 and a 6. According to several websites, her general positive traits include:

1   Strong leadership skills, pioneering spirit, creative force, idealistic, driven, individualistic, and courageous.

6   Artistic, imaginative, nurturing, loving, community-service oriented, and compassionate.

All of those traits describe Marie to a T. Now for the negatives:

1   Aggressive, impulsive, egotistical, loud, willful, overbearing.

6   Self-righteous, stubborn, bull-headed, outspoken, and domineering.

All of those traits describe Marie to a T.

The problem is, even the other number traits describe Marie to a T. 4's are scientifically minded, 5's are visionary, and 2's display a lot of self-consciousness. Marie can relate to those.

And we haven't even picked on Larry yet! Fours—positives include orderly, scientific, practical, amazing organizers, high achievers, major attention to detail; and negatives include lack of imagination, fixed opinions, overly serious, and argumentative. Marie can attest that Larry is NOT overly serious, and hates drama! Note from Larry: "I certainly don't agree with the 'lack of imagination' or 'argumentative' traits. It seems that many of the qualities ascribed to either of us could be widely and generally interpreted depending on ones personal beliefs, or even mood."

Some of the other numbers mention personality traits that fit Marie or Larry far more so than many of the above that fall within their "number." But perhaps the overall gist of numerology is to get the "essence" of a person's character. Marie's essence is mainly creative, strong, nurturing, and willful, with a huge ego and the tendency to dominate others. Note from Marie: "Say that again and I'll belt ya!" Larry's essence is scientific, achievement-oriented, highly organized, and a "do'er"—one who makes things happen. He also has a serious streak and stubbornness of opinion. Note from Larry: "Stubborn? Who me?"

But all of this is according to the interpretation of those divining the numbers. In a sense, it is also open to the interpretation of the person receiving the reading itself. If you want to believe you are a powerful leader, having your number state you are "bold and obnoxious" could easily be interpreted as such. Ask anyone and they might claim those same positive and negative essences as a 1 or a 4, yet actually be a number 3, 5, or 8. And nowhere does it say in the number descriptions that Marie likes to sing show tunes in Greek and Larry is an expert at mime (well, only on days that do not end in Y).

Ideally, a true numerological reading will get into much greater detail than what can be found on the many "do it yourself reading" Websites or the "Numerology for Dummies" type books that are in abundance in the New Age section of your local book store.

Character Destiny

Similar to astrology, some readings result in a one-page summary of character and destiny, while there are others that result in a 100-page, highly detailed diatribe that literally maps a person's past, present, and future with stunning and inimitable accuracy. One has to wonder, though, if this is more a statement about the person doing the reading than the actual method of divination or interpretation.

Similar to our zodiac signs (with their helpful and harmful influences), or our Chinese Year signs (with their positive and negative traits), we seek to match who we are with when we came into the world, and what we were called when we got here. As a Libra and Capricorn, the authors of this book (Ox and Dog according to Chinese astrology) have specific traits associated with our birth signs. Libras cannot make up their minds; Capricorns, thankfully, can. Libras are dreamy. Capricorns are more down to earth. Libras are outgoing. Capricorns are stable. The Ox is bold. The Dog is determined. The Ox is stubborn. The Dog is loyal. The Ox moves first, thinks later. The Dog thinks first, moves later. The Dog hikes his leg unsuspectingly…okay, just kidding. We wanted to make sure you were still paying attention.

Many of these traits allow us to form beneficial relationships with others who have "compatible" numbers, signs, or symbols. Ox and Dog, although both highly competitive, make a powerhouse team. (They better, or these two authors will never work together again!) Yet again, many of the associated birth-sign traits could not be further from the truth about who we might really be. Perhaps it's a combination of nature and nurture when all is said and done.

Fact or Fiction?

All over the world you will find many people living, loving, and working together who breach the code of "who goes together better," suggesting that perhaps these divination systems were meant to be more guideposts than full-on navigational systems one must follow to the last detail. The insightful Website Skepdic.com points out on their numerology page, "When you get your reading, you may find yourself ignoring the parts that don't fit you at all, and focusing on those parts that do seem to fit. They may actually fit you or they may fit your image of how you would like to be." This is a critical aspect of any divinatory art: telling the client what they want to hear, even if the reader is motivated by sincerity of purpose. Throughout the ages, seers, prophets, psychics, and clairvoyants alike have similarly utilized this psychological trait to great effect—providing convincing readings and interpretations to those so eager for answers.

So, can numerology be simply attributed to a psychological "pat on the back"? Should we simply construe it as a recreational diversion—holding little to no validity? In the authors' beliefs, no. Even the Skeptics at skepdic.com admit, "Nevertheless, numerology shouldn't be brushed off without a thorough examination of its underlying theory." Granted, they go on to say there does not seem to be any underlying theory to the skeptics, but those who know the true magic of numbers beg us all to look deeper.

There are several issues that scientists take against numerology, as well as every other divination method. The primary issue is the lack of cohesiveness to the system. Secondly, there are concerns regarding repeatability, empirical evidence, and often, sheer accuracy. There are so many different methods of calculating the matching numbers to letters: The English, Hebrew, Chaldean, Phonetic, Chinese, Indian, and Pythagorean are a few that come to mind. If one uses the Chaldean method, the letter W equals 6. In the English system, it equals 5, the total of 2 + 3 (23rd letter). These are significant differences that could result in totally inaccurate readings. The disparity is such that someone could go home thinking that they are destined for show biz, when perhaps the truth is quite the opposite, and their real life path is in the mortuary business. Although, some might argue that there is little distinction between the two disciplines.

Gematria

All humor aside, the art of numerology does have a foundation in esoteric knowledge, though, it goes back a long, long way.

One of the oldest references to the origin of numerology comes to us from the Hebrew Kabbalah. Known as "gematria," this Jewish mystical tradition associates numbers with letters from the Hebrew alphabet, then seeks hidden meaning in words that combine these letter/number forms. In gematria, entire words are converted into meaningful numeric associations; just as in numerology, a name is converted into a destiny or summation number by which divination occurs. But in gematria, similar words, with similar numeric values and contextual meanings are used to comment upon the original word, adding a richer depth to the system.

According to JewishEncyclopedia.com, gematria is:

A cryptograph which gives, instead of the intended word, its numerical value, or a cipher produced by the permutation of letters. The term first occurs in literature in the twenty-ninth of the thirty-two hermeneutic rules of R. Eliezer b. R. Jose, the Galilean (c. 200). In some texts the rule for permutative gematria is counted as a separate regulation—the thirtieth (comp. Königsberger's edition of the rules in his *Monatsblätter für Vergangenheit und Gegenwart des Judenthums*). Waldberg ("Darke ha-Shinnuyim"), who gives a list of 147 cases of gematria occurring in traditional literature, includes in this number cases of symbolical numbers, which properly belong to the twenty-seventh rule ("ke-neged").

Ancient Greeks are said to have used the system of gematria to help interpret dreams, associating a numeric value to the letters of the Greek alphabet. Gnostics used the system to find hidden meaning behind the names of deities such as Mithra. Early Christians, most likely influenced by the Hebrew Bible, associated the numeric value of the Greek letters for alpha and omega, beginning and end, with the Greek word for *dove* (a symbol of Christ), or peristera. That value is the number 801.

But it was the Kabbalists who developed gematria into a serious form of mystical knowledge, tradition, and divination, often utilized to seek the holy name of God, and to understand his ways and means via the numbers behind the words of their holiest of texts.

The word *gematria* comes from both Hebrew and Greek roots, with a link to the Greek word for *geometry*, and can be split into two traditions: "revealed" gematria, used in many forms of Rabbinic Judaism; and "mystical" gematria, more prevalent with those practicing Kabbalah. Gematria shares similarities with other numerological systems, namely the Greek version of isopsephy, numerology associated with the Latin language, and the Arabic Hisab al-Jummal. Some experts suggest gematria was first practiced by the Babylonian king Sargon II, in the eighth century BC Sargon II may have even used the divination method to help construct the wall of Khorsabad, which was 16,283 cubits in length, the exact numerical value of his own name.

The most common gematria tradition is the revealed form, with roots in both the Talmud and Midrash, as well as by many writers and commentators from later periods of time. This form focuses entirely on the power of assigning a numerical value to each letter of the Hebrew alphabet, with the end result being a word or combination of words that hold profound meaning, which were often said to be of a prophetic or divine nature.

The most widely studied tradition may be the mystical tradition that focuses on the 10 sefirot, or "fires of God," of the Kabbalistic tree of life, and the 22 letters of the alphabet. The mystical tradition, which was further evolved more extensively in the writings of Zohar, also seeks to associate the letters of the alphabet with the 22 solids formed by regular polygons (five are Platonic solids, four Kepler-Poisot, and 13 are Archimedean). One solid was associated with one letter.

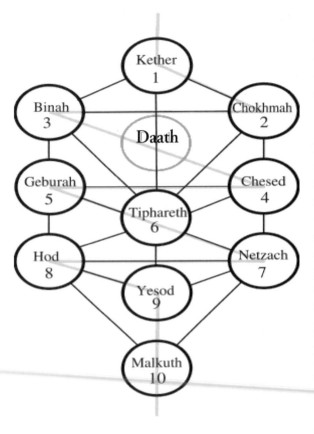

The Kabbalah Tree of Life corresponds the ten sefirot with letters of the Hebrew alphabet. Image courtesy of Wikipedia.

Thirteenth-century Kabbalists believed that there was a hidden code in the Old Testament, and that gematria could unlock the key that could read the code. This code was used to interpret whole verses by assigning numerical values to specific words. This practice was fine-tuned by the German scholar Eleazar of Worms, a commentarian writing during the same century.

Because much of gematria is based upon the interrelation of words and phrases, it naturally leaves much room for interpretation...or misinterpretation, as the case may be. Add to that the presence of diverse systems within the system, and different ways to calculate the equivalent value of an individual letter, and, similar to modern numerology, it appears that the outcome or end result can vary according to the person doing the "math."

According to the teachings of Harav Yitzchak Ginsburgh, a renowned authority on Kabbalah and Chassidut, who has been making the profound wisdom of the Jewish esoteric tradition accessible to seekers of Jewish spirituality for more than 25 years, the four calculation methods for assigning equivalent value are:

1. Absolute value—each letter has the value of its accepted numerical equivalent.
2. Ordinal value—each letter has the equivalent from 1 through 22.

3. Reduced value—each letter is reduced to a one-digit figure.

4. Integral reduced value—the total numerical value of a word is reduced to a single digit.

The name of God, from the Tikunei Zohar, *corresponds four calculation methods, four spiritual realms, and four letters of God's mystical name:*

Letter	Havayah Form of Calculation	Spiritual Realm
Yud	absolute value	emanation/atzilut
Hei	ordinal value	creation/beri'ah
Vau	reduced value	formation/yetzirah
Hei	integral value	action/asiyah

Adapted from *www.inner.org/gematria*

One thing to keep in mind is that this is just associated with one particular system of gematria. There are several, with other systems and sub-systems emphasizing varying decoding methods, such as the *notarikon*, which posits that the first letter of words can be combined to form new words; the opposite system, which takes the last letter of words to make new words or phrases; and the *temurah*, a complex system that organizes letters into tables that are then assigned specific mathematical values.

Even the early Christians felt the influence of the older Hebrew gematria. Theomatics, yet another numerology system, is based upon the Greek and Hebrew influences of the New Testament. The term, coined in the 1970s by Del Washburn, co-author (with Jerry Lucas) of *Theomatics: God's Best Kept Secret Revealed* and *Theomatics II : God's Best-Kept Secret Revealed,* is meant to bring together the words *mathematics* and *God,* and posits that God directly intervened in the writing of the Christian biblical texts. Basing itself on both Hebrew gematria and the Greek system of isopsephia, once again, a numerical value is given to each letter of both the ancient Hebrew and Greek alphabets, revealing distinct patterns that believers insist are not simply random or chance.

Ardent followers of theomatics claim that God himself placed the mathematical code into the biblical texts, and that each word of the Bible is spelled and placed into context with such intricate precision so as to literally document the entirety of past, present, and future. Names of people, names of locations, dates of events, and times of birth—were all orchestrated by this Divine Mathematician in an exact, predetermined location in the text to correspond with a numerical value meant for it and it alone. A Holy Magnum Opus.

The Bible Code

Most modern biblical scholars scoff at the idea of a coded Bible with a cipher that could unlock the mysteries of God and his intention and purpose. But that has not stopped others from looking for God in all the numeric places, and the Bible Code is the most recent of these attempts to find hidden patterns in holy books.

Similar to theomatics, which has a history dating back thousands of years in older numerological traditions, the much newer Torah Code, or Bible Code, also referred to as ELS, or Equidistant Letter Sequences, is a sort of numerology, but one that focuses on a particular technique of skipping letters to arrive at new words and phrases of prophetic meaning.

```
MYSTATUTESANDMYLAWSANDISAACDWELTI
NGERARANDTHEMENOFTHEPLACEASKEDHIM
OFHISWIFEANDHESAIDSHEISMYSISTERFO
RHEFEAREDTOSAYSHEISMYWIFELESTSAID
HETHEMENOFTHEPLACESHOULDKILLMEFOR
REBEKAHBECAUSESHEWASFAIRTOLOOKUPO
NANDITCAMETOPASSWHENHEHADBEENTHER
EALONGTIMETHATABIMELECHKINGOFTHEP
HILISTINESLOOKEDOUTATAWINDOWANDSA
WANDBEHOLDISAACWASSPORTINGWITHREB
EKAHHISWIFEANDABIMELECHCALLEDISAA
CANDSAIDBEHOLDOFASURETYSHEISTHYWI
FEANDHOWSAIDSTTHOUSHEISMYSISTERAN
DISAACSAIDUNTOHIMBECAUSEISAIDLEST
IDIEFORHERANDABIMELECHSAIDWHATIST
```

The Bible Code controversy began in early 1994, when three contemporary mathematician/scholars, Doron Witztum, Eliyahu Rips, and Yoav Rosenberg, published a paper in the *Statistical Science Journal* titled "Equidistant Letter Sequences in the Book of Genesis." This paper, which underwent several "rounds" of peer review and examination before publication, suggested that the book of Genesis contained within it a code that could be deciphered by looking at equidistant letters, whether forward, backward, straight across, or diagonally…and even other patterns that emerge upon intense scrutiny.

This method takes a particular starting point and looks for letters at a particular distance, say every third letter diagonally, or every fifth letter straight across, and finds patterns that create words or phrases of significant meaning. Words can even be spelled out backward and upside down.

Wikipedia offers a quite simple and understandable way to apply ELS to the Bible, or any other text if you saw fit:

> To obtain an ELS from a text, choose a starting point (in principle, any letter) and a skip number, also freely and possibly negative. Then, beginning at the starting point, select letters from the text at equal spacing as given by the skip number. For example, the bold (and underlined—authors' addition) letters in this sentence form an EL**S**. With a skip of -4, and ignoring the spaces and punctuation, the word SAFEST is spelled out backwards. Once you establish the first key word of the code you can then look for additional words to form phrases, even sentences that claim to prophesize about future events.

Even French mathematician Blaise Pascal wrote that "The Old Testament is a cipher," a thought amplified by the work of Sir Isaac Newton, who suggested that "the universe is a cryptogram set by the Almighty." Newton believed all events were a part of a Divine and previously ordained riddle that mankind has forever sought to decode. As far back as the 13th century, there is record of a Spanish Rabbi, Bachya ben Asher, who applied ELS to the Hebrew calendar.

The Bible Code gained popularity, and some notoriety, thanks to American journalist Michael Drosnin. Drosnin, author of two best-selling books that document the process in detail—*The Bible Code* in 1997 and the follow-up *The Bible Code II: The Countdown* introduced millions to the idea that the Bible held deeply embedded secrets that, when deciphered, might predict acts of violence, war, and catastrophe. Drosnin is attributed with predicting the assassination of Yitzhak Rabin, the Israeli prime minister, with his Bible Code, but his skeptics say that he was only capitalizing on the political tension of the times and making a prediction that anyone "in the loop" might imagine possible. In his second book, Drosnin made a vague prediction that we would see a nuclear holocaust as well as major natural catastrophes in 2006. Thankfully, that year passed with little fanfare, and Drosnin was forced to restate his belief that the Bible Code could be used for accurate predictions. In his recantation, he offered that it could merely offer probabilities rather than predictions.

Those who support the Bible Code usually focus on the Torah, which encompasses Genesis through Deuteronomy, and is known as the Torah Code. But many Bible Code followers ascribe the same mystery to the New Testament. And opponents of the Bible Code have suggested that when you want to find a pattern, you will. These opponents have also gone on to "codify" texts such as *Moby Dick*, finding all kinds of relevant references to the 9-11 terrorist attacks, the JFK assassination, and even the death of Princess Diana. Interestingly, Drosnin himself is quoted in the June 9, 1997 issue of *Newsweek* as saying, "When my critics find a message about the assassination of a prime minister encrypted in Moby Dick, I'll believe them." His critics did that and more, finding ELS mentions of many assassinations, including those of several prime ministers, Abraham Lincoln, JFK, and MLK. All in the context of a big tale about a big whale. Isn't it amazing what one can envision if they truly put their minds to it? One has to wonder if this very book you are reading contains amazing prophecies of death and destruction, and, most likely, it does if one had the time (and lack of a life) to look for them.

```
A R D S K I L L E D A T Y O U
H T O R T E N I N E A C H S W
A L M O S T S E E M E D T H A
P O I N T I N G D O W N A S W
I C T A I L T E N D O N I T I
N G A L O W A D V A N C I N G
A R E C A R R I E D B Y E V E
S I N G W H A L E A R E C U T
E I N L E I S U R E L Y S E A
L I Z I N G V I C I N I T Y T
```

The text of the classic novel Moby Dick *contains the ELS of Abraham Lincoln's death. Is it coincidence or the mark of a higher order behind all great literary works? Image courtesy of Wikipedia.*

We won't get into the pros and cons of the Bible Code here; but, suffice it to say, the controversy continues. Both sides of the debate argue their points convincingly, and with equal fervor and passion. There may indeed be a code in the Bible, as in many other books, but again we must ask, is it live or is it Memorex? Well, maybe we shouldn't ask that. Is it there for a reason, or is it our brain's never-ending ability to find patterns in all things? Is every work of literature one big word search puzzle?

Though the Bible Code has seemingly fallen out of public favor, it is only a matter of time before some new code system is offered up as proof that there is a divine order to all things, and most likely it will involve numbers (remember *The da Vinci Code*?).

Random Facts

W. Wynn Wescott, widely considered an extremely influential Satanist in the latter part of the 19th century explains in his book, *The Occult Power of Numbers*:

> The followers of Pythagoras...referred every object, planet, man, idea, and essence to some number or other, in a way which to most moderns must seem curious and mystical in the highest degree. "The numerals of Pythagoras," says Porphyry, who lived about 300 AD, "were hieroglyphic symbols, by means whereof he explained all ideas concerning the nature of things," and the same [numeric] method of explaining the secrets of nature is once again being insisted upon in the new revelation of the *Secret Doctrine* by H.P. Blavatsky. "Numbers are a key to the ancient views of cosmogony—in its broad sense, spiritually as well as physically considered, to the evolution of the present human race; all systems of religious mysticism are based upon numerals. The sacredness of numbers begins with the Great First Cause, the One, and ends only with the nought or zero—symbol of the infinite and boundless universe."

Our innate desire for learning about, and gathering information related to our personal and collective destinies, won't go away anytime soon. Numbers have become such an integral part of our daily life that it is expected that we would attempt to look for meaning behind them as well.

In *The United Symbolism of America*, Dr. Bob Hieronimus states, "Some of the best information comes from esoteric sources, which are not generally acknowledged by modern educators.... In the past few decades, the trend has been to discount these types of systems that are not based on empirical evidence. This is an old paradigm way of thinking, and I believe, as the new paradigm emerges, we will once again recognize the value of these divinatory arts...."

The paradigms just might be shifting, thanks in part to the growing number of people experiencing mysterious signs, sequences, and, the subject of the next chapter, synchronicities.

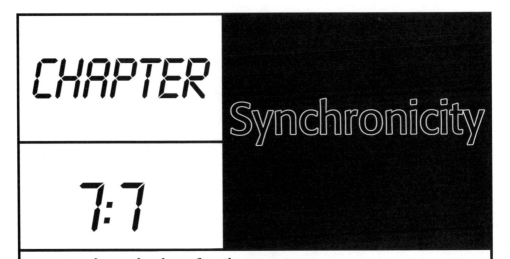

CHAPTER 7:7

Synchronicity

Another suburban family morning
Grandmother screaming at the wall
We have to shout above the din of our Rice Crispies
We can't hear anything at all
Mother chants her litany of boredom and frustration
But we know all her suicides are fake
Daddy only stares into the distance
There's only so much more that he can take
Many miles away
Something crawls from the slime
At the bottom of a dark Scottish lake
—*Synchronicity II*, The Police

For those of us who grew up in the '80s, it would be hard to disagree that the best-selling 1983 Police album *Synchronicity* represents the feelings and emotions of the era quite well. Millions of copies of this seminal album were purchased. To this day, the biggest hit on the album

"Every Breath You Take" is number 84 on the Rolling Stone list of the 500 Greatest Songs of All Time.

Perhaps not surprisingly, Sting was a big fan of Carl Jung, and penned the song as a tribute to his theory of synchronicity. In fact, Sting was so enamored with Jung's work that the cover graphic of the album depicts him reading a copy of Jung's work! As he explained the theme of the song to *Time* magazine: "Jung believed there was a large pattern to life, that it wasn't just chaos. Our song "Synchronicity II" is about two parallel events that aren't connected logically or causally, but symbolically."

As we have begun to see in the preceding chapters, number sequences can and often do have specific connective patterns. Similar to the song, numbers are also often used as symbolic representations. Oftentimes, there are hidden or repressed mathematical relationships that the creators may have purposely utilized as a means of permanence due to the eternal and unchanging nature of numbers.

The word *synchronicity* can be first attributed to Carl Jung, the noted Swiss psychologist who used the word to describe the "temporally coincident occurrences of acausal events." Jung also used the terms "acausal connecting principle," "meaningful coincidence," and "acausal parallelism" to describe events that seemed to be much more than sheer coincidence. The concept of synchronicity did not escape such luminaries as Albert Einstein, who was fascinated by this principle of connectivity of events that could not, it seemed, be explained away by simple scientific means.

Jung stated that these synchronicities served to link the subjective world with the objective world. Hidden mathematical relationships between events speak of this link, as though beneath the structure of visible reality there exists a complex and detailed infrastructure, or as we might say, "inner-frastructure." This implicate level of reality, to take a phrase from physicist David Bohm, may serve as a grid upon which all events occur, no matter their place in space or time, with some destined to occur simultaneously on several grid levels at a time.

Frank Joseph, editor-in-chief of *Ancient American* magazine and author of several books on Atlantis, wrote in a *New Dawn Magazine* article titled "Synchronicity: The Key of Destiny" that numbers were one of many categories of synchronicity that people experience throughout their lives. He believed number synchronicities "thread together mystical human experience, often with surprising results." Joseph chose to focus on the number 57, which appears throughout references to the history of the United States:

■ The last time the liberty bell rang was 57 years after Washington's 57th birthday.

- The closing paragraph of the Constitution following the seven articles constitutes 57 words.

- Throughout history 57 days, weeks, and months were found to separate major wars and military victories of Washington's army.

- In South Carolina's assault at Fort Ninety Six, 57 people were killed.

Joseph, akin to many others, believes that when two events or objects share an association with the same number, there is more than mere coincidence behind the scenes. This is especially so when that number turns up repeatedly, as does 11:11 and other time prompts and sequences discussed throughout this book. If it happens once or twice, it might be a lucky coincidence, but seven, nine, or 12 times? And in one day? Now that is just too strange to be anything BUT on purpose.

If the odds are a million to one against something occurring, chances are 50-50 it will.
—Anonymous

So, is the concept of random chance valid? Should such words as *arbitrary, accidental,* or *inadvertent* be stricken from the English language? Is there no such thing as luck, and should Marie stop picking up those dirty pennies and tossing them into wells?

Too Many 18's?

I was born on the 18th of May, 1962 (1 + 9 + 6 + 2 = 18). I was born at 9:54 a.m. (9 + 5 + 4 = 18). I was 18 inches long at birth. I was born in Louisville, Kentucky (Louisville has 10 letters and Kentucky has eight letters = 18 letters. I was officially adopted in the 18th month of my life (November 13, 1963). The number 18 is a 9-number in astrology, because 1 + 8 = 9. I turned 18 on May 18, 1980 (1 + 9 + 8 + 0 = 18). The last four digits of my Social Security Number add up to 18. My zip code ends with 18 (41018). At my job, I was originally hired as a shipper in the shipping department, and my shipper number given to me was 18. In 2000 our company installed a time clock for the first time, and my time-card barcode number adds up to 18.
—Contributed by "Jim"

Friedrich Schiller, the famed German poet and philosopher is quoted as saying "There is no such thing as chance; and what seems to us merest accident springs from the deepest source of destiny."

Numerology

As we explored in the preceding chapter, the study of numerology has been an accepted element of many cultures throughout the ages. According to our birth name and time, numerology suggests that our destiny is preordained and inevitable. Therefore numbers continue their role as a part of this hidden reality that we sense is there, but cannot put our finger on...until we wake up at the same time every night, and see the same digits on the clock staring back at us.

Stories of Synchronicity: Paranormal Numericals
By Scott Westmoreland

My wife and I married at 33 years of age, and as fate would have it, we conceived our first child on the wedding night. The very evening that we discovered she was pregnant, we were abruptly awakened by the ceiling fan over our bed, which came on "high," as well as the fan lights brightly filling the room. Startled, and a bit shaken, we glanced over at the clock radio and made note that it was 1:54 a.m. As our nerves calmed, we saw this as a sign of spiritual announcement of the beautiful baby boy who arrived some nine months later.

No other such "peculiarities" occurred throughout the next three years until (after a year of unsuccessful attempts to "augment" the family) we were once again jolted up from a sound sleep by the fan and its lights, blowing a mighty gust down on us, and brightly illuminating the pitch dark room. As before, we noticed the clock read 1:54 a.m. I recall saying, "OMG, its the same time it was the last time this happened!?" We were a bit less puzzled, as we viewed this occurrence with cautious optimism in anticipation of another pregnancy. Sure enough, the next day we found out we were having another child! That following night, we spent the night at my parent's house, and were once again awakened in the night by their clock radio alarm that had rudely sounded off. Fumbling in the darkness for the "off" button, my wife attentioned me that the numbers read 1:54 a.m.!? How and why could this be!? Is this purely a bizarre coincidence, this random time, this meaningless sequence of numbers? Or was it all a purposeful show of love and support from beyond? By the way, the alarm was set in the "off" position, and the pre-set wake-up time was set at 6 a.m.

As a follow-up, we did experience our fan and lights one more time (some three years after our wonderful daughter was born), during a popular television program that featured a plot line involving an unbeknownst pregnancy. In fact, at the very instant the character discovered she was pregnant, the fan and its lights came on full blast! This time, it was much earlier—not at 1:54 a.m. But we did learn the very next day (MUCH to our surprise) that we were expecting.

(As a footnote, Scott reported that the fan again came on twice on its own in one week, during times he calls "emotional nudges" that he gets from his grandmother and grandfather, both of whom are deceased. One was at 11:15 p.m., during a time he felt an overwhelming feeling of his grandmother's presence while he was brushing his teeth, and Scott later learned the next day that at the exact same time, 11:15 p.m., the night before, his parents' house was filled with the overwhelming odor of breakfast being cooked....)

The second was about two days later during an emotional viewing of old family slides on a 35-millimeter projector.

————

In another account, a woman we'll call "JL" was deeply saddened by the premature death of her son, Mark, from cancer. He was just in his mid-40s. A short time after his passing (prior to his memorial service), she began to awaken in the night with an overwhelming sense of his presence. She would glance over to the clock radio and notice it always read repeating numbers: 11:11 p.m., 12:12 a.m., 2:22 a.m., 5:55 a.m., and so on. This happened almost nightly, and sometimes during the day (always the same, always with repeating numbers). It seemed to take place whenever she felt his "emotional touch." It got to the point where she would just smile and say, "Hello, Mark." The fact that the feelings invariably coincided with the abnormal numerical sequence on the clock made it undeniably real, she says. This continued regularly for quite some time, and then dissipated throughout the years. Although he has been gone some 20 years now, she still experiences these moments with regularity, always knowing the contact will be accompanied by his leaving of a "numerical validation" on her digital clock radio.

Noted French author Anatole France believed that "Chance is perhaps the pseudonym of God when he does not wish to sign his work." This belief that synchronicities are signs or symbols originating from a higher power or being may be what forces us humans to give meaning to events occurring in unison. Meaning may not be necessarily implied in two number events colliding; rather, we imply the meaning to it. When this occurs, we marvel that, once again, we saw the number 876 nine times in one day, or had several run-ins with the number 62 in the last hour. Meaning is the element that we bring to a linked set of events the universe delivers to us.

In an online posting, we saw the following description: "Numbers, like images, cross the language barriers." Similar to music, numbers, or math, appears to be a universal means of communication, and one that might possibly cross more metaphysical lines as well.

Math seemingly knows no borders, and someone in Costa Rica can have a number synchronicity just as easily as someone in New Jersey. Upon closer reflection, our lives always seem to follow some kind of pattern, or play out like a puzzle, with interlocking pieces. During Carl Jung's study and treatment of patients who had been diagnosed with emotional and mental disorders, he determined that there was an uncanny relationship in many patients' dreams and events that occurred in waking life. One of the most famous and well-known cases involves a woman he treated who was difficult to break through. Jung listened intently as she described a strange dream involving a scarab beetle. At that very moment, one flew into the room and landed right before their eyes! This is a rare insect, and not common to their geographic region. This experience was all that particular patient needed to see in order to liberate her from her mental blocks and begin the healing process.

It was almost as if some higher force knew she needed the validation.

Pareidolia and Apoplexia

The human brain is hardwired to seek and find patterns wherever it can, in order to understand a complex situation or arrangement. This is a primitive survival mechanism remaining from our prehistoric ancestors, when it was important to discern a stampeding boar from a pet goat in the dense underbrush. This phenomenon, known as "matrixing," or more commonly "pareidolia," is a universal human response. The term *pareidolia*, according to Wikipedia, describes a "psychological phenomenon involving a vague and random stimulus (often an image or sound) being perceived as significant. Common examples include images of animals or faces in clouds, the man in the moon, and hidden messages on records played in reverse." Are you a tea drinker? If so, have you ever attempted to "read" the leaves in the bottom of the cup?

The term *apophenia* means the ability of the human mind to seek and find meaning and significance where there seemingly is none. Klaus Konrad coined this term in 1958, and defined it as the "unmotivated seeing of connections" accompanied by a "specific experience of an abnormal meaningfulness." The terms *apophenia* and *pareidolia* are often used to explain unknown or paranormal events. More than likely you have experienced this at some point in your life.

According to Dr. Martina Belz-Merk, "There is currently a controversial debate concerning whether unusual experiences are symptoms of a mental disorder, if mental disorders are a consequence of such experiences, or if people with mental disorders are especially susceptible to or even looking for these experiences."

Skepdic.com has lengthy descriptions of both apophenia and pareidolia. According to the site:

> The propensity to see connections between seemingly unrelated objects or ideas most closely links psychosis to creativity...apophenia and creativity may even be seen as two sides of the same coin. Some of the most creative people in the world, then, must be psychoanalysts and therapists who use projective tests like the Rorschach test or who see patterns of child abuse behind every emotional problem. Brugger notes that one analyst thought he had support for the penis envy theory because more females than males failed to return their pencils after a test. Another spent nine pages in a prestigious journal describing how sidewalk cracks are vaginas and feet are penises, and the old saw about not stepping on cracks is actually a warning to stay away from the female sex organ.

> Brugger's research indicates that high levels of dopamine affect the propensity to find meaning, patterns, and significance where there is none, and that this propensity is related to a tendency to believe in the paranormal.

> In statistics, apophenia is called a Type I error, seeing patterns where none, in fact, exist. It is highly probable that the apparent significance of many unusual experiences and phenomena are due to apophenia, e.g., ghosts and hauntings, EVP, numerology, the Bible code, anomalous cognition, ganzfeld "hits", most forms of divination, the prophecies of Nostradamus, remote viewing, and a host of other paranormal and supernatural experiences and phenomena.

The experience of apophenia is universal, and is experienced by many people throughout their lives. Skeptics argue that it seems highly likely that in the course of any long human life, linked events are bound to happen, and we, as humans, will find a way to label them as being relevant or important.

But, these same skeptics ask, how do we know the meaning we ascribe to them is the correct one? Is it personal, or a collective meaning from, as Jung believed, somewhere deep in the psyche ruled by archetype and symbol?

The writers of this book serve as an example. Yes, we like to make examples of ourselves. Better that than nuisances.

Let's propose that both Marie and Larry have a close encounter of the numerical kind. Steven Spielberg—are you listening? We can hear a sequel to *Close Encounters of the Third Kind* in the making. Anyway, instead of aliens arriving, it could be numbers! Okay, so, maybe we shouldn't quit our day jobs. Moving on, suppose that we both see the same number throughout the day. We both marvel at how it keeps popping up as we go about our business. We call each other and share our experiences. For each of us, synchronicity has occurred. But while Marie might take this as a negative sign related to her own emotional state that day, or other events that might have occurred during the day, such as her difficulty balancing her checkbook, Larry might interpret it in a totally positive light, go out and play the lotto with that number and find out he has the only winning ticket. Unfortunately, this is merely speculative, as Larry lives in a democratically repressed state that does not espouse recreational gaming.

If the 11:11 time prompts truly are a collective wake-up call, we have to entertain the notion that synchronicities happen on both an individual and collective level, with both individual and collective meanings. Because Jung believed that we access subconscious archetypes during these moments, we can postulate that there are number synchronicities that are meant to have meaning for the all as well as the individual.

Stories of Synchronicity: A Journal Entry of a Dream From May 11, 1999

I was teaching art in a big, beautiful school, and my art room number was 11. I was called out of the room by a janitor dressed all in white, and he pointed to the hallway wall where the number 11 was printed next to the room number. He looked at me very meaningfully, as if to say, what will you do about it?

Immediately I began looking for the key to the room. The key was gold, but—I thought in my dream—a little cheap-looking, so I could give it to the substitute teacher. I had to go teach in a bigger school near Milwaukee, so I got in a small, round white vehicle that floated on an air cushion and was steered with a mouse-like device and took off down the highway.

This dream occurred just after I had left a job teaching art in Lake Geneva because of the very heavy schedule it entailed. After the dream, I began to see 11:11 everywhere...digital clocks, license plates, road signs, you name it, until it was driving me crazy. Finally I Googled it and to my surprise, found that there was actually a Website dedicated to the phenomenon. Ever since, the double-11s seem to come in clusters, and I always know something profound, big, or crazy is about to happen. When I see clusters of higher doubles, like 44-44, it seems to be more about spiritual things.

For me, it all ties into the idea of God's universe as a synchronous whole, and as an alert Intelligence that reaches out to communicate to those who have "ears to hear."

And as a postscript, I did end up getting another teaching job, at a smaller school, but it was located right next to a highway sign that read 11:11, on Hwy. 11, which I had to see every time I drove there.

—*Linda S. Godfrey, author of* Strange Wisconsin, The Beast of Bray Road, *and* Hunting the American Werewolf

Two people experiencing the same number event, or one person experiencing the same number or event throughout a specific time period, suggests not just a link of minds, but of ideas and perceptions. There appears to be an underlying pattern that is part of the entire framework, which again harkens back to the concept of an intricate, hidden layer of reality beneath that which we see, hear, touch, taste, and feel. During a lecture in 1951, Jung detailed his version of this larger framework, which was then published as *Synchronicity— An Acausal Connecting Principle* in a volume with related research by Nobel Prize winner Wolfgang Pauli.

Time Prompts and Physics

Pauli, an Austrian-Swiss physicist, was intrigued by the links between physics and psychology, especially within the realm of quantum physics. He is noted for his work on spin theory, as well as for his discovery of the exclusion principle that links the structures of matter and chemistry. He also focused on the duality of the objective and subjective mind, with an emphasis on the impersonal nature of the objective mind. It was this mind that Jung suggested was the home of both the collective consciousness and collective archetypes, as well as the origin point of synchronistic experience.

Jung's fascination with symbol and archetype may have shaded his own personal interpretations of synchronistic events, but using the "keep it simple, stupid" (KISS) principle made famous by the tenet of Ockham's razor suggests that the simplest explanation is that these are, indeed, pure coincidence. Rather than attach all kinds of complex explanations to an experience, we look for the most simple, basic, fundamental cause—it just happened that way.

Medieval English philosopher and Franciscan monk William of Ockham (1285–1349) said, "Pluralitas non est ponenda sine necessitate." Translated, this means "Plurality should not be posited without necessity," and was a common principle in medieval philosophy. According to Skepdic.com, "Ockham's razor is also called the principle of parsimony. These days it is usually interpreted to mean something like 'the simpler the explanation, the better' or 'don't multiply hypotheses unnecessarily.' In any case, Ockham's razor is a principle that is frequently used outside of ontology, e.g., by philosophers of science in an effort to establish criteria for choosing from among theories with equal explanatory power. When giving explanatory reasons for something, don't posit more than is necessary." It is human nature to want to make things difficult, and add drama into situations where none need exist. Just look at your average marriage or love relationship to see proof of that!

Confirmation Bias

Random chance might lead to more connected experiences without an underlying meaning. What is referred to as "confirmation bias" is the likely culprit behind our resolute need to find or interpret information in a meaningful manner, all the while avoiding any evidence to the contrary. We believe what we want to believe, and hear and see what we want to hear and see, for personal reasons that often clash with what others believe, hear, and see. This is one of the main reasons for conflicts between religions and political parties (not to mention those pesky love relationships, too!).

Pauli was critical of this confirmation bias theory, thus his support for Jung's work. Many scientists struggle with their need to explain away coincidences as meaningless, all the while trying to reconcile the fact that the evidence sometimes points to these occurrences as being too obvious to be *anything but* meaningless.

Archetypes

The importance of archetypes cannot be understated here. Jung truly believed that nature itself contained patterns and symmetries of an archetypal sort. His beliefs are paralleled by those of physicist F. David Peat, who in his book *Synchronicity: The Bridge Between Mind and Matter* writes: "...nature contains certain archetypal patterns and symmetries that do not exist in any explicit material sense but are enfolded within the various dynamic movements of the material world." Peat further suggests that these subtleties of nature are "found to be further and further removed from simple mechanisms so that mind no longer appears to be alien to the universe. Likewise the synchronicities that form a bridge between matter and mind cannot be reduced to a single level of description."

Peat explains that during a synchronistic event, objects and events congregate to form an overall spatial and temporal pattern. This belief echoes a philosophy from the Middle Ages that was based upon correspondences and affinities between things such as plants, animals, minerals, and even the human body. Peat points to the work of writer Arthur Koestler, who felt these correspondences seem to be apparently disconnected events that happen together, but they are not dependent on traditionally understood Newtonian forces. Rather, as Koestler states, "certain things like to happen together."

Cosmic Giggles

Nature indeed consists of patterns, as we've discussed previously, and perhaps nature more than anything likes to pair things up. Terence McKenna, the prominent writer, philosopher, and ethnobotanist, referred to these events as "cosmic giggles," randomly moving "zones of synchronicity and statistical anomaly." McKenna's suggestion is that there may be a "science" to the synching of events, even if it appears utterly random while happening. For a great cosmic giggle it has long been suggested one listen to Pink Floyd's *Dark Side of the Moon* while watching *The Wizard of Oz*. Indeed, having done this a long, long time ago (Marie says, being of that particular era), the two seem to magically synch up. Whether this was intentional or a pure mystical coincidence, only the guys in Floyd know for sure! But this may be more a purposeful aligning of events than a random one, leading many people with way too much time on their hands to watch a host of old movies while listening to classic rock records, all in hopes of the next big "connection."

Time Prompts

People who experience time prompts and other synchronicities often refer to them as "miracles." Are they truly astonishing events, or are apophenia and pareidolia the explanation? Remember the KISS principle....

Cambridge University Professor J.E. Littlewood formed a new "law," known as Littlewood's Law, stating that the average individual can expect to experience one meaningful and significant event, that is, miracle, each month. This law, which he described in more detail in his *A Mathematician's Miscellany*, sought to put the kibosh on the "supernatural" nature of such events. His rule is directly related to a theory that we will examine more closely in Chapter 9:9, which basically suggests that if you take a large enough sample size of people, anything can (and usually does) happen!

Arguments aside, people are experiencing these linked events. They are ascribing meaning to them. And, in the case of popular numbers such as 11:11, they are assigning them a meaning ripe with collective significance.

Some people might view this as proof that our lives are predestined—set it in stone and unchangeable. They view the occasional synchronicity as a reminder of that inevitability every now and then. Others see these unusual events as proof of the power of nothing more than cause and effect. One step leading to another...and not necessarily along a predetermined path.

But even the mere cause and effect theory begs the question: how are the causes and effects so intricately linked that each has such profound impact on the other?

Entanglement

Perhaps we need to examine the issue at the molecular or subatomic level. Could theoretical or quantum physics hold the key? Within quantum physics, the theory of entanglement suggests that particles that come in contact with one another remain "entangled" even over vast distances of time and space. Eerily, while not physically connected, they can have an instantaneous effect on the other. This "spooky action at a distance" freaked out the likes of Einstein, who died before it became acceptable as a fact. Entanglement all but guarantees that cause and effect is happening constantly and instantly, and, if on a more macrocosmic scale, showing up as the synchronistic experiences in our lives.

If, as physicist David Bohm states, reality is comprised of different levels—the explicate being the reality we see and experience; the implicate being the one we do not see underneath it all; and the super implicate being the sort of "godlike" reality that encompasses the other two—then what appears to be coincidence may simply be an event in one reality leaking over into the other. The same could be said for the theories of alternate dimensions and parallel universes, which are two popular concepts of theoretical and quantum physics now gaining momentum with mainstream science. An event occurring on Plane A in sequence with one occurring on Plane B would seem random, yet in the bigger scheme of things, there is nothing random about it at all. We may not see what goes on in Plane A, so we don't rationally make the connection that this was, indeed, a cause and effect event. Just because you don't see the initial cause doesn't mean that it isn't there…somewhere.

In her 1998 book, *The Rainbow and the Worm,* Dr. Mae Wan Ho suggests that some coherent nature of space and time may provide a framework for another type of reality. "A coherent space-time structure theoretically enables 'instantaneous communications to occur over a range of time scales and spatial extents.' What this implies in practice is a vast, unexplored area, as the notion of non-linear structured time this entails is alien to the conventional, western scientific framework."

Resonance

The idea of resonance also suggests that coherence of frequency, whether between two particles, different systems of the human body, or any other vibratory matter, can create the illusion, or quite possibly the reality of phenomena that might be considered "paranormal." Two disparate events occurring simultaneously would fall into this theory of instant communication on a higher order of reality. Although the concept has been proven on a quantum level, it remains to be scientifically accepted on a grander scale.

Resonance may hold the key to a variety of unusual experiences, as we come to understand more and more about the role vibration plays in the makeup of matter and energy, as well as the way these things behave. The rate and intensity of vibrational frequencies of objects can create either harmony or discord between them, and perhaps it is when these frequencies complement each other, or synchronize, all matter of spooky action can occur, including paranormal events, psychic abilities, and strange coincidences that boggle the mind.

Symmetries

Once again, symmetries play a significant role in not just the fundamental nature of particles at the quantum level, but synchronicity, too. Werner Heisenberg, the "father" of quantum theory, believed that the most fundamental thing about nature was not necessarily particles, but particle symmetries. F. David Peat writes, "These symmetries could be thought of as the archetypes of all matter and the ground of material existence. The elementary particles themselves would simply be the material realizations of these underlying symmetries."

Heisenberg posited that these symmetries were the most fundamental level of our reality itself, something beyond mere photons and electrons, something that, as Peat words it, has "an immanent and formative role that is responsible for the exterior forms of nature." Peat goes on to ask, "Is it possible that archetypal symmetries of this nature could also manifest themselves in the internal structures of the mind?" What a great concept, in terms of how "without" can affect that which is "within" and vice versa, thus creating even more fertile ground for mysterious occurrences to take root.

Of course, the abstract natures of these symmetries have a mathematical aspect to them as they take place in "mathematically defined spaces." However, Peat points out, this is not necessarily an indication that particles "actually congregate together in space to form a pattern. Rather, it is their individual dynamic activity that, taken together, forms a pattern of mathematical transformations." And though we are talking about the dynamics of quantum matter, this same theory may apply to the manifestation of synchronicities in the macrocosmic world. Peat summarizes with this telling quote: "In this way it will be shown that there is no ultimate distinction between the mental and material so that synchronicities represent the explicit unfolding of deeper orders."

Because numbers are universal symbols, it makes sense that they should appear so often in synchronistic experiences. Again, from Peat, "It is only when certain aspects of the collective mind are projected into attention, clothed in the images and symbols of our particular culture, that we become aware of something universal that has come into the mind." This might explain the vast number of people who report thinking about an obscure, seldom-played song only to have it be played magically over the airwaves at just that instant. As long as the coauthor of this book, Larry, can remember, this has been a common occurrence for him. "I think about a song, and bang—it is often played as the next song! And, trust me, my musical taste is extremely atypical!" Marie can vouch for that. Russian clog dancing chants are not typical of your usual musical tastes nowadays.

Music, similar to math, is a collective language, an archetype we all operate from on a deeper implicate level. Finally, we close again with Peat, who said it so well: "Synchronicities are characterized by a unity of the universal with the particular that lies within a coincidence of events." The essence of this universal is seen in nature as patterns, symmetries, and even the laws of math that "interconnect a multiplicity of individual events." And indeed the possibility may exist that beneath this scientific framework lies a grid of creative and formative order Peat calls "the objective intelligence."

Objective Intelligence

This objective intelligence is present throughout nature, permeating the known laws with a mysterious presence of something higher at work than mere functionality. Behind every structure there is an architect. Both the quantum and cosmic worlds posit the importance of the observer, as well as the conscious mind. In terms of synchronicities, we must also take into account the collective and objective mind that acts as a potential repository field from which our personal experiences rise. In this objective mind, the links between event A and event B are formulated, to be experienced by the subjective mind and given meaning to. Out of the chaos of nature, patterns emerge, and we glom onto those patterns and offer our own personally tailored interpretation. When they happen as often as time prompts do, the meaning becomes ever more important and profound.

In his book *The Synchronized Universe: New Science of the Paranormal,* physicist Claude Swanson, PhD, talks about the role of synchronicity on both the quantum and cosmic scale, and its relationship to the manifestation of paranormal. Though his massive tome refers more to psi, ghosts, and remote viewing, his theory of a reality made up of layers of universes makes for interesting mental fodder. Swanson posits that paranormal events can alter the structure of otherwise random or quantum noise, and thus alter the probability of events. Though we first need a more clearly defined understanding of the nature of this quantum noise, the potential exists to "extend current physics theory to understand and explain paranormal phenomenon." Swanson discusses the Zero Point Field (ZPF) as a possible state of fundamental quantum reality from which all matter, form, and energy springs forth. According to the Calphysics Institute:

Quantum mechanics predicts the existence of what are usually called "zero-point" energies for the strong, the weak and the electromagnetic interactions, where "zero-point" refers to the energy of the system at temperature T=0, or the lowest quantized energy level of a quantum mechanical system. Although the term "zero-point energy" applies to all three of these interactions in nature, customarily (and hereafter in this article) it is used in reference only to the electromagnetic case. In conventional quantum physics, the origin of zero-point energy is the Heisenberg uncertainty principle, which states that, for a moving particle such as an electron, the more precisely one measures the position, the less exact the best possible measurement of its momentum (mass times velocity), and vice versa. The least possible uncertainty of position times momentum is specified by Planck's constant, h. A parallel uncertainty exists between measurements involving time and energy (and other so-called conjugate variables in quantum mechanics). This minimum uncertainty is not due to any correctable flaws in measurement, but rather reflects an intrinsic quantum fuzziness in the very nature of energy and matter springing from the wave nature of the various quantum fields. This leads to the concept of zero-point energy. Zero-point energy is the energy that remains when all other energy is removed from a system.

This Field, championed by the work of physicist Hal Puthoff, one of the founders of the earliest university-backed remote viewing studies, could be the generative, formative field from which objective intelligence operates. That the universe itself is filled with fluctuating energy of random photons virtually popping in and out of existence suggests a potential hotbed of anomalous phenomena that might exist as well. The field of all potentiality, as Deepak Chopra referred to it, might contain within it all the information needed to create the synchronistic events we call coincidence. In addition, in this landscape of the field, where past, present, and future exist all at once, we might also find the origins of those strange, related experiences of déjà vu.

Swanson also cites resonance as a key to the synching of levels of reality. This synchronization would theoretically allow communication between levels, as well as create a Synchronized Universe Model (SUM). In summary, this SUM assumes that "all particles in the universe interact with one another," yet takes it a step further to posit that distant matter communicates with local electrons via the motion of photons, a connection that embodies the Mach

Principle of distant matter determining local inertia and local forces. What does this have to do with seeing the number 10 50 times in one day? Swanson believed the Mach Principle was a fundamental insight into the connectivity of reality, matter, and energy. Local forces having their origin in the distant matter of space.

Swanson's description of a layered reality of universes that, through resonance and coherence, could "synch up" and allow for the crossing of matter and energy, not to mention the possibility of paranormal phenomena, also suggests that the ability of events that seem to occur in different spatial and even temporal frames could "synch up" and create a miracle or coincidence. Thus, time prompts could be coming to us from different dimensions of space, as well as different dimensions of time.

Swanson refers to a single synchronized universe "represented by one sheet of paper in a stack. Each sheet has its own unique frequency and/or phase that characterize the synchronized motion of the electrons in that system. Other sheets represent 'parallel realities' or other 'parallel dimensions' that may co-habit the same space and time and yet be unaware of one another." But in the phase-locking of two or more "sheets," there is interaction of a synchronized manner. When the sheets are not in synch, no cross-talk occurs, and things appear as normal, even as random chance, with no connectivity to boggle the mind and startle the senses. Consciousness, Swanson suggests, "interacts across these parallel dimensions. Thus it can affect and reduce the quantum noise. It can even synchronize motions between parallel realities. In this way higher forces (subtle energies) can be created, and energy can be extracted from these other dimensions."

When particles are in synch on their own "sheet," they obey the physical laws of that sheet. However, when they are in synch with those on a corresponding sheet, "the most dramatic paranormal effects are expected." It's an intriguing theory that does align with many concepts of both quantum and theoretical physics, and could also explain the ability of events to align and synch up at just the right place and time. If that is truly the case, then events may appear to have happened not at all by chance, but by some deeper design with deeper meaning. The mind or consciousness itself may even act similar to this sheet system, with thoughts and interpretations moving between the objective intelligent state into the subjective, where significance is then either formulated or tossed aside. Again, information comes at us from all angles, even other layers of reality, but we choose which is important and what we pay attention to, based upon our survival needs. Yet every now and then, a thought or interpretation may slip through the veil of distraction and grab us by the collar, waking us up to the possibility that there is more to reality than meets the eye.

In an upcoming chapter, we will play devil's advocate and argue a bit against the concept of synchronicity. But as author James Redfield wrote in *The Celestine Prophecy*, a book that has changed many minds and lives, there is, "The First Insight Theory: Mysterious coincidences cause the reconsideration of the inherent mystery that surrounds our individual lives on this planet."

As we were writing this book, one of the authors stumbled upon an article out of the blue about a gene on a particular chromosome in mice that might be involved in the repair of DNA. The number of that chromosome? 11. Coincidence? Perhaps. But while writing a book that focuses so intensely on the number 11, we might be moved to smile and ascribe some meaning to that "cosmic giggle." The timing is just too perfect.

And when it comes to synchronicities, timing is everything.

CHAPTER 8:8

Just Six Numbers?

God made the integers, all the rest is the work of man.
—Leopold Kronecker

Theories abound that the entire Universe is based upon a very small and select group of numbers—mathematical equations that describe the whole of reality with intricate beauty and amazingly efficient detail. Physicists have long attempted to discover the magical Theory of Everything (TOE). This elusive theory will hopefully bring a seamless connection between the four fundamental forces of gravity, electromagnetism, and the strong and weak nuclear forces. Other theories regarding a universal framework also exist. One such theory is IT—Information Theory. IT is the concept of the Universe as a computer, processing information in an increasing, compounding rate and spitting out new information to continuously expand what we see and experience as reality. Due to long-standing hesitance to change, scientists are only now beginning to openly discuss their belief in Information Theory.

But before we delve into Information Theory and attempt to show how the Universe seemingly behaves like a computer processor, with "reality" actually being comprised of "its and bits" that shape and mold matter, we need to examine the importance of numbers in the creation of the Universe itself.

Six Number Theory

In his book *Just Six Numbers*, Sir Martin Rees, the Royal Society Research Professor at Cambridge University and Astronomer Royal, makes a bold case for explaining how just six fundamental numbers can explain the entirety of the physical cosmos. These numbers, "constant values that describe and define everything from the way atoms are held together to the amount of matter in our universe," were imprinted during the Big Bang itself and began a process of cosmic evolution that allowed for the creation of stars and galaxies, as well as all of the necessary energy states that govern matter and force as we know it. "Mathematical laws underpin the fabric of our universe—not just atoms, but galaxies, stars and people," Rees writes. "Science advances by discerning patterns and regularities in nature, so that more and more phenomena can be subsumed into general categories and laws." The goal of theorists, Rees continues, is to one day "encapsulate the essence of the physical laws in a unified set of equations."

Rees, as well as the growing number of researchers who have picked up on his work, believes that these mathematical values are so sensitive that if any of them were "untuned," there could be no stars, and therefore, no life—at least not life as we know and recognize it today. The reason these six numbers are so critical, Rees states, is because "two of them relate to the basic forces; two fix the size and overall 'texture' of our universe and determine whether it will continue forever; and two more fix the properties of space itself...." Different choices of the six fundamental numbers, Rees tells us, would give us a much different universe...maybe even a sterile one.

The six fundamental numbers that shape the Universe, and helped make it in the first place, are:

1. Nu—"N," a critically huge number with the value of 1,000,000,000,000,000,000,000,000,000,000,000,000. This is a ratio of the strength of electrical forces holding atoms together, divided by the force of gravity (which is 10 to the 37th power) between them. If this number were smaller, even by a few zeros, it has been posted that the Universe's lifespan would be too short for biological evolution to occur. As Rees states, a short-lived universe would mean that no creatures could ever grow larger than insects, with no time for biological evolution to unfold. Thus, a buggy world indeed.

2. **Epsilon—0.007**—Another ratio, this time the proportion of energy released when hydrogen fuses into helium. This number defines how firmly atomic nuclei bind together and how all of the atoms one earth were made. The value of epsilon controls the power from the sun and how stars transmute hydrogen into all the atoms of the periodic table. Carbon and oxygen are common, and gold and uranium are rare, because of what happens in the stars. Were this number 0.006, or 0.008, Rees states that we could not possibly exist, again suggesting that the smallest tweaks would have resulted in a Universe far different than this one.

3. **Omega—The cosmic number 1** measures the amount of material in our Universe—galaxies, diffuse gas, and dark matter. Omega refers to the relative importance of gravity and expansion energy in the Universe. According to Rees, a universe with too high of an Omega level would have collapsed long ago; too low, no galaxies would have formed. The inflationary theory of the Big Bang says omega should be one, but astronomers have yet to measure its exact value. Some scientists point to the finely tuned initial speed of expansion as a hint of Creative Intelligence.

4. **Lambda**—The force of cosmic antigravity that was discovered in 1998. This is an extremely small number and appears to control the expansion of the Universe, however, it has no effect on scales of less than a billion light years. If lambda were any larger, its effect would have stopped galaxies and stars from forming, and cosmic evolution would have been "stifled before it could even begin."

5. **Q = 1/100,000**—The basic seeds for all cosmic structures such as stars, galaxies, and clusters of galaxies, all of which were imprinted in the Big Bang itself. The fabric—or texture—of our Universe depends on a number that represents the ratio of two fundamental energies. If Q were smaller, the Universe would be inert and without structure; if Q were much larger, the Universe would be a violent place where no stars or suns could exist, dominated by giant black holes.

6. **Delta—3**—The number of spatial dimensions in our world. Rees argues that life can only exist in three dimensions, not two or four. This number, it seems, has been known for hundreds of years, but is now being viewed in a whole new way, especially in

light of superstring theory, which posits that the most fundamental underlying structure are vibrating superstrings that operate in a potentially 10-dimensional "arena."

Just How Finely Tuned Is the Universe?

It is quite spooky to think that with some minor tweaks here and there, we would not exist. These are just some of the reasons why....

*If the strong nuclear force constant **was larger**: no hydrogen would form; atomic nuclei for most life-essential elements would be unstable; thus, no life. **If smaller**: no elements heavier than hydrogen would form; again, no life.*

*If the weak nuclear force constant **was larger**: too much hydrogen would convert to helium in big bang; stars would convert too much matter into heavy elements making life impossible. **If smaller**: too little helium would be produced and stars would convert too little matter into heavy elements, making life impossible.*

*If the gravitational force constant **was larger**: stars would be too hot and would burn too rapidly and too unevenly for life chemistry. **If smaller**: stars would be too cool to ignite nuclear fusion; thus, many of the elements needed for life chemistry would never form.*

*If the ratio of electromagnetic force constant to gravitational force constant **was larger**: all stars would be at least 40 percent more massive than the sun; stellar burning would be too brief and too uneven for life. **If smaller**: stars would be at least 20 percent less massive than sun and incapable of producing heavy elements.*

*If the ratio of electron to proton mass **was larger**: chemical bonding would be insufficient for life. **If smaller**: same as above.*

*If the ratio of number of protons to number of electrons **was larger**: electromagnetism would dominate gravity, preventing galaxy, star, and planet formation. **If smaller**: same as the previous reason.*

*If the expansion rate of the universe **was larger**: no galaxies would form. **If smaller**: the universe would collapse, even before stars formed.*

Adapted from Hugh Ross, PhD, The Creator and the Cosmos.

So far, Rees and his colleagues have been unable to find the one great undeniable link between all these numbers that would result in a mathematical Theory of Everything (TOE), if one such theory exists, but these fundamental ratios and numbers do build one upon the next to create a sort of cosmic blueprint. These "pieces of a puzzle" may possibly be used to describe the nature of the Universe and its forces, and certainly speak to the idea that beneath it all there is a grand plan or design that works. We humans are proof of that.

Reasons for the Universe

In Rees's opinion, there are three explanations for the finely tuned Universe in which we seem to live, one that is dependent upon the previously discussed six numbers. First, we must consider sheer coincidence. It is certainly a possibility that we are here just because that's the way the numbers were tuned with no deeper meaning attached. Secondly, many scientists suggest that the specific tuning of these six numbers, so intricately perfect, lends itself to the argument in favor of a Creator—or "intelligent design." This theory is gaining ground with reputable scientists as a viable alternative to the longstanding belief in evolutionism. According to the official Website of ID (intelligentdesign.org):

> Intelligent design refers to a scientific research program as well as a community of scientists, philosophers and other scholars who seek evidence of design in nature. The theory of intelligent design holds that certain features of the universe and of living things are best explained by an intelligent cause, not an undirected process such as natural selection. Through the study and analysis of a system's components, a design theorist is able to determine whether various natural structures are the product of chance, natural law, intelligent design, or some combination thereof. Such research by observing the types of information produced when intelligent agents act. Scientists then seek to find objects, which have those same types of informational properties that we commonly know, come from intelligence. Intelligent design has applied these scientific methods to detect design in irreducibly complex biological structures, the complex and specified information content in DNA, the life-sustaining physical architecture of the universe, and the geologically rapid origin of biological diversity in the fossil record during the Cambrian explosion approximately 530 million years ago.

At the very least, this Creator wanted us humans to show up, and tuned the Universe with that specific intention in mind. "If you imagine setting up the universe by adjusting six dials, then the tuning must be precise in order to yield a universe that could harbor life," Rees states. The question is: who or what is responsible for the tuning? (See Chapter 10:10 for more on this!)

Last, but certainly not least, is the idea that we are not alone in terms of being the only Universe to have experienced a Big Bang. Other universes may exist, each with their own rate of cooling, their own fine-tuning, and their own laws, which are defined in the end by a different set of numbers. As Rees puts it, "This may not seem an 'economical' hypothesis—indeed, nothing might seem more extravagant than invoking multiple universes—but it is a natural deduction from some (albeit speculative) theories, and opens up a new vision of our universe as just one 'atom' selected from an infinite multiverse."

The intricate omega, for example, which simply describes the density of the universe, is so precise that, as a result, we are all able to exist. It boggles the mind to think that were this value just a tiny bit higher, our infant Universe might not have begun expanding, and gravitational forces would have run amok, causing what some describe as a "great crunch" instead of a "big bang." And if the amount of mass present was any lower, gravity would never have had a chance to allow particles to connect and interact, forming into objects, and ultimately life. Were these tunings just the result of the way matter and energy blew apart during the Big Bang itself? Was this intricacy coded somehow into the pre-Bang singularity from which the Universe was formed? When was the plan written...and by whom or what? Let's look at "N."

N

"N" dictates how big the Universe is allowed to get, and beyond that, or below that value, the gravitational force might exceed the electric force, and the Universe would not exist. Were gravity significantly stronger than we know it, our reality might be very different, and we would likely be seeing a lot more black holes around us. Definitely not a good thing! The relationship between electromagnetism and gravity is, again, so finely tuned as to allow for things to be just as they are, from the smallest to the largest objects, governed by laws that keep things in a cohesive state. One minor tweak, and it would be utter chaos.

Each of these six fundamental numbers would seem to be utterly critical to the absolute "rightness" of the Universe that we live in, a rightness that allowed for all the perfect combinations, events, and interactions to lead to life, at least on our little planet. English astronomer James Jeans said, "The universe appears to have been designed by a pure mathematician." The laws that govern motion, gravitation, force, and matter are all, at their foundation, mathematical laws that give order to nature and form the bedrock of all physical reality. The word *astronomy* itself means "law of the stars," and those laws have their basis in mathematics. Even the esteemed 13th-century scholar Roger Bacon recognized that natural laws were fundamentally mathematical laws. According to the classic *Encyclopedia*, Bacon's *Opus Majus* states:

"Part IV" (pp. 57–255) contains an elaborate treatise on mathematics, "the alphabet of philosophy," maintaining that all the sciences rest ultimately on mathematics, and progress only when their facts can be subsumed under mathematical principles. This fruitful thought he illustrates by showing how geometry is applied to the action of natural bodies, and demonstrating by geometrical figures certain laws of physical forces. He also shows how his method may be used to determine some curious and long-discussed problems, such as the light of the stars, the ebb and flow of the tide, the motion of the balance. He then proceeds to adduce elaborate and sometimes slightly grotesque reasons tending to prove that mathematical knowledge is essential in theology, and closes this section of his work with two comprehensive sketches of geography and astronomy. That on geography is particularly good, and is interesting as having been read by Columbus, who lighted on it in Petrus de Alliaco's Imago Mundi, and was strongly influenced by its reasoning.

In his book *The Goldilocks Enigma: Why is the Universe Just Right For Life?* author and physicist Paul Davies states "The ancients were right: beneath the surface complexity of nature lies a hidden subtext, written in a subtle mathematical code. This cosmic code contains the secret rules on which the universe runs." Davies, also the author of *The Mind of God*, reminds us that early scientists such as Galileo and Newton believed that by exposing the patterns behind the fabric of nature, they could somehow get a glimpse the mind of God. This religious quest parallels the more modern belief by today's scientists, many of them by no means religious, where Davies says "an intelligible script underlies the workings of nature, for to believe otherwise would undermine the very motivation for doing research, which is to uncover something meaningful about the world that we don't already know."

Davies believes that science has indeed "uncovered the existence of this concealed mathematical domain." We humans, he goes on, have been made "privy to the deepest workings of the universe," and, unlike the animals who simply observe these workings, we humans alone have the power to try to explain them.

Numbers or Turtles?

There is a story often attributed to both Bertrand Russell and to the 19th-century American philosopher William James. The story revolves around a lecture being given about the nature of the universe. Halfway through the lecture, a woman stands up in the back of the room and denounces the lecturer, proudly claiming that she knows the exact nature of how the Universe is put together. Her claim? That the Earth rests on the back of a giant elephant that is, in turn, standing on the back of a giant turtle. Stunned, the lecturer asks her what the turtle is standing upon. The woman shouts back, "You must be a very clever young man, but you can't fool me! It's turtles all the way down!"

Many theories and explanations regarding the nature of the Universe exist, and like the turtle theory in the sidebar, there must be what is called the "termination of the chain of explanation." To explain a theory, there must be a beginning and an end. A start and a finish. The woman at this lecture apparently felt that a bottomless chain of turtles was a perfectly rational and reasonable explanation, or perhaps, as Paul Davies suggests in *The Goldilocks Enigma*, there is a levitating super-turtle upon which the chain of turtles stands. Of course, we can laugh at this concept, but it illustrates the difficulties that come along with theorizing anything about the nature of reality itself! Perhaps the joke is on us.

This Universe...and Beyond!

As we continue to make further advancements into the study of cosmology, and our ability to see into the heart of deep space improves, other ratios and numbers may be added to complete the architectural framework of the cosmos. These six initial and fundamental numbers also may provide for the possibility of multi dimensional strings and parallel universes. Rees himself is a proponent of the multiverse theory, and the idea is growing in popularity among theoretical and quantum physicists. According to the *International Journal of High-Energy Physics*, "The idea of multiple universes is more than a fantastic invention. It appears naturally within several theories, and deserves to be taken seriously." The journal further states: "This multiverse—if true—would force a profound change of our deep understanding of physics. The laws reappear as kinds of phenomena; the ontological primer of our Universe would have to be abandoned. At other places in the multiverse, there would be other laws, other constants, other numbers of dimensions; our world would be just a tiny sample. It could be, following Copernicus, Darwin, and Freud, the fourth narcissistic injury."

In fact, quite simply, different universes would have formed at different rates, cooled at different rates, and therefore be governed by different laws, numbers, and ratios from our own. Thus, our Big Bang could have been one of many (part of M-theory) that was created with its own specific set of mathematical components at the core of its expansion and evolution. In our Universe, these six cosmic numbers are the only thing that keeps us from being one of those badly tuned universes where nothing expands, forms, coheres.... Talk about being in the right place at the right time! The subatomic forces that shape and mold our very reality exist because of such a honed, perfected tuning of the rate of expansion after the Big Bang. The sensitivity to these six numbers seems apparent in the physical laws that governed the processes behind the formation of galaxies, stars, and planetary systems.

Undoubtedly, this raises more questions than answers. The biggest questions the mathematical nature of order begs are: can there then be an "intelligence" behind these numbers? Is this a stable system and is there room for such concepts as entropy, disorder, and chaos? The idea that these numbers are attuned, and create a potential formula that links them together, then begs the question: who or what "attuned" them? The mathematical formulas behind all six values are so perfectly deliberate one would think that the creative force of the entirety of reality was a gigantic calculator...or perhaps a computer. We will first look at the concept of the Universe as a computer, which again will ask those pesky questions: Who is the Master Programmer? Who developed the initial language?

The Universe as a Computer

The question on the lips of many cutting-edge mathematicians, cosmologists, astronomers, and physicists is:

Could the Universe simply be a massive quantum computer?

In order to explain the vast complexities of our Universe, many scientists look to the technology age as a guide to just what might account for the sheer volume of "stuff" that fills our world. The basis of this theory starts with the idea that particles and their interactions are not solely responsible for transferring energy, but information as well. Bits of information.

Its and bits.

"The Universe is the biggest thing there is and the bit is the smallest possible chunk of information. The universe is made of bits. Every molecule, atom, and elementary particle registers bits of information. Every interaction between those pieces of the universe processes that information by altering those bits...the Universe is a quantum computer," writes Professor Seth Lloyd in *Programming the Universe: A Quantum Computer Scientist Takes on the Cosmos*. In an interview with the Edge Foundation, Professor Lloyd states:

> It's been known for more than a hundred years, ever since Maxwell, that all physical systems register and process information. For instance, this little inchworm right here has something on the order of Avogadro's number of atoms. And dividing by Boltzmann's concept, its entropy is on the order of Avogadro's number of bits. This means that it would take about Avogadro's number of bits to describe that little guy and how every atom and molecule is jiggling around in his body in full detail. Every physical system registers information, and just by evolving in time, by doing its thing, it changes that information, transforms that information, or, if you like, processes that information.

Is it possible, that like a giant information processing system, the Universe computed itself into existence via the Big Bang? Once this initial computation is complete, perhaps it then compounds the amount of initially programmed information with newly computed information...then "it" begins the task of processing it all over again in a cyclical pattern. The result is a snowball effect of continuously created "stuff," the variety of which is ever-increasing, ever-expanding.

The formation of atoms and other elementary particles, then, would consist of specific amounts of information in the form of its and bits, and as the universe processes this information to create more particles and matter, it also corresponds to the laws of physics, chemistry, and biology—all of our known laws that govern structural behavior and other physical elements. Similar to a huge computational system, the Universe appears to some to have a "scripted quality" that suggests, as Seth Lloyd states, "the same astral dramas are played out again and again by different stellar actors in different places."

In a computational universe system, entropy acts as the "information required to specify the random motions of atoms and molecules." These motions are too small to be seen or measured, so Lloyd posits that entropy can also be described as that information in a physical system that we cannot see—one that remains outside of our visible awareness. Entropy also determines the amount of thermal energy in a system that has usefulness. Entropy is an integral part of the second law of thermodynamics, which states that the entropy of the universe does not decrease as a whole, but rather the amount of unusable energy increases. One way to think about the concept of entropy is to picture it corresponding in quantity to the number of bits required to describe or quantify the jiggle of atoms. Heat itself is the energy behind the jiggle; entropy describes the information behind the jiggle.

As a giant computer, the its and bits of information that are required to process anything and everything into existence that we can see—that is, a planet—prove staggering in number. But even the materials required to form an electron requires a staggeringly large number of pieces of information, again, most of which remains beyond our visibility. "Ultimately," Lloyd writes, "information and energy play complementary roles in the universe: Energy makes physical systems do things. Information tells them what to do."

This interplay between the physical and the informative, physics, and information, is the dance of the "computational nature" of the Universe itself. In the mid-20th century, such notable scientists such as Harry Nyquist, Claude Shannon, Norbert Wiener, and their colleagues devised and formulated the theory behind the mathematical nature of this interplay with the utilization of mathematical arguments to create actual amounts of information that would be required to do specific things. An example of this would be in the number of bits required to send a communication down a telephone line. These researchers formulated what is now "Information Theory," which was later refined by James Clerk Maxwell and Ludwig Boltzmann.

In an interview with Jason Cosmowiki of *Strange Ideas*, Seth Lloyd described the Universe as "one big honking quantum mechanical computer," suggesting that the Universe itself is simply a simulation. A representation that is so exact that one could not distinguish it from reality. Although this sounds very "Matrix-esque," the idea that the universe acts as a quantum computer suggests that decoherence is the key to what we then see as reality. When quantum bits decohere, or choose one path over another in the processing progression, specific structures arise and form. According to adherents of the quantum universal model, this is what gives the Universe the appearance of being "programmed." The suggestion is that specific choices are made within the system as they would be in a computer, where certain its and bits of information are utilized above others, with the end result being what we see and perceive as everything from atoms to black holes. Different choices suggest a different universe.

In his book *Decoding the Universe: How the New Science of Information Is Explaining Everything in the Cosmos, From Our Brains to Black Holes* (which wins the grand prize for world's longest book title!), author Charles Seife examines this concept of a Cosmic Computer. Seife, like a growing number of research-ers, believes that this computer has programmed itself and all of reality into existence. Pretty heady stuff!

Seife looks at Information Theory as a way to possibly understand the odd principles at play in the Universe by focusing on the physicality of informa-tion. Information, he suggests, is a "concrete property of matter and energy which is quantifiable and measurable." Yet this information is subject to physical laws, and these laws, as in any other area of natural science, do dictate the behavior of mass and energy as information.

All of this information has to be transmitted and communicated, and this process of transmitting its and bits through space uses energy, all of which is measurable and precisely programmed to deliver a specific coded set of infor-mation that will eventually be a planet or star. The Universe, thus, could in-deed be the fastest and most efficient computer ever dreamt of by those who follow Moore's Law. Moore's Law was created in 1965 by Gordon Moore, co-founder of Intel, and states that the total number of transistors per square inch on integrated circuits (IC) had doubled every year since the IC was invented. As a measurement of computing power, Moore's Law basically states that com-puting power doubles roughly every two years. Imagine the amount of com-puting power within the universal computational system doubling at such a rate! The sheer volume of information would be staggering, snowballing into more information with farther reaching capabilities. It truly boggles the mind to think of the potential power and speed of this system.

But again, all of this begs the question, who or what is doing the programming?

And going back to the multiverse theory, one might also ask, does each Universe have its own program/programmer, or is there a Master Program/ Programmer behind the curtain, as in Oz? These are the challenges of Informa-tion Theory's leading proponents, who seek to comprehend and understand the power of the its and bits.

Pi

Six numbers and its and bits aside, there is another number that seems to speak of a nature far more profound than its quantitative value. Pi, or 3.14, is nothing more than the ratio of the circumference of a circle to its diameter. Pi is the 16th letter of the Greek alphabet. In the system of Greek numerals it has a value of 80.

The symbols for pi are universal, as is the meaning behind the symbols.

Based on the Greek word *periferia*, meaning "circumference," and represented by the Greek letter *p*, this simple irrational number has origins so ancient that some scholars say they may be untraceable to the source. Pi is not only an irrational number, meaning that it is unable to be expressed as a ratio of two different integers and that its decimal expression never ends and never starts recurring, but it is also what is known as a "transcendental number." These numbers are described by Wikipedia as "a complex number that is not algebraic, that is, not a solution of a non-zero polynomial equation with rational coefficients. In other words, transcendental numbers are numbers that do not arise from ordinary algebraic expressions."

Although Pi is certainly an interesting number, its mystique likely comes from the fact that it is one of the oldest mathematical quantities that we can trace throughout history. Some scholars attribute Archimedes with the first real theoretical work involving pi, with other mathematicians adding to the growing body of understanding this simple number throughout the ages. One of the most fascinating aspects of pi is its ability to calculate the circumference of a circle around massively large sized spheres. This computation can be performed to a very high degree of accuracy thanks to its infinite decimal expansion.

Pi is one of those unusual numbers, as are omega, delta, and the others about which Sir Martin Rees writes that would no doubt be the same for an alien from another universe. It represents a relationship, a ratio that is always going to be the same value, no matter what universe you are in, and no matter the size of the object of measurement. Pi is pi no matter where you go. This type of constant is literally a part of the fabric of our Universe, and perhaps many others as well.

Pi has a reputation as being somewhat of a "controversial" number, with several alternate interpretations being hypothesized. According to Michael Hayes, author of *The Hermetic Code in DNA: The Sacred Principles in the Ordering of the Universe*, pi associated with music, harmonics, and DNA itself. The "mathematical convention pi," as he refers to it, corresponds with the numerals 22/7, a symbol of the "triple octave," and a formula fully known about by ancient Egyptians, who incorporated it into their daily activities, as well as with the building of the pyramids. This same relationship is also apparent in the pyramid structures of Teotihuacán, Mexico, and, as Hayes states, even England's Stonehenge. Does this sound suspiciously like a sacred number?

Pi's musical association is, according to Hayes "designed to express the law of seven and the law of three—the triple octave, composed of 22 notes." Each of the three individual octaves is also composed of three "inner" octaves, Hayes proposes, totaling nine octaves and "exactly 64 fundamental notes, the square of the constant number 8." Hayes calls this the "Hermetic Code," and states it is a universal formula found everywhere, including the structure of our own DNA.

The "mathematical" pi has a value closer to 3.14159. The "classical" pi value is 3.142857.... Regardless, the universal symmetry Hayes and other researchers have found between pi and the fundamentals of harmonics also seems present in the structure of the genetic code, which we will discuss further in Chapter 10. Hayes states, "The Hermetic Code, as we know, is primarily an expression of the law of triple creation, which holds that everything is composed of trinities within trinities. This means that the three individual octaves embodied within pi are in themselves triple octaves, making nine octaves in total, or sixty-four notes—precisely the number of RNA codon combinations."

This has very far-reaching implications, and as Hayes writes:

Where this conclusion leaves us, the human race, we can but speculate, but the fact that the genetic code of the microcosmic world of the cell, and the hermetic code in the macrocosmic world of the human mind are absolutely identical is surely significant. It, in fact, brings to mind the principal dictum of Hermes Trismegistus, which was inscribed on the legendary Emerald Tablet: "As above, so below."

The implication one immediately draws from this is that the only difference between the DNA helix and a fully-functional human brain is simply one of scale. And if the human brain is a kind of metaphysical "helix," then presumably it is also an integral component—a cell-nucleus—in the body of an infinitely greater, multidimensional "organism"—our own galaxy, perhaps.

Pi's magnificence suggests again that behind all of what we see and don't see, there is a structured measurement with mathematical principles. The very fabric, and foundation, of our existence, and how we measure the world of reality around us, is entirely dependent on numbers. Yet, this dependency hints so deeply at a force behind the math of such vast and precise intelligence and order. In Chapter 10:10 we will take a deeper look at the mysterious creative and formative nature of numbers, and why some might say God or the Creative Force itself is a number. But first, let's play devil's advocate and ask a possibly leading question: Are numbers really that big of a deal, or are we making mountains out of molehills?

CHAPTER 9:9

The Trouble With Numbers

The last function of reason is to recognize that there are an infinity of things which surpass it.
—Blaise Pascal

As we have seen in the preceding chapters, numbers and mathematical modalities play an integral role in virtually all aspects of our existence. Mathematical law may even serve as the foundation for all of reality. The Universe could probably be described within the confines of just six numbers. The laws of physics might actually be the laws of the land. Wouldn't the seeming simplicity of that concept be a refreshing change from our complex and busied existence? If we could take numbers and their properties at face value, life might be so much less...well....intricate.

But that suggestion doesn't necessarily mean that numbers are always the magical, mystical, and mysterious miracles that we imagine them to be. Any good writer, or writing team, in this case, worth its weight in gold (and with the economy the way it is, gold value is soaring!) would be remiss to pass up the chance to play devil's advocate and present the opposing viewpoint. Even when it comes to numbers and the profound mystique they suggest, we have to understand that there are other laws that take the complex and swap it for the simple. Remember our friend William of Ockham and his principle of

179

Ockham's razor? With all other things being equal, generally the simplest possible explanation is the correct one.

Many of the more mundane laws involving numbers were discovered out of the sheer curiosity of mathematicians and scientists who were simply not satisfied with the "magical" properties ascribed to specific patterns and rates of frequency that were uncovered during their research.

Pascal's Triangle

Consider Pascal's Triangle. This is a geometric arrangement of digits that describe the "binomial coefficients" in a triangle. In plain English, that means that "In mathematics, the binomial coefficient is the coefficient of the $x k$ term in the polynomial expansion of the binomial power $(1 + x) n$. In combinatorics, it is often called the choose function of n and k; it is the number of k-element subsets (the k-combinations) of an n-element set; that is, the number of ways that k things can be 'chosen' from a set of n things." That description, from Wikipedia, would take a textbook to explain, but our interest in Pascal's Triangle goes far beyond what it helps determine the value of.

This intriguing Triangle was named after Blaise Pascal, who first wrote about his use of the Triangle to solve problems in probability theory back in 1655. But the Triangle had been studied and written about much earlier, even as far back as the 10th century in commentaries written about the ancient Sanskrit *Chandas Shastra*. This work initially dates the use of the Triangle back to the fifth century BC, with the Indian mathematician Bhattotpala later

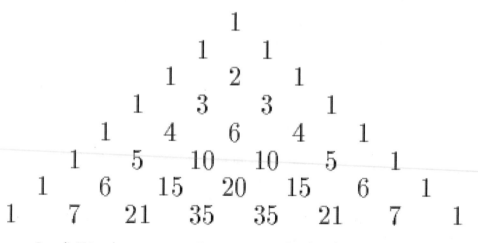

Pascal's Triangle up to row 7. Image courtesy of Wikipedia.

expanding upon the rows of the Triangle. Persian mathematician Al-Karaji and astronomer-mathematician Omar Khayyam further expounded upon the Triangle between 953 and 1131 AD, thus the added name of "Khayyam's Triangle."

Thanks to mathematician Yang Hui in the 13th century, the Chinese had their own version, today known as "Yang Hui's Triangle." Later, Italian algebraist Niccolo Fontana Tartaglia put his own spin on the Triangle, developing a formula for solving cubic polynomials—100 years before Pascal began his own work! Of course, Italians refer to it as "Tartaglia's Triangle" in homage to their countryman.

The interesting point is that, similar to pi, Pascal's Triangle is a formulaic sequence, a numeric description of repeating patterns that can look quite magical, especially when it was discovered by some of those ancient math wizards that the Fibonacci numbers were embedded within the Triangle. But similar to pi, there are sound mathematical properties underlying what some might look upon as a "number mystery."

Pascal's Triangle does indeed contain some eye-opening patterns:

- If one looks at the odd numbers only, you get what closely resembles the fractal known as Sierpinski Triangle, and the closer to infinity you get in the number of rows, the more it matches the Sierpinski Triangle.

- The value of each row, if each number in that row is considered as a decimal place and numbers over 9 are carried over, is a power of 11. Here again, the number 11 plays a significant role in mathematical patterns.

- By skipping over certain numbers at specific angles you get sums of Fibonacci numbers.

- Diagonals along the left and right edges contain only 1's.

- Diagonals next to the edge diagonals contain natural numbers in order.

- In rows where the second number is prime, all the terms in that row except the first 1's are multiples of that same prime number.

According to goldennumber.net, a few more interesting properties of Pascal's Triangle include:

- Horizontal rows add to powers of 2 (that is, 1, 2, 4, 8, 16, and so on).

- The horizontal rows represent powers of 11 (1, 11, 121, 1331, and so on).

- Adding any two successive numbers in the diagonal 1-3-6-10-15-21-28... results in a perfect square (1, 4, 9, 16, and so on).

- It can be used to find combinations in probability problems (if, for instance, you pick any two of five items, the number of possible combinations is 10, found by looking in the second place of the fifth row. Do not count the 1's.)

- When the first number to the right of the 1 in any row is a prime number, all numbers in that row are divisible by that prime number.

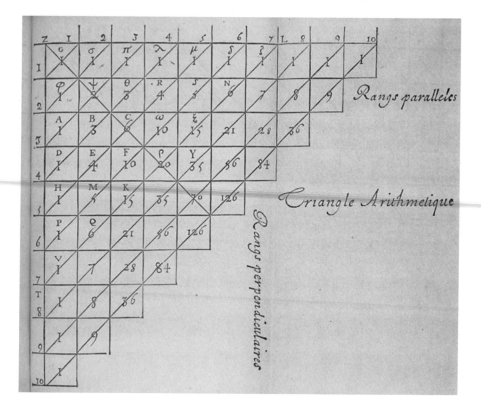

Blaise Pascal's formula for the Pascal Triangle in his own handwriting. Image courtesy of Wikipedia.

Similar to the Fibonacci Sequence, Pascal's Triangle does hint at a "higher" intelligence behind its construction. Although numbers seem to have their own laws and rules, many mathematicians and scientists refuse to ascribe mystical powers to them. Perhaps they are being short-sighted, for it seems that neither sacred numbers nor time prompts are enough to convince them of the magical powers of numbers. Or could it be that perhaps these rules and laws are blander than we would like to think?

Here is a challenge we found on a Website called Plus.Maths.org. Look up a bunch of naturally occurring numbers, such as the lengths of some of the world's rivers, the population sizes in Peruvian provinces, or the figures in Bill Clinton's tax return. Take a sample of those naturally occurring numbers and look at their first digits (ignore zero for now). Then count how many numbers start with 1, how many start with 2, then 3, and so on.

Benford's Law

As you might expect, the end result would be that the same number of numbers begin with each differing digit, and that the proportion of numbers beginning with any of the specific digits between 1 and 9 would be 1/9. Right? Is that your final answer?

Wrong. The distribution of first digits is not so spread out, and, in fact, the most common starting digit will always be 1, while the least common is 9. Believe it or not, there is actually a formula that describes this, a law. Benford's Law, also known as "First-Digit Law." This law basically states that groups or lists of numbers from real-life sources will follow a specific pattern of leading digit frequency.

Canadian-American astronomer and mathematician Simon Newcomb (1835–1909) is credited as the first person to take notice of this amazing law. He wrote about it in his 1881 paper "Note on the Frequency of Use of the Different Digits in Natural Numbers." While Newcomb's observation was important, it was physicist Frank Benford in 1938 that, upon seeing the same patterns in his own research, finally put two and two together. Benford conducted some real-world experimental sampling, which was intended to prove the law that would later be named after him. He collected vast sums of data, including the addresses of the first 342 people listed in *American Men of Science*. In his analysis, he found that approximately 30 percent began with 1, 18 percent with 2, and so on. This pattern was repeatable with other sets of data, similar to baseball statistics, death rates, stock prices, street addresses, and electricity bills, but even Benford was at a loss to explain exactly why it worked.

Fast forward to around 1961, when American mathematician Roger Pinkham took the issue on. Pinkham believed that a potential explanation for this pattern could be explained. He supposed that there was indeed a law of "digit frequencies," and suggested that this law had to be universal—regardless of what form the digits were in, that is, prices in dollars or Drachma, or measurements in inches, cubits, or meters. Pinkham called this universality "scale invariant," and was the first to show that Benford's Law is, indeed, scale invariant. It works both ways, too. If a law of digit frequencies is scale invariant, it has to be Benford's Law.

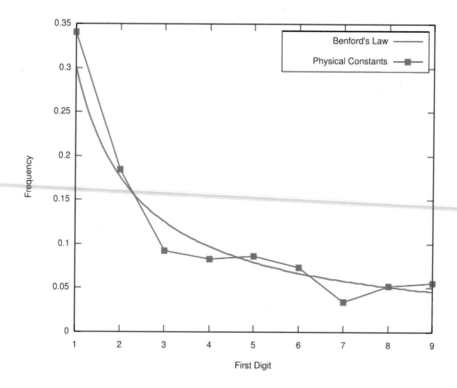

A plot of Benford's Law vs. the first significant digit of a set of physical constants. Image courtesy of http://physics.nist.gov/constants.

Benford's Law in Base 10 shows the percentage rate for each leading digit from 1 to 9.

1–30.1 percent

2–17.6 percent

3–12.5 percent

4–9.7 percent

5–7.9 percent

6–6.7 percent

7–5.8 percent

8–5.1 percent

9–4.6 percent

Further experimentation with Benford's Law has been done on everything from business statistics and annual turnover rates to fundamental physical constants, but the law has some constraints. Numbers cannot be random, as in lottery picks (sorry!), and cannot be overly constrained where the range of possibilities is way too narrow. So while you cannot pick the winning numbers for next week's $50 million Power Lotto, you could use Benford's Law in other important ways.

Researchers are working on ways to use the law to detect fraud in tax returns and financial data (Bill Clinton's tax return was scrutinized by accountancy professor Dr. Mark Nigrini using this law and, surprisingly, no fraud was detected!) as well as other useful functions, such as checking irregularities in clinical study trials and verifying demographic models.

Similar to all good things, the law does have specific limitations. Although it cannot apply to certain sets of numbers, it is an intriguing example of a mathematical formula that can be used to explain what might appear to some as "mysterious circumstances" involving the appearance of one digit over another in large sets of data.

Laws, Rules, and Constants

There are literally dozens of such laws and rules that use numbers to define, categorize, and validate everything from computer processing to widescale distribution to human behavior. We don't have time to get into all of these in one chapter, but, to name a few:

- *Apery's constant*—A curious mathematical constant that arises in a variety of physical problems. The number of known digits of Apery's constant has increased dramatically during the last decades due to the utilization of computers and algorithmic enhancements.

- *80-20 rule*—The Pareto principle, the law of the vital few and the principle of factor sparsity, states that, for many events, 80 percent of the effects come from 20 percent of the causes. According to About.com, "In 1906, Italian economist Vilfredo Pareto created a mathematical formula to describe the unequal distribution of wealth in his country, observing that twenty percent of the people owned eighty percent of the wealth. In the late 1940s, Dr. Joseph M. Juran inaccurately attributed the 80/20 Rule to Pareto, calling it Pareto's Principle."

- *Power Law*—Any polynomial (a mathematical expression involving a sum of powers in one or more variables multiplied by coefficients) relationship that exhibits the scale invariance property, power laws are involved in a huge number of natural patterns.

- *Zipf's Law*—Named for linguist George Zipf. It shows that the probability of occurrence of words or other items starts high and then decreases by tapering off. Thus, a few occur often while others occur rarely.

Again, these are just a few of the many laws, rules, and constants used in science, computing, business, physics, and even the determination of frequencies of particular earthquakes! Because this book deals so heavily with number patterns and synchronicity, we did find some specific laws that deal with things of a coincidental nature—things we often apply spiritual and personal meaning to.

Did you know that there is a law that says each of us can expect a miracle to occur in our lives at a rate of about one per month? Marie can't speak for Larry, but she is definitely on arrears! Littlewood's Law makes just such a statement. First published by Cambridge University professor J.E. Littlewood in *A Mathematician's Miscellany*, this law was initially developed to actually debunk supernatural or paranormal claims about the phenomenon of miracles. Littlewood's Law is directly related to the Law of Truly Large Numbers, which posits that when you get a sampling that is large enough, anything can happen. Consider it the Murphy's Law of Math.

Littlewood defines a miracle as "an exceptional event of special significance occurring at a frequency of one in a million; during the hours in which a human is awake and alert, a human will experience one thing per second (for instance, seeing the computer screen, the keyboard, the mouse, the article, and so on); additionally, a human is alert for about eight hours per day; and as a result, a human will, in 35 days, have experienced, under these suppositions, 1,008,000 things." Accepting this definition of a miracle, one can be expected to observe one miracle every 35 consecutive days or so. Therefore, miracles may not be as miraculous as originally thought! With so many people experiencing so many events throughout so many days, this seems not only logical, but far less "paranormal" than we've been led to believe by religious institutions that insist we have to beg, plead, and petition for just one miracle in a lifetime.

Again, the authors of this book can't quite vouch for the effectiveness of this law in our own lives, but the Law of Truly Large Numbers does allow for strange coincidences, such as someone winning the lottery three times in a year. Yet there has actually been multiple studies conducted that help explain how this could easily happen. One of the most notable was conducted by statisticians Stephen Samuels and George McCabe of Purdue University after the *New York Times* ran a story of a woman who won the lottery twice, against staggering odds. According to their research, the odds of someone winning the lottery twice are actually about 1 in 30 in a four-month period, and better odds throughout a seven-year period. Not staggering at all. This is likely due to the fact that players tend to buy multiple tickets every week, upping their odds of winning considerably.

With more than six billion people on this planet, the odds are actually high that someone else, maybe even 10 million someone elses, will be dreaming of the exact same thing you are tonight. Perhaps they will be having the same dinner. Or sharing the same birth date. The larger the sample number, the more frequently these "coincidences" seem to occur, which appears astounding to us until we realize that just as many millions can share the same event, they can also share the same "meaningful coincidence," and apply the same personal significance to that event.

Thus, according to Littlewood's Law and the Law of Truly Large Numbers, each of us should be experiencing some strange, coincidental events, some even potentially miraculous, every single day. This would no doubt include seeing 11:11 on the digital clock or noticing the constant appearance of the number 23 throughout one's day, especially when our brains take the first few coincidences we experience and create patterns around them, amplifying their importance and setting us up to see even more and more of them appear. So, is this the explanation for the time prompt phenomena?

Coincidence

Coincidence is described by author David Marks in his book *Psychology of the Psychic* as odd matches when two events occur that are perceived to contain a similarity. But as we have seen, Littlewood's Law and the Law of Truly Large Numbers dictate that these odd matches should actually be occurring all the time, just by the sheer size of our populace alone. Linked events happen every day, and the claims of paranormal or conspiratorial relationships may be overblown by the mere fact that life, and ultimately history, as mathematical laws suggest, repeats itself all the time. Statistically, coincidences must happen; they are inevitable.

> *History repeats itself. That's one of the things wrong with history.*
> —Clarence Darrow, U.S. defense lawyer (1857–1938)

Matrixing

Perhaps much of the reason humans apply so much meaning to these coincidences comes from our tendency toward matrixing, seeking patterns where there may or may not be any. Matrixing, which is technically called pareidolia, is an important concept as it is an explanatory basis for many unexplained phenomena. If you recall, we talked briefly about the concept in a previous chapter, but, we wanted to further expand upon it now. According to the *Weird Encyclopedia*, "Pareidolia refers to the human habit of looking for the familiar in the unfamiliar. The electrical socket isn't a face—we know that. Our brains tell us it is impossible, it's simply a piece of plastic and the holes are where the metal plugs go. But that doesn't stop us from seeing something more human in the configuration. Likewise, listening the monotonous spraying of water while we shower can give us a tendency to hear other things behind the "white noise" of our bathing ritual. We may know the front door is locked as we bathe at home alone, but sometimes we wonder if someone has broken in, taking advantage of our moment of helplessness. Sure, it never happens, but—oh, was that the phone ringing? Guess not.

Blessed Virgin Mary Pareidolia can take on amazing and even absurd forms, especially when some of us believe in supernatural things such as ghosts, angels, blessed virgin Marys (bvM's), and so forth. Visually, it's an easy concept to reckon: we look for faces and other familiar patterns in the things we see. Babies instinctively know to concentrate on mom and dad's eyes, almost as soon as they're able to focus their own; children lie on their backs in the summer and seek out cool shapes in the clouds. We amuse ourselves with computer-generated pictures where familiar objects are hidden in seemingly random patterns of color, or we scour books to find a guy in glasses named Waldo amid hundreds of similar characters. The effect is the same.

Not just religious icons are appearing in unexpected places these days (and yes, we are counting Elvis as a religious figure). The great abundance of ghost photographs appearing on the Internet appears to consist mainly of light blobs on photo negatives, camera straps, and wisps of steam or clouds of dust; these aren't exactly good examples of pareidolia, but people are still making them out to be the spirits of the undead—and are sometimes pointing out human faces to be found within the light blobs (or orbs), which they reckon to be the souls of those deceased persons still floating around here on earth. A few ghost photographs are also apparently oddly shaped tree knots, curling flames, and vague shapes that show up on processed photographs. Some of them look kind of spooky, but they're a far cry from the spirit beings wearing period clothing that we've been reading about for years. Why doesn't somebody take a really good ghost photo for a change?

Biases

It's natural for our brains to do this, especially when faced with events or occurrences that appear to have remarkable timing or frequency. It may also be our tendency toward "confirmation bias," where we naturally interpret information according to our personal perceptions and avoid information that goes against or challenges those perceptions.

Ever have a spouse or loved one yell at you, "You only hear what you want to hear"? May we have a show of hands? I (Larry) have been accused of practicing such "selective hearing" on more than one occasion! This is a prime example of information bias in personal relationships—where we tend to tune out details or ignore red flags. Described as an "error of inductive inference, or a form of selection bias toward confirmation of the hypothesis under study or disconfirmation of an alternative hypothesis," the authors of this book have seen confirmation bias in action in our paranormal research, from folks on both sides of the fence. Believers shut out information that challenges their beliefs. Skeptics shut out information that challenges their disbelief.

Also referred to in psychology and cognitive science as "belief bias," "selective thinking," and "hypothesis locking," this variety of preconceived belief often lacks any supportive evidence, yet seems to again be related to our brain's ability to matrix and find relationships where none might really exist. We are sure that by now you won't be surprised to know that there is even a Murphy's Law of Research that states "enough research will tend to support your theory!"

This is similar to the "polarization effect," which is seen in politics and involves the use of evidence that can be described as neutral to shore up an established and biased existing point of view. The polarization of red versus blue state beliefs is a perfect example of moving sides further and further apart as they cling for dear life onto confirmation biases that they perceive to support their beliefs. Again, we turn to the human brain and the five senses, which rapidly evaluate information and then "choose sides," so to speak, by filling in the gaps of unavailable, or shaky, information with a pre-existing subconscious bias. Once the brain processes and accepts the bias as true, it becomes incredibly difficult to shake that bias, even upon presentation of true and valid information. Have you ever tried to convince a die-hard skeptic of something—even with undeniable proof? It is usually like talking to a wall.

Religious beliefs, traditions, personal values, and cultural ideologies all contribute to the confirmation bias and polarization effect that we see in everyday life. Our perceptions of everything from the political arena to our own interactions with others are colored by these notions.

These same dynamics occur when we consider whether or not we "believe" in psychics, ghosts, UFOs, and even whether we believe that numbers such as 11:11 have mystical meanings and connotations. But it would not be fair or accurate to say that people view evidence with bias. Rather, extensive research into cognitive studies has shown that it is in the "reading" of the evidence that the bias, which already exists, appears. This may explain why children are so pure and unbiased toward truth. If you look ugly, they tell you. They have not yet trained their brain to "not say anything if you can't say anything nice." Ahhh, to be young again. Imagine how much different of a world we might live in if everyone was brutally honest and forthright!

Geneticist David Perkins coined the phrase "myside bias" to refer to thinking "my" side of an argument is the correct one. This kind of thinking can lead to all sorts of negative psychological traits such as delusion, paranoia, and even self-aggrandization, however, here we are concerned with whether or not these biases are placing false assumptions on synchronistic events.

The tragic thing about these types of psychological biases is that even when someone is handed pure proof of evidence to the contrary, the human will to always "be right" usually kicks in, and we end up with often large groups of people following false leads and buying into inaccurate assumptions. Again, as paranormal researchers, we both see this happening every day, whether with people refusing to think orbs are nothing more than airborne particulate matter, or rigid scientists refusing to acknowledge that millions of people through time have seen ghosts, experienced time anomalies, or been visited by angelic beings in the dead of night.

Perhaps the most interesting and amusing example of this bias comes from Glenn R. Morton, a theistic evolutionist. In 2002, Morton wrote about "Morton's Demon," which he believed was an evil spirit that stands ready at the gateway to a person's five senses and takes in only facts that agree with the person's beliefs. This is analogous to "Maxwell's Demon," an 1871 thought experiment by Scottish physicist James Clerk Maxwell. In it, Maxwell described a demon that chooses the outcome of a physics experiment according to bias that possibly violates the second law of thermodynamics.

The real demon, then, might be our own need to associate meaning to something quite mundane in mathematical terms. This subjective validation of evidence may be shared by millions of people, giving the impression of a larger and grander mystery than might be the case, but it still begs the question: do we get what we expect?

Recent studies into the brain's ability to tell time suggest that we may have an intricate internal clock within our brains. Our brain cell network might even evolve throughout long periods of time to respond to stimuli with neural connections that allow us to tell time without a clock. Research at UCLA's David Geffen School of Medicine by a team of neurobiologists and psychiatrists is delving into the brain's ability to generate and count regular fixed movements and use that information to encode time. External cues provide the needed information, such as changes in light, melatonin levels, and the actual time on the clock on the wall.

According to Dean Buonomano, associate professor of neurobiology and psychiatry at the David Geffen School of Medicine, and a member of the university's Brain Research Institute, "Many complex human behaviors—from understanding speech to playing catch to performing music—rely on the brain's ability to accurately tell time. Yet no one knows how the brain does it." Buonomano further posits that "Our results suggest that the timing mechanisms that underlie our ability to recognize speech and enjoy music are distributed throughout the brain, and do not resemble the conventional clocks we wear on our wrists."

The body's Circadian rhythms of sleep and waking cycles definitely seem to be regulated by the brain. Studies in the 1970s associated this inner regulatory point with the suprachiasmatic nucleus, a cluster of cells in the hypothalamus, the region of the brain that also regulates appetite and biological states.

These studies suggest the brain's ability to not only construct patterns based upon evident information, but also, to place a time upon them. To wake up once at 11:11 would mean little, but if the brain makes a neural connection after waking up twice at that specific time, that connection would then become an embedded time code that will continue to manifest. Think of the times you have forgotten to set the alarm only to wake up exactly at the same time you normally would in order to prepare for work.

If indeed the brain can tell time, and if the brain engages in the matrixing of meaning in an attempt to discern a pattern, how can we then know whether a time prompt is just a time prompt, a sheer coincidental event dictated by the Law of Truly Large Numbers and doled out significance to by a brain habitually trained to do so, or a real and meaningful wake-up call that we should, and must, pay attention to?

"Pseudomathematics" is a term used to describe mathematical-type stuff that doesn't normally fit within purely mathematical frameworks or follow mathematical models. Sacred geometry, numerology, and even time prompts themselves can be categorized as a form of pseudomathematics, for none truly follow strict laws without treading into the realm of the mysterious or metaphysical. Pseudomathematics often disregards proven mathematical laws and rules, using non-mathematical means to bolster its arguments, yet can often contain some solid math around the perimeters, so to speak.

One of the most common uses of pseudomathematics is in an attempt to solve classical problems with formulas and standards considered mathematically impossible. Additionally, twisting or modifying existing mathematical methods to apply a new meaning or standard to them would be considered pseudomathematics. Pure mathematics would state that it is impossible to square a circle, double a cube, trisect an angle, or place a true meaning on the concept of infinity. Yet, in the world of sacred geometry, we have seen attempts to do just those things. Many similar attempts have been made in the field of physics with attempts to disprove classical truths with pseudomathematical means, thus labeling those who try as "cranks," if not worse.

But the only way we can really discern the magical properties of numbers, and again, even Pythagoras and his ilk expounded upon them, is by suspending a little belief. We must engage in a little controlled confirmation bias and assume that behind the Laws that seem to work with such precision—and shock with stunning accuracy—there had to have been a mind, a truly mathematical master genius, thinking all this stuff up.

Is God a number?

CHAPTER

10:10

Is God a Number?

> *The great book of nature can be read only by those*
> *who know the language in which it was written.*
> *And this language is mathematics.*
>
> —Galileo

I s God a number? At first glance, this might appear to be a loaded question that might be expected to elicit a similar response to the question "Is God a male or female?"

Of course, because Western religious traditions already insist that the answer to that controversial question is that God is male, let us attempt to transcend personal belief, and study the inquiry from a socio-religious perspective. Before doing so, however, it is important to recognize and comprehend the underlying idea and concept of God.

Mohandas Karamchand Gandhi's poem "The Meaning of God" is a beautiful sonnet that describes God's ever-present nature:

There is an indefinable mysterious Power that pervades everything.

I feel It, though I do not see It.

It is this unseen Power that makes Itself felt and yet defies all proof, because It is so unlike all that I perceive through my senses.

It transcends the senses....

That informing Power or Spirit is God....

*For I can see that in the midst of death life persists, in the midst of un
truth, truth persists, in the midst of darkness light persists.*

Hence I gather that God is Life, Truth, Light. He is love.

He is supreme good.

But he is no God who merely satisfies the intellect

If He ever does.

God to be God must rule the heart and transform it.

—Mohandas Karamchand Gandhi (Young India, October 11, 1928)

Nearly every culture on Earth believes in the existence of some type of supreme higher power. From Yahweh to Yoda and the Force, the many changing faces of God remind us of the need to put our faith and belief in a bigger power that can watch over us, protect us, and guide us.

Although degrees of faith differ, the belief in "God" or a "Creator" is ubiquitous. Mankind's need for a foundational deity is universal, and has often been credited with the creation and destruction of whole cultures. The "my God vs. your God" battle continues to this day, with no apparent end in sight.

Those who do believe in a God, though, strive to describe or define it, usually as an entity or figurehead, and a deity that oversees the creation it manifested from its own desire to express itself. Omniscient, omnipotent, omnipresent—an all-encompassing force that, according to cultural belief, is either benevolent like a loving father or judgmental and harsh like a taskmaster.

Much has been written about various numbers that have been attributed to God throughout the ages. Among others, the numbers 1, 7, 40, 66, 180, and 360 have all been ascribed to be holy numbers with sacred meaning. The number 3, representing the triune nature of God, as well as the triune nature of reality itself, is found in a variety of religious traditions and creation myths, describing a three-fold nature to the creative force from which all else manifests; the seen and the unseen.

However, the idea that God itself could be described in numeric form seems almost blasphemous. To place divine power upon mere digits hints at heresy, as well as the blending of science with religion, which many feel go together about as well as oil and water. There do seem to be, though, certain numbers that hint at a significance far beyond ordinary mortal numbers. Aside from that, the creative force itself acts through various physical laws, and all laws have a mathematical component that cannot be denied at the fountain.

Constants

In Chapter 8:8, we examined the cosmological constants of the six numbers that must be finely tuned to allow for life as we know it to exist. Add to this the cosmological constant of the presence of dark energy, a force that increases as the size of the Universe increases, and we have measurable and demonstrable values that make up for all the matter, or lack of it, in the Universe.

To fine-tune the physical constants present in the Universe, including the four fundamental forces of gravitation, electromagnetism, and the strong and weak nuclear forces, as well as the ratio of electrons and protons present, requires something, or someone, to do the tuning. Could it all be a random accident that things worked out the way they did? Would that be easier to believe than the concept of a higher master mathematician at play, working out the equations that underlie the values that create stars, form galaxies, and allow for the birth of the elements from which life is made?

Many of the past and present leading scientists believe there is a God behind the number, if not a number behind the God. Here is a sampling of some quotes we found, with sources.

■ Fred Hoyle (British astrophysicist): "A common sense interpretation of the facts suggests that a super intellect has monkeyed with physics, as well as with chemistry and biology, and that there are no blind forces worth speaking about in nature. The numbers one calculates from the facts seem to me so overwhelming as to put this conclusion almost beyond question." (*Wall Street Journal*, "Science Resurrects God," 12-27-97.)

■ George Ellis (British astrophysicist): "Amazing fine tuning occurs in the laws that make this [complexity] possible. Realization of the complexity of what is accomplished makes it very difficult not to use the word *miraculous* without taking a stand as to the ontological status of the word." ("The Anthropic Principle," G.F.R. Ellis, 1993.)

■ Paul Davies (British astrophysicist): "There is for me powerful evidence that there is something going on behind it all.... It seems as though somebody has fine-tuned nature's numbers to make the Universe.... The impression of design is overwhelming." (*The Cosmic Blueprint: New Discoveries in Nature's Creative Ability to Order the Universe*, 1988.)

- Alan Sandage (winner of the Crawford Prize in astronomy): "I find it quite improbable that such order came out of chaos. There has to be some organizing principle. God to me is a mystery but is the explanation for the miracle of existence, why there is something instead of nothing." (*New York Times*, "Sizing Up the Cosmos," 03-12-91.)

- Arno Penzias (Nobel Prize in physics): "Astronomy leads us to a unique event, a universe which was created out of nothing, one with the very delicate balance needed to provide exactly the conditions required to permit life, and one which has an underlying (one might say 'supernatural') plan." (*Cosmos, Bios, and Theos*, Margenau, H. and R.A. Varghese, 1992.)

- Stephen Hawking (British astrophysicist): "Then we shall…be able to take part in the discussion of the question of why it is that we and the universe exist. If we find the answer to that, it would be the ultimate triumph of human reason—for then we would know the mind of God." (*A Brief History of Time*, 1988.)

- Alexander Polyakov (Soviet mathematician): "We know that nature is described by the best of all possible mathematics because God created it."("Fortune," S. Gannes, 1986.)

- Ed Harrison (cosmologist): "Here is the cosmological proof of the existence of God—the design argument of Paley—updated and refurbished. The fine-tuning of the universe provides prima facie evidence of deistic design. Take your choice: blind chance that requires multitudes of universes or design that requires only one…. Many scientists, when they admit their views, incline toward the teleological or design argument." ("Masks of the Universe," E. Harrison, 1985.)

- Arthur L. Schawlow (professor of physics at Stanford University, 1981 Nobel Prize in physics): "It seems to me that when confronted with the marvels of life and the universe, one must ask why and not just how. The only possible answers are religious…I find a need for God in the universe and in my own life." (*Cosmos, Bios, Theos*, Margenau and Varghese, 1992.)

■ Wernher von Braun (pioneer rocket engineer): "I find it as difficult to understand a scientist who does not acknowledge the presence of a superior rationality behind the existence of the universe as it is to comprehend a theologian who would deny the advances of science." (*The Skeptical Enquirer*, T. McIver, 1986.)

Though not all scientists would agree, this is but a sampling of those who are open to the presence of a higher force at play in the design of this finely tuned mechanism we call our Universe. Most do agree that there is a numeric aspect, a degree of this fine-tuning required, and it can be described in numeric terms. And if these numbers are off by even the slightest amount, we cease to exist, or to ever have existed.

Rubik's Cube

The numbers involved might be described better as the structure of the Universe. These numeric values define laws, how things work, how they come about in the first place. We want to ask the questions: Is God a number, too? And if so, what number?

One of the most amusing and curious quests to find God's Number involves a retro toy that is once again becoming all the rage. Remember Rubik's Cube? This little block of good fun was a huge hit in the 1980s, and required the player to try to solve the puzzle by getting all the same colors on the same side of the cube. The world record for "cubing" is currently set at 9.86 seconds, set in 2007 at the World Cube Association competition in Spain. Yes, there are Olympics for cubing.

According to Northeastern University researchers, who attempted to find the minimum number of moves possible to solve the cube (Ockham's razor meets Rubik's Cube), there are more than 43 quintillion possible arrangements to slush your way through. But a doctorate student named Dan Kunkle, and a professor of computer science named Gene Cooperman, have announced that they found the "God Number," and it is 26. As part of a National Science Foundation grant, these two men solved Rubik's Cube in only 26 moves, what they call "God's Number," because "God would always use the fewest moves possible to solve the puzzle." (This assumes God has time to play with cube toys.)

The two plan to whittle down that God's Number, and they insist that the number is not what is important. Rather, the concept of finding the simplest and fastest way to solve a problem, with the use of technology, of course, as a powerful overseeing creator might.

Other Possibilities

The 1980s toys aside, there just might be a more serious number associated with the divine. The God numeral, according to physicist Scott Funkhouser, could be an unimaginably big number, say 10^{122}, or 10 times itself 122 times. This number seems to show up in some very critical cosmic instances, appearing first in the late 1990s when scientists began researching the presence of dark energy. This energy is believed to be behind the accelerating rate of expansion we see in our Universe. This same number, albeit with a give-or-take of a factor of 10, appears in other important ratios, such as the ratio of mass of the observable Universe to that of the smallest "quantum" of mass, which is 6×10^{121}; and one of the measurements of entropy that determines the many ways particles in the current Universe can be spatially arranged, which is 2.5×10^{122}.

Again, even to see these common ratios show up five or six times is stunning to most physicists and cosmologists. It seems highly unlikely that chance is behind this repetition of ratios involving huge numbers, or that rolling the dice and playing a huge game of cosmic craps. Sir James Joyce, considered by many to be one of the founders of astrophysics, once wrote that the Universe seemed to him more like a great thought than a great machine. This begs the question: Who or what is thinking the great thought?

Teleological Argument

This desire to find evidence of an existence of a creator or Godlike power in the perceived order and design of nature is called a "teleological argument," or an "argument from design," and is based upon the Greek word *telos,* meaning "end" or "purpose." The argument consists of four basic components:

1. Nature appears too orderly, complex, and purposeful to be random or accidental.
2. Nature must have been created by an intelligent, wise, and purposeful entity.
3. God is intelligent, wise, and purposeful.
4. God exists, and nature is proof.

The problems arise, though, when the argument extends into a definition of intelligence, and the religious connotations become involved. In our discussion of Information Theory we looked at a theory that offers a compromise. The Universe looks ordered and purposeful because it is a giant computer computing itself. Most people might not equate a computer with God, but this theory allows for intelligence to the design behind the numbers and values that make up our Universe, as well as a non-religious sensibility. The teleological argument buys into the Anthropic Principle, which proposes that the finely tuned constants are set to specifically allow for life as we know it; namely, intelligent life that evolves into human beings.

The main forces behind the Anthropic Principle are John D. Barrow and Frank J. Tipler, authors of *The Anthropic Cosmological Principle*, published in 1986. They propose that the intricacy of design that leads to life is so utterly improbable and must be on purpose, compared to the vast and possibly infinite range of possible conditions that could have led to the opposite result: no life at all. But other scientists argue that statistics could be manipulated to define a number of natural situations that have that same level of improbability, yet happened anyway. Life may, then, not be as improbable as we think. Thus, maybe the conditions that arose on earth as sustainable to life were quite simply luck…just as picking a one in a million lottery ticket might be.

Proponents of the teleological argument must therefore prove that only intelligent design, and not sheer luck, could account for a universe so perfectly tuned and masterfully thought out, and opponents suggest that even if there is an intelligent force behind this whole mathematically inclined reality, it does not mean that designer is God, or in the words of author Richard Dawkins (*The God Delusion, The Blind Watchmaker*), it is only required that the designer be at least as complex and purposeful as the designed object. This does not imply the designer be God, and French philosopher Voltaire himself echoed this sentiment in his belief that the teleological argument suggested a powerful intelligence, but not necessarily the *most* powerful one.

There is even argument over the nature of the designer itself. According to Quentin Smith, author of *The Anthropic Coincidences, Evil and the Disconfirmation of Theism*, we should not even assume that the designer of any intelligent universe would even be a good guy. Instead, he warns us "it is reasonable to conclude that God does not exist, since God is omnipotent, omniscient and perfectly good and thereby would not permit any gratuitous natural evil. But since gratuitous natural evils are precisely what we would expect if a malevolent spirit created the universe…if any spirit created the universe, it is malevolent." The Universe, Smith argues, is a hostile environment indeed, with most of its conditions not at all gently attuned to the emergence of life.

This hostility is evident even examining the way nature works on our own planet, with the survival of the fittest and the food chain. It's not necessarily a dog-eat-dog world, but it definitely is one where shark eats fish, leopard eats gazelle, and humans eat whatever they fancy. On a more macrocosmic level, the hostility of the environments on other planets do not even lend themselves to life, and one can only imagine how difficult it would be for anything to survive the extremes of heat and cold to be found in the outer reaches of our universe.

On a blog called Cosmic Variance, created by a group of physicists and astrophysicists including Mark Trodden, Risa Wechsler, Sean Carroll, JoAnne Hewett, Julianne Dalcanton, John Conway, and Daniel Holz, the following blog post spoke to the potential non-"divine" origins of the Universe.

Special pleading that the universe is essentially different from its constituents, and (by nature of its unique status as all that there is to the physical world) that it could not have either (1) just existed forever, nor (2) come spontaneously into existence all by itself, is groundless. The only sensible response such skepticism is "Why not?" It's certainly true that we don't yet know whether the universe is eternal or whether it had a beginning, and we certainly don't understand the details of its origin. But there is absolutely no obstacle to our eventually figuring those things out, given what we already understand about physics.

A Higher Nature

As the battle rages on over whether or not the universe was designed with purpose, intent, and even intelligence, pitting science against religion in a most current sense, there are compromises being offered between those who walk in either world. Some scientists and religious leaders see no conflict between the concepts of evolution and intelligent design, rather choosing to view the existence of life on Earth as something potentially arising from a creator-deity who utilizes evolution as the means of allowing life to unfold and emerge and evolve.

With continued conflict and controversy surrounding the basic existence of God, it would seem even more impossible to quantify the nature of God, especially in mathematical terms. But numerologists and those involved with Sacred Geometry think that there are sequences, such as the God Number of 112358134711, which speak of a higher and more profound nature. This number, linked to the Kabbalah and the Fibonacci Sequence discussed earlier, always come back to the master number of 11. You start with the number 1, and then add each number to the one before it to get the next number. 0 + 1 = 1. 1 + 1 = 2. 2 + 1 = 3. 3 + 2 = 5. 5 + 3 = 8, and so on and so on to 7 + 4 = 11, and then the whole thing repeats itself. Numerologists claim if you add up the series of numbers 1123581347 (which we visited in an earlier chapter), without the final 11, you get 8, the number of eternity and infinity, and if you allow the 11 to repeat all the way to the end, you end on 10, the divine number and a magical number rife with symbolism in the Kabbalah, Gematria, and even the Tarot. While this speaks volumes to numerologists, to others it seems as though any end number could be given some mysterious, even divine, significance.

Divine 7

Again, we think of the Fibonacci sequence that shows up beautifully in the intricacies of nature, art, architecture, and sacred design. Perhaps God is more than one number. Perhaps God is all numbers. Perhaps God is an equation or a pattern that contains the entirety of numbers within its infrastructure. Few would argue in the Judeo-Christian tradition of the importance of number 7 appearing throughout the texts, including in divisible forms. There are 21 Old Testament writers—3 × 7. There are seven of those named in the New Testament. The numeric value of those seven names adds up to 1,554, which is 222 × 7. God describes man's years as three score and 10, 70. God formed man in Genesis 2:7 from the dust of the earth, and we know that the human body is made of the same elements found in that same dust of the earth—14, or 2 × 7.

These could be nothing more than a collection of evidential situations found in the texts that point to the number 7. Call it confirmation bias. Perhaps the same perusal of the texts turns up just as many references to the number 42. Or 12. Or 11. But no matter how many numbers repeat how many times, one cannot help but feel there is significance to the constant repetition of just a handful of numbers, over and over, and how often they seem to link science and spirit, universal structure, and the nature of the divine. Mind and matter. The pot of gold at the end of the rainbow, and the rainbow itself.

There are seven colors in the rainbow, after all.

333

Christians also point to the number 333 as being the number of God. We recall 666 is the number of God's adversary, the Beast of Revelation, the anti-Christ of the Apocalypse. The number 333 is considered holy because of the divine nature of the triune, tripled. The number 3, as presented in earlier chapters, holds such a high place in the numerological hierarchy of numbers, and tripled imbues it with a profound holiness and power. God becomes "three times holy" as in Isaiah 6:3.

777

Perhaps the God Number exists far closer to home than the outer reaches of an expanding universe. In the first chapter of this book, we looked at time prompts and how they might be wake-up calls meant to, as one theory states, activate our "junk DNA." If the Universe is a giant computer spitting out its and bits of information to create reality, then our DNA is a personal computer doing the same thing, only the its and bits it spits out make…us.

Others involved in Bible Code interpretation and sacred numbers in the Old and New Testament suggest that perhaps God's Number should be 777, the triplicate of the divine and lucky number 7.

Geometric Harmony

Author Sarah Voss writes in her book *What Number is God? Metaphors, Metaphysics, Metamathematics, and the Nature of Things*, that the concept of a divine number might be more metaphorical than literal. She agrees that all of life is deeply imbued with the presence of sacred numbers, geometry, and patterns, and that we might need to take a more metaphorical approach to seeking a distinct divine numeric association with the higher intelligence thought to be behind all of creation. She quotes Dutch mathematician B.L. van der Waerden, in reference to the Pythagorean Greeks who revered numbers as divine, as saying, "Mathematics formed a part of their religion. Their doctrine proclaims that God has ordered the universe by means of numbers. God is unity, the world a plurality, and it consists of contrasting elements. It is harmony which restores unity to the contrasting parts and which molds them into a cosmos. Harmony is divine. It consists of numerical ratios."

The geometric harmony spoken of, Voss continues, is present throughout the physical world, in symmetries and proportions evident throughout nature. These proportions are mirrors of the grander, greater macrocosmic reality, symbols of the cosmos seen in the intricacies of a spiraled face of a flower or a Nautilus shell. But she suggests that Pythagoras, Plato, and others may have been speaking metaphorically when they described nature and natural laws in terms of geometrical ratios and proportions. Yet many of the scientists of the past have acknowledged that this link between macro and micro, between numbers and nature, does also exist in a literal sense, even though it may have been written about and philosophized about in more symbolic terms.

DNA

One of the most enduring symbols that suggest a higher intelligence instilled in the structure of manifest reality is within our own bodies. DNA operates a lot like a computer, and the human genome consists of the equivalent of 750 megabytes of information or data. A very small percentage of that data, perhaps 3 percent, is involved in the composition of the 22,000-plus genes that make each of us the person that we are. The other 97 percent is like a blank hard drive, ready to be encoded with information to store in the genome.

This non-coding DNA is often referred to as "junk DNA," although in recent years it has been determined to be anything but, both by the scientific community and the metaphysical community. A question on one intelligent-design Website begs for more argument: "Why would a perfect God create flawed DNA which is primarily composed of useless, non-coding regions?" Yet, as mentioned earlier, God does indeed create flaws throughout nature—if we interpret them to be so. Maybe what we see as flaws are really all a part of a bigger picture to which we are only given a tiny glimpse.

We look at the 3 percent of DNA that works with amazing and intricate precision to create the correct elements of our bodies, from cells to major organs, and then directs those elements in just the precise manner. To someone with a religious bent, the fact that our bodies are mechanisms of the highest and most profound design and order are Godlike enough. DNA makes each of us who we are; unique expressions of life itself, yet in the most fundamental way, all pretty much the same.

But it's the junk stuff that interests those who are having time prompts, and it's the junk stuff that suggests there might be more to us humans than we ever imagined, more to us than our blue eyes and brown hair and long legs and crooked smiles. Most geneticists agree that the non-coding DNA is necessary for the proper functioning of the coded DNA. They are just not sure how. There are many theories as to why the non-coding DNA appears inactive, even suggesting it provided no selective advantages or that it was once a necessity and lost its coding ability somewhere along the way. Truth is, it is still within us, and the quest is on to determine what it just might be capable of doing if activated.

Also known as "secondary DNA," many studies have shown that this former junk stuff plays a functional role in the structure of the nucleus of a cell, and that the amount of this non-coding DNA was directly proportional to the size of the cell. Other studies showed that heterochromatin, once believed to be junk DNA, actually has a role in suppressing genes, and that actual gene expression during development is also related to non-coding DNA. This DNA seems to have more functionality than ever imagined, providing regulation of certain roles in development and proper framing of translation of proteins. Further research is revealing even more amazing functions of what was once thought to be dormant or inactive stuff, and its role in making sure our metabolic system works as it should.

Humans aren't the only holders of junk DNA. A study by David Haussler of UC California, Santa Cruz, reported by the BBC in May of 2004, showed that humans, rats, and mice share "many identical chunks of apparently 'junk' DNA." The team Haussler led compared the genome sequence of humans with that of mice and rats, and they were literally astonished by the identical stretches of DNA they found across the three species. Furthermore, they found that the patterns matched closely with chickens, dogs, and fish sequences.

These "ultra-conserved elements" that did not seem to do anything of value suggested that their function was indeed of great importance, most likely, as Haussler stated, by controlling "the activity of indispensable genes and embryo development." The study led many scientists to rethink their opinion of this junk stuff, prompting Professor Chris Ponting of the UK Medical Research Council's Functional Genetics Unit to state, "I think other bits of 'junk' DNA will turn out not to be junk. I think this is the tip of the iceberg, and that there will be many more similar findings."

For many people who have time prompts, the theory is that the awakening of a deeper consciousness and awareness is one of those findings lying just beneath the tip of the iceberg. There is even a hint of a "language" to this non-coding DNA, as pointed out in a *Science* magazine article in 1994 by F. Flam, which suggested that the sequence of the "syllables," or the nucleotides in DNA, should be completely random, but are not. They in fact have a striking parallel with human language, and are now believed to contain some kind of coded information. The authors of this paper, called "Hints of a Language in Junk DNA," actually employed a series of linguistics tests to analyze the junk DNA and found amazing similarities to human language. Again, the cry arose that there would be no beneficial reason for an organism to carry around so many useless, junk molecules that seemingly served no purpose. There must be a code. There must be a purpose to that code. The quest is on to determine what that code is trying to tell us, and how it will change us or transform us, once awakened into its full capacity.

This code, and its purpose, is not yet fully understood in the science community. But the spiritual community is hard on the case, suggesting that this non-coding DNA is the home of psychic abilities, paranormal manifestation, and higher levels of conscious awareness waiting to be awakened in humankind. From seeing ghosts to being able to know what another person is thinking, to locating a missing child using psi abilities, this code might hold the key to the realm of the unknown that we have long relegated to the fringes of science, or, better yet, the world of pseudoscience.

Though there is no physical evidence for this, many people feel strongly that this part of the makeup of the human body is where the "key" to higher levels of being lies, and that the door is a trigger event, perhaps the coming year of 2012, that will activate this DNA and allow it to fulfill its purpose, thus allowing us as a species to fulfill ours. This may also turn out to be the case for the other living species that share with us the secret of junk, or unfulfilled, DNA. We may not be the only ones ascending!

The Hermetic Code

In his book *The Hermetic Code in DNA: The Sacred Principles in the Ordering of the Universe*, Michael Hayes suggests there is a mathematical-based code embedded throughout ancient religions and traditions and science, a code that is mirrored in our own DNA structure. He calls it the Hermetic Code, and states, "The Hermetic Code is much more than a mathematical tool. It is a universal blueprint for all evolutionary or creative development, and its distinctive inner symmetry is to be found in the biomolecular and physical structures of all form of life."

The Hermetic Code is based upon the "sixty-four word/twenty-two note amino acid 'scale of resonance' but also, for example, in the overall physiology of human beings with their three nerve complexes responsible for sensation, emotion, and perception, and their eight sets of endocrine transformers...." Hayes, also the author of *The Infinite Harmony*, posits that all living beings are "hermetically composed; they are all in their relative scales evolutionary 'triple octaves' with the inherent potential to achieve a state of 'optimum resonance.'" It is this optimum resonant state many believe will be the result of our junk DNA being triggered into activity.

Hayes also asks the important question of "who or what told DNA how to behave?" His theory of an association between our DNA and a higher mathematical code that shows symmetries between what goes on "above" in the cosmos and what goes on "below" in our own physiology is behind the idea that it is possible, through "transcendental evolution," for human individuals to emulate the living cell and to achieve a similar condition of optimum resonance.

Though quick to admit that the evolution of DNA on earth has been a bit dicey, and often erratic, Hayes states, "...underlying all this apparent random, selective evolution is the symmetry of DNA and the genetic code" and compares that symmetry to fundamental laws found in nature, especially those found in harmonics that make up the "music" of life. The harmonic ratios of music mirror the ordering principles of the universe...and our own DNA. As above, so below...as if a "fundamental cosmic harmony" was behind it all. And of course, this harmony is based upon numbers. He even quotes physicist Paul Davies, who said, "We can therefore regard the spectrum of light from an atom as similar to the sound of a musical instrument," and takes it one step further by describing a range of musical relationships between atoms and their components, even referring to the theory of quantum chromodynamics, which suggests that beneath the material of an atom "there are other essentially musical symphonies being played by nature."

Anyone who has studied music theory knows of the prominence of mathematics in scales, octaves, and such. "The Hermetic Code, as we know, is primarily an expression of the law of triple creation, which holds that everything is composed of trinities within trinities. This means that the three individual octaves embodied with pi are in themselves triple octaves, making nine octaves in total, or sixty-four 'notes'—precisely the number of RNA codon combinations."

Okay, so God may be both a mathematician AND a musician, not to mention a geneticist and computer programming whiz! DNA molecules work with four chemical components, known as bases of the genetic code, which construct molecules known as RNA triplet codons. Each of those comprises three bases, serving as templates, Hayes explains, for the production of amino acids, which in turn assemble into complex protein chains. All of this follows the musical structure evident in the formula pi, and seen throughout nature and the cosmos on an even grander scale. But Hayes also suggests that this hermetic is genetic, and that "certain fundamental aspects of consciousness—ideas, concepts, revelations, and so forth—are metaphysical genes and are produced in exactly the same way as are amino-acid chains."

This more metaphysical attribute to both non-coded DNA and the idea of a higher intelligence behind man and nature alike is what those who experience 11:11 time prompts believe will lead to a coming age of higher reality. If DNA serves to evolve us physically, could the secrets it holds within its own "King's Chamber" serve to evolve us spiritually and consciously as well? The concept of resonance, of the links between vibration and levels of consciousness, cannot be ignored either. Are we all on the cusp of a spiritual revolution that will be brought about by the activation of our 97 percent non-coding DNA, where a Hermetic Code based upon the fundamentals of music and harmony sits?

If the Universe is indeed "one song," maybe this is the song we are all about to sing, once we all find our individual and collective voice.

Bond of Number

Throughout this book, it has been made clear the underlying dynamics of nature and even humanity as based upon mathematical laws. These laws may make up part of the Theory of Everything sought after by physicists, yet go one step further, as stated by John Michell in *The Dimensions of Paradise*. Ancient scientific metaphysics had a similar but wider function. It attempted to describe not merely the nature of the physical Universe, but human nature also, and in the same terms, linking the two together as macrocosmic and microcosmic aspects of the one primordial act of creation. The Universe, human nature, and the mind of the Creator were made commensurable by number, which Plato called the "bond holding all things together."

This bond of number was seen in ancient traditions as being applicable to both individual human existence and the greater design of the cosmos, and it was just as functional and present in the DNA that makes us who we are, as it was in the fine-tuned structure of the planets and galaxies and stars. This rather sacred concept, as Michell concludes, is a "synthesis of the proportions and harmonies in the field of number, it depicts the essential structure of the universe and the human mind alike...." It describes the dimensions of both a pyramid and the heavens themselves, and dictates the form of human and animal and plant, all according to a great and grand design that includes both randomness at times, and perfect order at others, as part of a whole working to create life. Successfully, we might add!

In our research to try and pin a number on God, we came across so many ideas and theories and even facts that do suggest we are dealing with a Master Programmer, or at least to be fair, a Master Program. We also came across an even more astounding discovery with much more modern technological implications, because most everyone owns a phone. God is not just a potential number or sequence or harmonic code. God might even *have* a number. *A phone number.* In a June 2003 article for the BBC News titled "Man Shares God's Phone Number," a man named Andy Green of Salford, England, kept getting strange phone calls after the movie *Bruce Almighty* was released. The movie starred Jim Carrey as a man who met God and got his private phone number. That number was the same at Green's, and soon the sandwich shop manager was getting calls from people asking to speak to the Big Cheese himself. "One guy said he had no money, so I told him to get a job," Green told the news agency, commenting on the weird assortment of characters who dialed the divine digits with questions, requests, and petitions.

Whether this is proof of belief in the close association of a divine being with mathematical laws, or just proof of the stupidity of the average movie-going audience is open for debate. Numbers influence us and govern our lives. They have their own power, and that power just might be divine in nature. They shape the laws that shape us, and, amplified by the meaning we give them, make our reality real. God may not be a particular digit, sequence, or even code. Instead, the creative and intelligent foundation from which all reality springs forth appears to be enamored of numbers, using them to shape the laws that shape form, matter, and energy, and dictate the way things appear to be, seen and unseen, in this and any other Universe.

God is not a number. God is all numbers...and numbers are everything.

CHAPTER 11:11

Why Numbers Matter

I could never make out what those damn dots meant...
—Lord Randolph Churchill, on
figuring out decimal points

When we began this book, neither of us truly had any idea just how important numbers were. Of course we knew they played a role in our everyday lives, especially when we pulled out our ATM card or checkbook, dialed in a critical cell phone number, or filled in our Social Security number on an application. We were certainly aware of the proliferation of numbers all around us. What we weren't fully cognizant of was the magnitude. Numbers literally are anywhere and everywhere.

Throughout our research and discussion with others, we came away with a new appreciation for numbers, as well as a stunning discovery: numbers are truly magical, and they matter. Sometimes more than we ever imagined. Numbers have the power to shape, form, describe, manifest, and transform. Numbers truly are the key to the universe.

As we wrote this book, a huge concert called "46664" took place in London's Hyde Park to honor the 90th birthday of Nelson Mandela, the anti-apartheid activist and former president of South Africa. Mandela spent 27 years in prison for crimes committed while he spearheaded the struggle against apartheid. While incarcerated, his prison I.D. number was 46664. Known as the "digits of despair," they represented the oppression and suffering of being behind bars for more than two decades until his release on February 11, 1990.

Today, the numbers 46664 are now the name of Mandela's new HIV/AIDS foundation, dedicated to raising global awareness and research, and represented by five simple digits that symbolize the long, hard road from oppression to freedom, evil to good, fear to courage, and despair to hope.

Numbers have the power to transcend suffering and usher in a new era of possibilities. But, similar to miracle diets or mail-order brides, there is a catch.

In her book *Numbers*, written with David Boyle, Dame Anita Roddick reminds us that "we are measured, counted and recorded every time we buy anything. We are summed up, averaged out and cross-sectioned by academics and officials in surveys and screeds of government statistics that suck us dry of our individuality. We are part of a gigantic experiment that believes everything can be measured..." But Roddick did go on to emphasize that numbers are magic—if, and only if, we remember that what they quantify and represent is us. Humanity. The measure of a man or a woman.

And therein lies the catch: The best things in life are not only free, but immeasurable. Love. Freedom. Passion. Hope. Beauty. Goodness. Humor. Character.

Perhaps it is best to think of numbers the same way that we do the houses in which we live. They provide a foundation and shelter within which we move and live and have our being. They give us structure, familiarity, and a sense of home. Outside of their walls, we find those things to which even numbers can only allude. The mysteries of life that, when reduced to mathematical equations, suddenly lose their mystery and mystique.

Thus, the question: With all of the technological gadgetry at our disposal, and our dependence on money, stock performances, dates, and times...with all of our obsession with ages and years and breast size and waist width and how many hairs remain on our heads, are we placing too much importance on the numbers, and not enough on the actual things they measure? Are we forgetting about life itself?

For all of us who have had unusual experiences with numbers, especially those mysterious and sometimes annoying time prompts, we need to remember that it is not the digits themselves that matter, but what the digits are alerting us to. Pay attention. Wake up. Take notice.

So, having made it to the end of the book (unless you cheated and skipped directly to this part...in which case shame on you!) we can finally reveal to you the mystery of the book's namesake.

11:11

Seeing 11:11 on the clock day after day, night after night, is not coincidental. It is not just a random event that miraculously keeps repeating. It happens for a reason. Unfortunately, we still don't know what that reason is. The authors of this book have had their own experiences with time prompts.

Marie D. Jones

I've woken up many nights at 11:11 p.m., 2:22 a.m., 3:33 a.m., and so on, and this has repeated over and over again during the last six months or so. I never gave any thought to these strange repetitive times, until I was asked to write this book. Now I notice them all the time, and so does my son, who often yells at me across the room "Hey, mom, it's 11:11!" Friends of mine, who know I am writing this book, point out to me while out for dinner or drinks, "Hey, it's now 11:11 p.m.!" Yet the earth never moves beneath my feet, and I have yet to feel a sense of total awakening. In fact, I've never had anything of interest happen during those time prompts, other than a fleeting sense of amusement, and a little annoyance that I can never seem to sleep through one damned night without waking up a zillion times, and that my friends now drive me crazy telling me what time it is! I am now more aware than ever of these time prompts. But I have to be, because of this book. Because of my focus. So, the question I must ask myself is this: Is it happening now because this is when my junk DNA has chosen to be activated, and it is sheer coincidence I also happen to be writing about a subject I never even thought about a year or two ago? OR is it happening because my brain has created a new connection as a result of my research and is now paying close attention to clocks, dials, and read outs as a result? Again, I am reminded of the concept of buying an orange Hummer with green doors because you think nobody else has one, then suddenly noticing they are everywhere...and rather ugly to boot. I suppose the best way to deal with a mystery like this is to keep paying attention to what is happening to me when it happens, even if it seems like nothing is happening at the time. As they say, one day, all shall be revealed. Maybe it will be revealed to me one wake-up call at a time.

Larry Flaxman

Like my counterpart, I too have had my own share of time prompts and repetitive numeric sequences. While I never really paid much attention to them, I have always maintained a conscious awareness that "something" unusual might be going on due to the fact that the same numbers kept popping up. Time and time again these same patterns have consistently played a part in my life in one form or fashion. My rational, often skeptical, left-brained scientific brain tried to justify them as it has to be coincidence; however, I knew that, statistically, the odds were against that. Regardless, I had always intended to dedicate some time to researching the phenomenon; however, with the hustle and bustle of daily life it always seemed to get pushed to the back burner in favor of more pressing, higher priority items. To be completely honest, until we started to do the research for this book, I had thought my experiences were completely isolated and singular. I was not aware that this was actually a widespread phenomenon, and that other rational, scientifically minded people were also having similar experiences! I quickly discovered that everyone seems to have a story to tell about their own experiences. As the stories, ideas, and thoughts came in from those we solicited, I was reminded of the quintessential desire and need for "connection" to our fellow humans. Expanding upon that concept a bit further, what if these events were a form of validation or verification that there truly is some sort of quantum "connection" or link that exists between us? An invisible, yet ever-present bond that inextricably links us together. Much has been written about the Akashic Records, morphic fields, the quantum mind, as well as many other esoteric cosmologies. While I tend to take a very careful, guarded approach to most new-age mysticism, there appears to be sufficient evidence that some form of causal connection does exist. Are these common experiences trying to tell us something? Are they the cosmic equivalent of the annoyingly loud alarm clock that always seems to go off when you least expect it to? Perhaps. While I have never experienced enlightenment, Zen-awareness, altered states of consciousness, or transcendence during my own time prompt events, they have definitely helped to open my eyes to the possibility that reality is truly a mesh which interconnects all.

■

Peter A. Gersten Esq., former director of Citizens Against UFO Secrecy (CAUS), discusses his views on his Website, *www.pagenews.info*.

What people found was that the 11:11 experience was as a shared experience.

It is simply an occurrence where at 11:11 (a.m./p.m.) their attention would be pulled to a clock, not to see what time it was, but one simply gets an impulse to look at the clock. One is not looking to see what time is it. It is almost an unconscious glance.

The other aspect is where a significant event occurs at 11:11, as some kind of indicator.

It can be more than that when my cat was dying from kidney failure, there was nothing we could do except make him comfortable and hold his paw. My daughter was there with me when he took is last breath. She walked out, came back in, and said it is 11:11. She knew nothing of the 11:11 phenomena. It is almost like an indicator, or trigger.

But the millions of people who have been "triggered" still struggle to understand why. As one woman so succinctly wrote on Angelscribe.com, "I have been having some weird experiences with the 1111, 111, and others. I have been noticing them for about a week now. It is so weird. I will look at the clock and it's 1:11. Today I was trying to change some properties on my web browser and the file size was 1111 bytes! That was really weird. I went back and looked again and it was different! Weird! I have seen a lot of the double numbers and numbers with the 111's. Obviously, someone is trying to tell me something. I figure I will learn that something soon."

Yes, we all may learn "that something" soon. Maybe, when we learn "that something," it will transform us and enlighten us, both individually and collectively. Perhaps it will change our physical appearance. Is it beyond the realm of probability to speculate that it might even change the whole planet?

Then again, maybe it won't change anything at all. Perhaps it will be a "non-event" like Y2K?

Whatever these time prompts mean, and whatever these strange signs, sequences, or synchronicities are trying to tell us, the bottom line is, no matter what the circumstances, we must pay attention to our lives. We must live in the now.

Something or someone is trying to get us to look away from the cell phones, "Crack Berries," iPods, and MP3 players, computers, video games, and awful reality shows where we watch people play out their own lives for the camera, while ignoring the sheer potentiality of our own. It is truly incredible to think that the "someone" or "something" may be an internal influence originating within our own brains, or perhaps it is a subconscious poke in the side from some higher (or lower!) dimensional being. Remember this the next time your cell phone rings or your e-mail beeps.

The "who" or "what" matters not—the fact that we are being prompted in the first place is the truly important facet of the equation.

Throughout the centuries, man has carefully recorded the measurement of time using a variety of methods and units. From the motion of the sun across the sky, the phases of the moon, the emission of radioactive cesium atoms, and "Like Sands Through the Hour Glass, So are the Days of Our Lives" ...oh wait, that was from a cheesy soap opera.

At times, most of us have viewed the construct of time as both a blessing and a curse. We measure our yesterdays, todays, and tomorrows with marks on a calendar as if we are desperate to leave our own indelible mark. Yet, too often, the time within those days slips by unattended to, because we are so singularly focused on the dates rather than the present moments that make up every waking moment of our lives. Hourglasses don't have numbers, but they do make us all too painfully aware, one grain of sand at a time, of how quickly our lives pass us by. Live your life by the Epicurean philosophical quote of *"Dum vivimus, vivamus,"* or "While we live, let us live."

Unlike our number-centric society, in some cultures, numbers don't mean a thing. A recent article titled "Tribe Living Without Numbers" in the July 18, 2008 Metro.co.uk Newssite reported on a recently discovered tribe living deep in the Amazon rain forest. This particular tribe, the Piraha, had, according to Professor Edward Gibson of MIT, never learned to use numbers because, quite simply, they did not need them. "This group could learn, but it's not useful in their culture, so they've never picked it up." Other similar studies by linguists reported similar findings; tribes such as the Piraha did have words for "one," "two," and even "many," but nothing beyond this rather infancy-stage skill level of counting and quantifying. Nor did this primitive culture have the skill for drawing, which might have added to their lack of desire to develop a system of indicating numbers.

But most of us do not live in simple tribal villages, working off the land in harmony with nature's flow and pace, with little use for numbers. Most of us live with time constraints, deadlines, and schedules. In our culture we are taught from an early age that a healthy respect for numbers is an absolute necessity. Again, they govern much of our outer lives and they hold mysteries and secrets that unlock our inner lives as well. From the mundane to the sacred, numbers matter. Numbers count (pardon the pun).

Although explorers, scientists, and researchers have mounted concerted searches for the elusive fountain of youth, we are not any closer. As a result of our aging bodies, we are not the same at the age of 90 that we were at 10. We don't look the same at 300 pounds as we do at 165. We are not the same people at midnight that we were at noon.

Inside, where it counts, we must remember that we have no structure to be measured. We are infinite, eternal, and beyond all boundaries. The "essence" of who we are does not age, never gains weight, or loses hair. As Whitman so succinctly said, we are large. We contain multitudes. Had he said instead, "hmmm, I'd say we are about 180 miles wide and oh, about twice that long in length," his words would not have held the power they did, and still do hold today. Those multitudes he spoke of went as far inside us as they did outside us. How do you measure or quantify the landscape of a human soul? Is there width, height, and depth to a life? As we discussed in Chapter 9:9, even our own DNA operates in the language of numbers, so behind it all there is always the math.

If God and the forces behind reality do indeed speak to us in numbers, it is only because, like music, it is a form of language that we can wrap our minds around. No matter where we come from, we can all recognize the one from the many. As for our hearts and souls, we seek to look beyond the digits and equations and hone in on what they stand for, what they represent. The authors of this book had no idea when we started just how deep, mysterious, and intriguing numbers could be. Now we both agree that they are truly as paranormal as ghosts, UFOs, and strange creatures that go bump in the night. They are a treasure to be discovered by following clues left behind in every aspect of reality. Add them, divide them, subtract, and multiply, and they lead us to a greater understanding of how things are the way they are...and maybe even why.

So, as we draw to a close there still remains one lingering question. The grand enchilada. The giant pita. We previously alluded to the fact that we believe these number sequences are not coincidental, and they are occurring for a reason. Statistical improbabilities aside, are they simply random chaotic patterns? As authors, we would love nothing more than to present you with some spectacular, all-encompassing external proof. Unfortunately, we cannot do so in good conscious. Like you, we admit that we don't know what the actual answer is. We have provided you with a variety of facts, ideas, and theories to help you form your own position or hypothesis. Rather than look for external causative explanations, perhaps we need to turn our focus inward. It may not be "supernatural," "paranormal," or even "extraordinary," but rather the brain's newfound attention on an otherwise oft ignored moment in time.

To summarize the theories that may be behind these time prompts:

1. An outside, external trigger or wake-up call coming from a higher intelligence that wishes to guide us, direct us, or alert us to a need for paying more attention to our lives, our futures, and our destinies

2. Sheer, random coincidence based upon laws, such as Littlewood's Law and the Law of Truly Large Numbers, that state when you have enough people around, coincidences are bound to happen...and happen often.

3. The brain's need and ability to create patterns from otherwise random events, or take small coincidences and matrix them into meaningful situations, thus alerting the mind to see even more and more of these events.

4. A combination of one or more of the above.

There seems to be evidence pro and con for each of the examples, with the most rational emphasis on the brain doing the job of seeking out information and creating patterns and meaning from that information.

But perhaps there is something prompting the brain to do this. What is to say that these mysterious events are not the attempts of higher beings to shake us out of our zombie-like existence and get us off our butts before it is too late? Think about it. In an age when we are both overly attentive to something and suffering severe attention deficit disorder in others, what better way for a higher power to get us to take notice? We authors believe, after doing the research, hearing the stories, and, well, crunching the numbers, that these time prompts happen for a reason, just like anything else in life. They happen because we are all connected, by some invisible grid-like structure that encompasses the whole of reality. We cannot see it, yet we have many names for it. The Akashic Records. Zero Point Field. Book of Life. Dark Matter. The Void.

It is our conclusion that these time prompts happen to trigger within us the realization that there is a bigger picture to be seen. A larger force at play, and that, because it is happening to so many people, we are linked, each of us potentially triggering others to wake up and take notice even as we are experiencing the mystery of numbers in our lives. This collective phenomenon, then, has a two-fold purpose. It happens to many of us, maybe even to all of us. Time prompts may be occurring in the life of every human being every day, but not every human being pays the needed attention. With all of the background noise and static in our lives, it's quite probable that the vast majority just aren't aware because they have mentally "tuned" them out, just as many of us tune out other synchronicities.

With our brain's mental equivalent of TIVO selectively "blocking" or suppressing this noise, it might even be an automatic response. We can only absorb so much information in one day, at one time, and our basic survival needs must come first. The tragic thing is, by ignoring these "higher" bits of potential information, we might be shooting ourselves in the foot on a much grander scale. Do we live just for getting by in the present, or with one eye on the future? Do we merely survive, or attempt to thrive?

The fact that these time prompts happen to each of us in a personalized and individualized manner that holds a specific meaning is critical. Whatever is behind this, brain or divine, it knows just what each of us needs to actually wake up and take notice, and will continue to prod and poke at us until we do take notice. Imagine millions of souls moving forward, each of them on a separate path all their own, yet linked by an invisible cord.

The time prompts are the cord.

Time prompts occur in the place that a higher intelligence realizes we will actually look as we go about our days—clocks, microwave ovens, cell phones, dashboards—all of the places that represent the faster-paced reality we live in today, one that is quickening with alarming speed and leaving us more exhausted, disconnected, and unsatisfied by the minute. For those of us who love to read, we even see them in those ancient antiquities called books. The time prompts just might be our last chance to pay attention, to sit up, stand up, step up, wake up, and take notice...before we get so busy and preoccupied and distracted that we never see what is right before our very eyes.

Life.

The Holy Grail so many seek may have a height, a width, and even a depth. Yet no number or equation could ever measure what the Grail holds within.

Truth.

Just as a huge and ornately designed treasure chest is no match for the gold it contains within. As long as we remember that we are the contents of the Grail, we will continue to use numbers, signs, synchronicities, and sequences to our advantage. And no matter where they are coming from, we will let them lead us to the truth, like some cryptic code left behind by ancient wise ones eager to see if we are up to the task.

Vita non est vivere sed valere vita est. (Life is more than merely staying alive.)

APPENDIX

Number Trivia and Anomalies

efore we ended this book, we simply could not resist a little fun with numbers. Because as mysterious and enigmatic as they are, they can boggle the mind and even bring out a gasp of awe or a chuckle or two. Following are some of the amazing anomalies we found on the Web and in other sources that show, indeed, that there are more to numbers than originally meets the eye.

0 to 100—Unique Number Facts

- 0 is the additive identity.

- 1 is the multiplicative identity.

- 2 is the only even prime.

- 3 is the number of spatial dimensions we live in.

- 4 is the smallest number of colors sufficient to color all planar maps.

- 5 is the number of Platonic solids.

- 6 is the smallest perfect number.

- 7 is the smallest number of faces of a regular polygon that is not constructible by straightedge and compass.

- 8 is the largest cube in the Fibonacci sequence.

- 9 is the maximum number of cubes that are needed to sum to any positive integer.

- 10 is the base of our number system.

- 11 is the largest known multiplicative persistence.

- 12 is the smallest abundant number.

- 13 is the number of Archimedian solids.

- 14 is the smallest number n with the property that there are no numbers relatively prime to n smaller numbers.

- 15 is the smallest composite number n with the property that there is only one group of order n.

- 16 is the only number of the form $xy = yx$ with x and y different integers.

- 17 is the number of wallpaper groups.

- 18 is the only number (other than 0) that is twice the sum of its digits.

- 19 is the maximum number of fourth powers needed to sum to any number.

- 20 is the number of rooted trees with six vertices.

- 21 is the smallest number of distinct squares needed to tile a square.

- 22 is the number of partitions of eight.

- 23 is the smallest number of integer-sided boxes that tile a box so that no two boxes share a common length.

- 24 is the largest number divisible by all numbers less than its square root.

- 25 is the smallest square that can be written as a sum of two squares.

- 26 is the only positive number to be directly between a square and a cube.

- 27 is the largest number that is the sum of the digits of its cube.

- 28 is the second perfect number.

- 29 is the seventh Lucas number.

- 30 is the largest number with the property that all smaller numbers relatively prime to it are prime.

- 31 is a Mersenne prime.

- 32 is the smallest non-trivial fifth power.

- 33 is the largest number that is not a sum of distinct triangular numbers.

- 34 is the smallest number with the property that it and its neighbors have the same number of divisors.

- 35 is the number of hexominoes.

- 36 is the smallest non-trivial number that is both square and triangular.

- 37 is the maximum number of fifth powers needed to sum to any number.

- 38 is the last Roman numeral when written lexicographically.

- 39 is the smallest number that has three different partitions into three parts with the same product.

- 40 is the only number whose letters are in alphabetical order.

- 41 is a value of n so that $x2 + x + n$ takes on prime values for $x =$ 0, 1, 2, ... n-2.

- 42 is the fifth Catalan number.

- 43 is the number of sided seven iamonds.

- 44 is the number of derangements of five items.

- 45 is a Kaprekar number.

- 46 is the number of different arrangements (up to rotation and reflection) of nine non-attacking queens on a 9 × 9 chessboard.

- 47 is the largest number of cubes that cannot tile a cube.

- 48 is the smallest number with 10 divisors.

- 49 is the smallest number with the property that it and its neighbors are squareful.

- 50 is the smallest number that can be written as the sum of of two squares in two ways.

- 51 is the 6th Motzkin number.

- 52 is the 5th Bell number.

- 53 is the only two digit number that is reversed in hexadecimal.

- 54 is the smallest number that can be written as the sum of three squares in three ways.

- 55 is the largest triangular number in the Fibonacci sequence.

- 56 is the number of reduced 5 × 5 Latin squares.

- 57 = 111 in base seven.

- 58 is the number of commutative semigroups of order four.

- 59 is the number of stellations of an icosahedron.

- 60 is the smallest number divisible by 1 through 6.

- 61 is the third secant number.

- 62 is the smallest number that can be written as the sum of three distinct squares in two ways.

- 63 is the number of partially ordered sets of five elements.

- 64 is the smallest number with seven divisors.

- 65 is the smallest number that becomes square if its reverse is either added to or subtracted from it.

- 66 is the number of 8 iamonds.

- 67 is the smallest number which is palindromic in bases five and six.

- 68 is the 2-digit string that appears latest in the decimal expansion of ˉ.

- 69 has the property that $n2$ and $n3$ together contain each digit once.

- 70 is the smallest weird number.

- 71 divides the sum of the primes less than it.

- 72 is the maximum number of spheres that can touch another sphere in a lattice packing in six dimensions.

- 73 is the smallest multi-digit number that is one less than twice its reverse.

- 74 is the number of different non-Hamiltonian polyhedra with a minimum number of vertices.

- 75 is the number of orderings of four objects with ties allowed.

- 76 is an automorphic number.

- 77 is the largest number that cannot be written as a sum of distinct numbers whose reciprocals sum to 1.

- 78 is the smallest number that can be written as the sum of four distinct squares in three ways.

- 79 is a permutable prime.

- 80 is the smallest number n where n and $n+1$ are both products of four or more primes.

- 81 is the square of the sum of its digits.

- 82 is the number of six hexes.

- 83 is the number of strongly connected digraphs with four vertices.

- 84 is the largest order of a permutation of 14 elements.

- 85 is the largest n for which $12 + 22 + 32 + ... + n2 = 1 + 2 + 3 + ... + m$ has a solution.

- 86 = 222 in base six.
- 87 is the sum of the squares of the first four primes.
- 88 is the only number known whose square has no isolated digits.
- 89 = 81 + 92.
- 90 is the number of degrees in a right angle.
- 91 is the smallest pseudoprime in base 3.
- 92 is the number of different arrangements of eight non-attacking queens on an 8 × 8 chessboard.
- 93 = 333 in base 5.
- 94 is a Smith number.
- 95 is the number of planar partitions of 10.
- 96 is the smallest number that can be written as the difference of two squares in four ways.
- 97 is the smallest number with the property that its first three multiples contain the digit 9.
- 98 is the smallest number with the property that its first five multiples contain the digit 9.
- 99 is a Kaprekar number.
- 100 is the smallest square which is also the sum of four consecutive cubes.

Visit *www.stetson.edu/~efriedma/numbers.html* for factoids about numbers up to 1,000.

Number Facts You Don't Really Need but Are Cool Anyway...

The skin of a human being varies from 0.5mm in the eyelids to 6.0mm or more in the palms, soles of the feet, and between the shoulders.

The following are the elements that make up a 154-pound man:

- 100 pounds of oxygen

- 27.72 pounds of carbon

- 15.4 pounds of hydrogen

- 4.62 pounds of nitrogen

- 2.31 pounds of calcium

- 1.54 pounds of phosphorous

- 0.54 pounds of potassium

- 0.35 pounds of sulfur

- 0.23 pounds of chlorine

- 0.23 pounds of sodium

- 0.007 pounds of magnesium

- 0.0006 pounds of iron

- 0.0045 pounds of manganese

- Tiny traces of zinc, copper, fluorine, silicon, and iodine

More Fun Factoids

- Only one thunderstorm in 800 produces hailstones as large as walnuts, and one in 5,000 produces hailstones as large as baseballs.

- In one year the average human heart circulates from 770,000 to 1.6 million gallons of blood through the body.

- The Rubik's Cube can be turned into more than 43 quintillion (43,252,003,274,489,856,000) different configurations.

- The average ejaculate contains as many as 787 million sperm.

- On average, a Twinkie will explode in a microwave in 45 seconds.

- If you were to count continuously every moment of every day, it would take 31,688 years to count to one trillion.

- From a 52-card deck it is possible to deal 2,598,960 different five-card poker hands.

- The total amount of money in a standard Monopoly game is $15,140.

- A dime has 118 ridges around the edge.

- It takes approximately 4,000 folds to tear a U.S. dollar bill.

- The average lead pencil will draw a line 35 miles long or write approximately 50,000 English words.

- Though there are only 52 cards in a typical deck of cards, they can be arranged in just about 80,660,000,000,000,000,000,000, 000,00,000,000,000,000,000,000,000,000,000,000,000,000,000 different ways.

- 123456787654321 is 11,111,111 multiplied by itself.

- On a bingo card of 90 numbers there are approximately 44 million possible ways to make bingo.

- The number 2,520 can be divided by 1, 2, 3, 4, 5, 6, 7, 8, 9, and 10 without having a fractional leftover.

- The chances of an exact duplication of fingerprints are about 64 billion to 1.

- The odds against a royal flush in poker are exactly 649,739 to 1.

- A sneeze can travel as fast as 100 miles per hour.

- If you had $10 billion in $1 bills and spent one every second, it would take 317 years to spend them all.

- Six eight-stud Lego pieces can be combined 102,981,500 ways.

- If you had 15 cubes numbered 1 to 15 and you tried to line them up in every possible sequence, and if you made a change every minute, it would take you 2,487,996 years to do it.

- Here are the odds of rolling various combinations with two dice in a game of Craps:

Roll:	Odds:
2 or 12	35 to 1
3 or 11	17 to 1
4 or 10	11 to 1
5 or 9	8 to 1
6 or 8	6.2 to 1
7	5 to 1

- Except for 2 and 3, every prime number will eventually become divisible by 6 if you either add or subtract 1 from the number. For example, the number 17, plus 1, is divisible by 6. The number 19, minus 1, is also divisible by 6.

- If you were to go on vacation for 11 days, you'd have less than one million seconds to enjoy it.

- The number of possible ways of playing just the first four moves on each side in a game of chess is 318,979,564,000.

- There are 24 known "perfect" numbers. These are numbers that equal the sum of all its divisors except itself. For instance, 6—the lowest of these numbers—is divisible by 1, 2, or 3 and 1 + 2 + 3 = 6. The largest of the known "perfect" numbers has 12,003 digits.

- The numbers on opposite sides of a die always add up to 7.

For more mindless number trivia, go to *www.mindlesscrap.com/trivia/stats.htm*

The Magical Bell Curve

One of the more practical number anomalies that was discovered recently was the bell curve. This relates entirely to lotto draws. It was found that if the winning numbers in 6 number lotto draws were added together, then 80 percent of all wins would fall in the range between 100 and 176.

The easiest way to explain this is for you to locate your latest lotto results. Now add the six prime winners together (ignore the supplementaries) and you will probably find that the resultant sum lies between 100 and 176. If you had the patience to sit down and work out the eight million odd combinations possible in a lotto then added each of these individual combinations together, starting with the smallest group (1 + 2 + 3 + 4 + 5 + 6=21) and finishing with the largest group is (40 + 41 + 42 + 43 + 44 + 45 = 255), you would find to your amazement that most winning lotto draws fall around the central point of 138. The closer your selected lotto numbers are to this central figure of 138, the better your chances of capturing a major prize. This applies to any six number lotto draw anywhere in the world. If you plotted the resultant shape of this curve out on graph paper, you would end up with the shape of a bell. Hence, the name Bell Curve.

For example, if you happened to think that 1, 3, 8, 19, 21, and 32 were your luckiest numbers, you might be somewhat dismayed to find that they add up to 84, which is way outside the Bell Curve preferred range of 100–176. Your chances of capturing a major win with this combination of numbers would probably be something like four to five times less than with, say, 8, 15, 17, 19, 35, and 44, which add up to 138. So if you have favorite groups of six numbers that you enter in the lotto, you might like to add each group up to see what they come to. The closer your number groups get to the central 138, the better your chances.

There is a computer program available that automatically "knocks out" all number groups that don't fall within the preferred range. We use it on our customized lotto systems. It simply means that all "unlikely" games are left out, which can reduce the playing cost by 25 percent or more, without greatly reducing your chances. Occasionally, a maverick group adding up to only 70 or so wins (or maybe 200 or more), but this is the exception.

Unusual Relationships of Phi

- Square phi and you get a number exactly 1 greater than phi: 2.61804...: $\varnothing^2 = \varnothing + 1$

- Divide phi into 1 and you get a number exactly 1 less than phi: 0.61804...: $1 / \varnothing = \varnothing - 1$

- Take the square root of 5, add 1, and then divide by 2, and you also get phi. $(5^{1/2} + 1) / 2 = \varnothing$. Which can also be expressed all in 5's as: $5 \wedge .5 * .5 + .5 = \varnothing$

Spooky Coincidences

The Lincoln-Kennedy Links

- Abraham Lincoln was elected to Congress in 1846.

- John F. Kennedy was elected to Congress in 1946.

- Abraham Lincoln was elected president in 1860.

- John F. Kennedy was elected president in 1960.

- Both were particularly concerned with civil rights.

- Both presidents were shot on a Friday.

- Both presidents were shot in the head.

- Lincoln's secretary was named Kennedy.

- Kennedy's secretary was named Lincoln.

- Both were assassinated by Southerners.

- Both were succeeded by Southerners named Johnson.

- Andrew Johnson, who succeeded Lincoln, was born in 1808.

- Lyndon Johnson, who succeeded Kennedy, was born in 1908.

- John Wilkes Booth, who assassinated Lincoln, was born in 1839.

- Lee Harvey Oswald, who assassinated Kennedy, was born in 1939.

- Both assassins were known by their three names.

- Both names are composed of 15 letters.

- Lincoln was shot at the theater named "Ford."

- Kennedy was shot in a car called "Lincoln" made by Ford.

- Lincoln was shot in a theater, and his assassin ran and hid in a warehouse.

- Kennedy was shot from a warehouse, and his assassin ran and hid in a theater.

- Booth and Oswald were assassinated before their trials.

- A week before Lincoln was shot, he was in Monroe, Maryland.

- A week before Kennedy was shot, he was with Marilyn Monroe.

- Lincoln's name has seven letters.

- Kennedy's name has seven letters.

- In Lincoln's and Kennedy's names the vowels and consonants fall in exactly the same place; in the order c, v, c, c, v, c, c.

- War was thrust upon Lincoln almost immediately after inauguration.
- War was thrust upon Kennedy almost immediately after inauguration.
- Lincoln ordered the Treasury to print its own money.
- Kennedy ordered the Treasury to print its own money.
- International bankers may have arranged the assassinations of Lincoln and Kennedy.
- Lincoln gave negroes freedom and legalized equality.
- Kennedy enforced equality for negroes.
- Lincoln delivered the Gettysburg Address on November 19, 1863.
- Kennedy was assassinated on November 22, 1963.
- Lincoln was sitting beside his wife when he was shot.
- Kennedy was sitting beside his wife when he was shot.
- Rathbone, who was with Lincoln when he was shot, was injured (by being stabbed).
- Connally, who was with Kennedy when he was shot, was injured (by being shot).
- Rathbone's name has eight letters.
- Connally's name has eight letters.
- Lincoln's bodyguard was away from his post at the door of the President's box at the theatre.
- Kennedy's bodyguards were away from their posts on the running-boards of the President's car.
- Lincoln didn't die immediately after being shot.
- Kennedy didn't die immediately after being shot.
- Lincoln and Kennedy died in places beginning with the initials P and H.

- Lincoln died in Petersen's house.

- Kennedy died in Parkland Hospital.

- There were conspiracy theories that Johnson had knowledgeable about Lincoln's assassination.

- There were conspiracy theories that Johnson had knowledgeable about Kennedy's assassination.

- Days before it happened, Lincoln told his wife and friends about a dream he'd had of being shot by an assassin.

- Hours before it happened, Kennedy told his wife and friends it would be easy for an assassin to shoot him from a crowd.

- Shortly after Lincoln was shot, the telegraph system went down.

- Shortly after Kennedy was shot, the telephone system went down.

- Kennedy's father had been the Ambassador to England at the Court of St. James's.

- Lincoln's son became the Ambassador to England at the Court of St. James's.

- Lincoln's wife tastefully and expensively redecorated the White House.

- Kennedy's wife tastefully and expensively redecorated the White House.

- Lincoln loved great literature and could recite poetry by heart.

- Kennedy loved great literature and could recite poetry by heart.

- Lincoln had young children while living at the White House.

- Kennedy had young children while living at the White House.

- Lincoln's sons had ponies they rode on the White House grounds.

- Kennedy's daughter had a pony she rode on the White House grounds.

- Lincoln lost a child (12-year-old son) while president.

- Kennedy lost a child (newly born son) while president.

- Lincoln had two sons named Robert and Edward. Edward died young and Robert lived on.

- Kennedy had two brothers named Robert and Edward. Robert died young and Edward lived on.

- Lincoln's funeral train traveled from Washington, D.C., to New York.

- Kennedy's brother's funeral train traveled from New York to Washington, D.C.

- The man running alongside Kennedy's car snapping pictures with his 35mm camera was a salesman of Lincoln cars.

- Kennedy bought a Virginia home that was the 1861 Civil War headquarters of Lincoln's first general-in-chief, McClellan.

- Jefferson Davis was the name of the president of the Confederate states while Lincoln was president of the Union states.

- Jefferson Davis Tippit was the name of the police officer killed allegedly by Kennedy's alleged assassin.

- Lincoln was sitting in a rocking chair at Ford's Theater when he was shot.

- Kennedy had a special rocking chair he sat in at the White House.

- Henry Ford bought the rocking chair Lincoln died in and put it in his museum in Dearborn.

- Kennedy's seat in the Lincoln he was sitting in when he was shot is in Ford's museum.

- Lincoln's seat in the Ford he was sitting in when he was shot is in Ford's museum.

Every 20 years

- 1840: William Henry Harrison (died in office).

- 1860: Abraham Lincoln (assassinated).

- 1880: James A. Garfield (assassinated).

- 1900: William McKinley (assassinated).

- 1920: Warren G. Harding (died in office).

- 1940: Franklin D. Roosevelt (died in office).

- 1960: John F. Kennedy (assassinated).

- 1980: Ronald Regan (survived assassination attempt).

- 2000: George W. Bush (survived assassination attempt by a grenade in Russia).

History Repeats Itself...a Theory

by Jim Snell

I have discovered a 49-year cycle in history:

- 1812: Percival, the prime minister of Great Britain is "assassinated," and War of 1812.
  Then, 49 years later...

- 1861: Beginning of the Civil War, and assassination of Abraham Lincoln in 1865.
Then, 49 years after 1865...

- 1914: Assassination of the Arch Duke of Austria, Franz Ferdinand, which triggers beginning of World War I.
Then, 49 years after 1914...

- 1963: Assassination of John F. Kennedy, and we were in the very beginning of Vietnam at that time.
Then, 49 years after 1963...

- 2012: Will we have yet another assassination of a "World Leader," and maybe the beginning of World War III? Will the "49 year cycle" be broken, or are we going to witness the beginning of the "Mother of All Wars"? We shall see!

Also, note that every other "assassination" was an *American President*...

Dyscalculia—A Number Disease?

Dyscalculia is a type of specific learning disability (SLD) involving innate difficulty in learning or comprehending mathematics. Dyscalculia is a lesser-known disability, similar and potentially related to dyslexia and Developmental Dyspraxia. Dyscalculia occurs in people across the whole IQ range, and sufferers often, but not always, also have difficulties with time, measurement, and spatial reasoning. Current estimates suggest it may affect about 5 percent of the population. Although some researchers believe that dyscalculia necessarily implies mathematical reasoning difficulties as well as difficulties with arithmetic operations, there is evidence (especially from brain damaged patients) that arithmetic (for example, calculation and number fact memory) and mathematical (abstract reasoning with numbers) abilities can be dissociated. That is (some researchers argue), an individual might suffer arithmetic difficulties (or dyscalculia), with no impairment of, or even giftedness in, abstract mathematical reasoning abilities.

The word *dyscalculia* comes from Greek and Latin, which means: "counting badly." The prefix *dys* comes from Greek and means "badly." *Calculia* comes from the Latin "calculare" which means "to count." That word *calculare* again comes from "calculus," which means "pebble" or one of the counters on an abacus. Frequent difficulties with arithmetic, confusing the signs: +, ", ÷ and ×.

Other signs:

- Inability to tell which of two numbers is the larger.

- Difficulty with everyday tasks such as checking change and reading analog clocks.

- Inability to comprehend financial planning or budgeting, sometimes even at a basic level; for example, estimating the cost of the items in a shopping basket or balancing a checkbook.

- Difficulty with times-tables, mental arithmetic, etc.

- Require logic rather than formulae, until a higher level requiring calculations is obtained.

- Difficulty with conceptualizing time and judging the passing of time.

■ Problems differentiating between left and right.

■ Having a poor sense of direction (that is, north, south, east, and west), potentially even with a compass.

■ Difficulty navigating or mentally "turning" the map to face the current direction rather than the common North = Top usage.

■ Having difficulty mentally estimating the measurement of an object or distance (for example, whether something is 10 or 20 feet [3 or 6 meters] away).

■ Inability to grasp and remember mathematical concepts, rules, formulae, and sequences.

■ An inability to read a sequence of numbers, or transposing them when repeated, such as turning 56 into 65.

■ Difficulty keeping score during games.

■ Difficulty with games such as poker with more flexible rules for scoring.

■ Difficulty in activities requiring sequential processing, from the physical (such as dance steps) to the abstract (reading, writing and signaling things in the right order). May have trouble even with a calculator due to difficulties in the process of feeding in variables.

■ The condition may lead, in extreme cases, to a phobia of mathematics and mathematical devices.

The Most Pathetic Facts in Math

■ If you multiply 1089 by 9, you get 9801. It's reversed itself! This also works with 10989, 109989, 1099989, and so on.

■ 1 is the only positive whole number that you can add to 1,000,000 that gives you an answer that's greater than if you multiply it by 1,000,000.

■ $19 = 1 \times 9 + 1 + 9$ and $29 = 2 \times 9 + 2 + 9$. This also works for 39,49,59,69,79,89, and 99.

- 153, 370, 371, and 407 are all the sum of the cubes of their digits. In other words, $153 = 1^3 + 5^3 + 3^3$.

- If you divide any square number by 8 you get a remainder of 0, 1, or 4.

- 2 is the only number that gives the same result added to itself as it does multiplied by itself.

- If you multiply 21,978 by 4, it turns backward.

- There are 12,988,816 different ways to cover a chessboard with 32 dominoes.

- $69^2 = 4,761$ and $69^3 = 328,509$. These two answers combined use all the digits from 0 to 9.

- You can chop a big lump of cheese into a maximum of 93 pieces with 8 straight cuts.

- In the English language, 40 is the only number whose letters appear in alphabetical order.

- $1 \div 37 = 0.027027027...$ and $1 \div 27 = 0.037037037...$

- $13^2 = 169$ and if you write both numbers backward you get $31^2 = 961$. This also works with 12 because $12^2 = 144$ and $21^2 = 441$.

- $1/1089 = 0.00091827364554637281...$ (And the numbers in the 9 times table are 9,18,27,36...)

- 8 is the only cubed number that is 1 less than a squared number.

- To multiply 10,112,359,550,561,797,752,808,988, 764,044,943,820,224,719 by 9 you just move the 9 at the very end up to the front. It's the only number that does this (thank goodness!).

- The number 4 is the only number in the English language that is spelled with the same number of letters as the number itself.

- $1 \times 9 + 2 = 11$, $12 \times 9 + 3 = 111$, $123 \times 9 + 4 = 1111$, and so on.

297 and 11

- For example, if you take the number 54.54 + 45 = 99.99 + 99 = 198.

- 19 + 98 + 89 + 91 = 297. If you try this with any number between 11 or 999 and do the same equations, you always arrive back at the number 297.

- If you do it with 297 by itself, you still end up with 297.

- Some of the numbers have longer equations than others. Some take four lines to reach 297.

- Some take six lines to reach 297. I still think it has something to do with the number 11.

What Are the Odds?

Sociologists have found that individuals typically have around 150 people whom they regard as "close." Therefore, each of us typically has an entourage of around 23,000 "friends of a friend." Then say we have about five acquaintances for each close friend, the number swells to 600,000.

Fancy seeing you here! The chances of meeting someone on a train with whom you share an acquaintance are therefore surprisingly high: for the population in the United Kingdom, it's around 1 in 100. If you also include socio-economic factors that boost the numbers of people from particular backgrounds traveling by train to particular destinations, the chances rise even higher. Take another "coincidence": discovering you share the same birthday as someone. How big a gathering of people do you think you'd need to get odds better than 50:50 that at least two shared your birthday? As there are 365 possible birthdays, you might guess the answer to be about half of 365—about 180 people. In fact, you need just 23.

This is because you're not asking for a match between a specific birthday—say, April 12th. All you want is a match between any two birthdays and any two people. This reduces the numbers of people needed to produce the "coincidence." To find at least two people born on April 12th, you'd need more than 250 people to give odds better than 50:50. The less specific you are about what you want, the more likely coincidences become. There is another effect at work behind some coincidences. They often seem surprising because we mix up two different probabilities: (1) the chances of something interesting happening; and (2) the chances of something interesting happening *after it has been given many opportunities to occur.*

For example, the chances of getting a winning "double 6" in a single throw of two dice is 1 in 36. But the probability of getting at least one from 25 attempts is 50:50. The more you try, the better your chances, but it's easy to forget the number of "tries" involved in real-life coincidences. Psychologists' research shows that people judge the chance of coincidences using simple—and apparently very sensible—rules. Roughly speaking, if one coincidence is twice as "outlandish" as another, people regard it as twice as unlikely. But probability theory shows that the likelihood of coincidences varies in a more complex, non-linear way. "It's not surprising we're poor at assessing coincidences," says psychologist Dr. Susan Blackmore. "We acquire skills by constant practice, but we don't go around all day deliberately seeking out coincidences. If we did, we'd soon realize that we live in a sea of them and would be far less surprised when they popped up." Although scientists regard everyday coincidences with contempt, they treat them seriously when they occur in science.

Human Coincidences

The lives of Thomas Jefferson and John Adams, two of America's founders, are quite similar. Jefferson crafted the Declaration of Independence, showing drafts of it to Adams, who (with Benjamin Franklin) helped to edit and hone it. The Continental Congress approved the document on July 4, 1776. Surprisingly, both Jefferson and Adams died on the same day, July 4, 1826—exactly 50 years after the signing of the Declaration of Independence.

Mark Twain was born on the day of the appearance of Halley's Comet in 1835, and died on the day of its next appearance in 1910. He himself predicted this in 1909, when he said: "I came in with Halley's Comet in 1835. It is coming again next year, and I expect to go out with it."

Oregon's *Columbian* newspaper announced the winning Pick 4 lottery numbers for June 28, 2000, in advance. The newspaper had intended to print the previous set of winning numbers but erroneously printed those for the state of Virginia, namely 6-8-5-5. In the next Oregon lottery, those same numbers were drawn.

Do Try This at Home

This is really strange. Try it!

Get a calculator:

1. Key into the calculator the first three digits of your phone number (the exchange, not the area code).
2. Multiply by 80.
3. Add 1.
4. Multiply by 250.
5. Add the last four digits of your phone number.
6. Add the last four digits of your phone number again.
7. Subtract 250.
8. Lastly, divide by 2.

Is this your phone number?

Bibliography

Barrow, John D. and Frank J. Tipler. *The Anthropic Cosmological Principle.* New York: Oxford University Press, 1986.

Bolton, Alain de. *The Architecture of Happiness.* New York: Vintage International, 2008.

Boyle, David and Anita Roddick. *Numbers.* White River Junction, Vt.: Chelsea Green Publishing, 2004.

Cheiro, Count Louis Hamon. *Cheiro's Book of Numbers.* London: Barrie & Jenkins, 1978.

Davies, Paul. *The Goldilocks Enigma: Why Is the Universe Just Right For Life?* New York: Mariner Books, 2008.

Dawkins, Richard. *The God Delusion.* New York: Houghton Mifflin, 2006.

Haughton, Brian. *Haunted Spaces, Sacred Places.* Franklin Lakes, N.J.: New Page Books, 2008.

Hayes, Michael. *The Hermetic Code in DNA: The Sacred Principles in the Ordering of the Universe.* Rochester, Vt.: Inner Traditions, 2008.

———. *The Infinite Harmony.* London: Weidenfeld & Nicholson, 1994.

Heath, Richard. *Sacred Number and the Origins of Civilization.* Rochester, Vt.: Inner Traditions, 2007.

Hieronimus, Robert. *The United Symbolism of America: Deciphering Hidden Meanings in America's Most Familiar Art, Architecture and Logos.* Franklin Lakes, N.J.: New Page Books, 2008.

Ifrah, Georges. *The Universal History of Numbers: From Prehistory to the Invention of the Computer.* New York: John Wiley and Sons, 2000.

Joseph, Frank and Laura Beaudoin. *Opening the Ark of the Covenant; The Secret Power of the Ancients, The Knights Templar Connection, and the Search for the Holy Grail.* Franklin Lakes, N.J.: New Page Books, 2007.

Jung, Carl J. *Synchronicity: An Acausal Connecting Principle.* New York: Bollingen Foundation, 1960.

Kenyon, J. Douglas, et al. *Forbidden Religion: Suppressed Heresies of the West.* Rochester, Vt.: Bear & Co., 2006

Kenyon, J. Douglas, et al. *Forbidden Science: From Ancient Technologies to Free Energy.* Rochester, Vt.: Bear & Co., 2006.

Kenyon, J. Douglas, et al. *Forbidden History: Prehistoric Technologies, Extraterrestrial Intervention and the Suppressed Origins of Civilization.* Rochester, Vt.: Bear & Co., 2005.

Kosminsky, Isidore. *Numbers: Their Meaning and Magic.* New York: Puttnam and Sons, 1927.

Lloyd, Seth. *Programming the Universe: A Quantum Computer Scientist Takes on the Cosmos.* New York: Vintage, 2006.

Malkowski, Edward F. *The Spiritual Technology of Ancient Egypt: Sacred Science and the Mystery of Consciouness.* Rochester, Vt.: Inner Traditions, 2007.

McTaggart, Lynne. *The Field: The Quest for the Secret Force in the Universe.* New York: HarperCollins, 2002.

Michell, John. *The Dimensions of Paradise: Sacred Geometry, Ancient Science and the Heavenly Order on Earth.* Rochester, Vt.: Inner Traditions, 2008.

Naudon, Paul. *The Secret History of Freemasonry—Its Origins and Connection to the Knights Templar.* Rochester, Vt.: Inner Traditions, 1991.

Peat, F. David. *Synchronicity: The Bridge Between Mind and Matter.* New York: Bantam New Age Books, 1987.

Rees, Martin. *Just Six Numbers: The Deep Forces That Shape the Universe.* New York: Basic Books, 2000.

Roberts, Courtney. *The Star of the Magi: The Mystery That Heralded the Coming of Christ.* Franklin Lakes, N.J.: New Page Books, 2007.

Schwaller de Lubicz, R.A. *Sacred Science.* Rochester, Vt.: Inner Traditions, 1988.

Talbot, Michael. *The Holographic Universe.* England: Grafton Books, 1991.

Voss, Sarah. *What Number is God? Metaphors, Metaphysics, Metamathematics and the Nature of Things.* New York: State University of New York Press, 1995.

Westcott, W.W. *Numbers: Their Occult Power and Mystic Virtue.* England: Theosophical Publishing House, reprint 1974.

Index

About the Authors

Marie D. Jones has been involved with science, metaphysics, and the paranormal for most of her life, which led to a fascination with quantum physics and the writing of her popular and highly regarded book, *PSIence: How New Discoveries In Quantum Physics and New Science May Explain the Existence of Paranormal Phenomena.* Marie is also author of *2013: End of Days or a New Beginning—Envisioning the World After the Events of 2012,* which features essays from some of today's leading thinkers and cutting-edge researchers. She also coauthored *Supervolcano: The Catastrophic Event That Changed the Course of Human History,* with her father, geophysicist Dr. John Savino. Marie is a New Thought/metaphysics minister and spiritual counselor with a background in metaphysical studies. She worked as a field investigator for MUFON (Mutual UFO Network) in Los Angeles and San Diego in the 1980s and 1990s, cofounded MUFON North County, and currently serves as a consultant to ARPAST, the Arkansas Paranormal and Anomalous Studies Team.

Marie began her extensive writing career as a teenager by writing movie and video reviews for a variety of national magazines, as well as short stories, including award-winning science fiction and speculative fiction for small press genre and literary magazines. She is now a widely published author with hundreds of credits to her name.

Her first nonfiction book, *Looking For God in All the Wrong Places,* was chosen as the Best Spiritual/Religious Book of 2003 by the popular book review Website, RebeccasReads.com, and the book made the Top Ten of 2003 list at MyShelf.com. Marie has also coauthored more than 36 inspirational books for Publications International/New Seasons, including *100 Most Fascinating People in the Bible, Life Changing Prayers,* and *God's Answers to Tough*

Questions. Her essays, articles, and stories have appeared in *Chicken Soup for the Working Woman's Soul, Chicken Soup to Inspire a Woman, If Women Ruled the World, God Allows U-Turns, UFO Magazine, The Book of Thoth, Paranormal Magazine, Light Connection Magazine, Alternate Realities, Unity Magazine, Whole Life Times, Science of Mind Magazine,* and many others. She is also a popular book reviewer for such Websites as BookIdeas.com and CurledUp.com.

Her background also includes more than 15 years in the entertainment industry as a promotions assistant for Warner Bros. Records, film production assistant, and script reader for a variety of film and cable TV companies. She has also been an optioned screenwriter, and has produced several nationally distributed direct-to-video projects, including an award-winning children's storybook video.

In her capacity as an author and researcher, Marie has appeared at several major conferences, including CPAK and the Queen Mary Ghost Hunting Weekend. She has been interviewed on more than 100 radio talk shows including *Coast To Coast* with George Noory, NPR, KPBS Radio, Dreamland, and the *Shirley MacLaine Show,* and has been featured in dozens of newspapers, magazines, and online publications all throughout the world. She lives in San Marcos, California, with her son, Max.

Larry Flaxman has been actively involved in paranormal research and hands-on field investigation for more than 10 years, and melds his technical, scientific, and investigative backgrounds together for no-nonsense, scientifically objective explanations regarding a variety of anomalous phenomena. He is the president and senior researcher of ARPAST, the Arkansas Paranormal and Anomalous Studies Team, which he founded in February of 2007. Under his leadership, ARPAST has become one of the nation's largest and most active paranormal research organizations, with more than 150 members worldwide dedicated to conducting research into the paranormal using the most stringent scientific methodology. ARPAST is also now a proud member of the TAPS family (The Atlantic Paranormal Society). Larry supervises a staff of fully trained researchers and more than $250,000 worth of top-of-the-line equipment. Widely respected for his expertise on the proper use of equipment and techniques for conducting a solid investigation, Larry also serves as technical advisor to several paranormal research groups throughout the country.

Larry has appeared in numerous print interviews, including features in local and regional newspapers, magazines, and online publications such as *The Anomalist, Times Herald News, Jacksonville Patriot, ParaWeb, Current Affairs*

Herald, Unexplained Magazine, and *The Pine Bluff Commercial.* He has been interviewed for several local and regional news television outlets such as *Ozarks First,* as well as national cable television, most recently appearing in a two-part special on ARPAST for MudTruck TV. He has been interviewed on dozens of radio programs, including *X-Zone, Ghostly Talk, Eerie Radio, Crossroads Paranormal, Binall of America,* and *Haunted Voices.*

Larry has authored several published articles regarding science and the paranormal, and is a regular columnist for *The Paranormal Awareness Society* Newsletter. He is also cocreator (with Marie D. Jones) of ParaExplorers.com, devoted to the exploration of ancient and modern unknown mysteries, and is developing a line of related books and products. In addition, Larry is cocreator of the popular new ParaTracker software program for documenting data from paranormal investigations. His own ARPAST online research database system, SOCIUS, is considered one of the most comprehensive in the field. His enthusiasm for education and training in the paranormal field has also garnered many requests for special events and seminars, including popular charity investigations at haunted locations throughout the South, lectures on paranormal awareness for the Breckenridge Movie Theatre chain, and Teen Technology Night at the Nixon Library.

Larry also currently works in law enforcement/information technology. He is married and lives in Little Rock, Arkansas.